EDUCATIONAL ADMINISTRATION

Leading with Mind and Heart
Second Edition

Robert H. Palestini

Rowman & Littlefield Education
Lanham, Maryland • Toronto • Oxford
2005

KH

A ROWMAN & LITTLEFIELD EDUCATION BOOK

Published in the United States of America
by Rowman & Littlefield Education
A Division of Rowman & Littlefield Publishers, Inc.
A wholly owned subsidary of The Rowman & Littlefield Publishing Group, Inc.
4501 Forbes Boulevard, Suite 200, Lanham, Maryland 20706
www.rowmaneducation.com

PO Box 317
Oxford
OX2 9RU, UK

British Library Cataloguing in Publication Information Available

Library of Congress Cataloging-in-Publication Data

Palestini, Robert H.
    Educational administration : leading with mind and heart / Robert H. Palestini.— 2nd ed.
        p. cm.
    Includes bibliographical references and index.
    ISBN 1-57886-234-5 (pbk. : alk. paper)
    1. School management and organization. 2. Educational leadership. I. Title.
    LB2805.P288 2005
    371.2—dc22

                                                                    2005004851

9/15/05

CONTENTS

PREFACE

This is a book about school administration. And, in my view, school administration is primarily about leadership. The conventional wisdom is that leaders are born, not made. I disagree! My experience and, more importantly, scholarly research indicate that skills can be learned. Granted, some leaders will be superior to others because of genetics, but the basic leadership skills are learned and can be cultivated and enhanced. The first eleven chapters speak to the so-called science of administration, while the last chapter deals with the "art" of administration and leadership. One needs to lead with both mind and heart to be truly effective.

The effective building blocks of quality school leadership are the skills of communication, motivation, organizational development, management, and creativity. Mastering the theory and practice in these areas of study will produce high-quality leadership ability and, in turn, produce successful school administrators; doing so with "heart" will result in highly successful administration.

There is another assumption that many educational practitioners make regarding effective administration that I would also dispute. Namely, that "nice guys (and gals) finish last." To be a successful administrator, the belief goes, one needs to be firm, direct, even autocratic. Once again, scholarly research, as well as my own experience, indicates that no one singular leadership style is consistently effective in all situations and at all times. Empirical and experiential studies indicate that effective leaders vary their styles depending on the situation. This situational approach is a recurring theme in this book. In the concluding chapter, we argue that effective leaders use both their minds and their hearts in the leadership process, and that, in fact, nice guys and gals oftentimes do finish first.

Some twenty-five years ago, when I was coaching high school basketball, I attended a coaching clinic where the main clinicians were Dean Smith, coach of North Carolina University, and Bobby Knight, coach of Indiana University. Both coaches were successful then, and three decades later, they remain successful and, in one case at least, revered.

In the morning session Bobby Knight explained how *fear* was the most effective motivator in sports. If your want your athletes to listen to you and you want to be successful, you need to instill fear in the players. In the afternoon session, Dean Smith explained how *love* is the most effective motivator in sports. If you want to win and be successful, you must engender love in the athletes.

You can understand my sense of confusion by the end of that clinic. Here were two of the most successful men in sports giving contradictory advice. As a young and impressionable coach, I was puzzled by these apparently mixed messages. Over the intervening years, I have often thought about that clinic and tried to make sense of what I had heard. After these many years, I have drawn two conclusions from this incident, both of which have had a significant impact on my philosophy of leadership and on this book.

The first conclusion has to do with the *situational* nature of leadership. Bobby Knight and Dean Smith impressed upon me the truism that there is no one singular leadership style that is effective at all times and in all situations; and, second, that despite reaping short-term success, the better style for ensuring long-term success is one that inspires love, trust, and respect. Just as athletes become robotic and are fearful of making mistakes when fear is the motivator, so are employees who are supervised by an autocratic manager. Initiative, creativity, and self-sufficiency are all stymied by the leader who instills fear in his or her subordinates. Thus, I arrived at my conclusion that effective school administration and leadership begins with love, trust, and respect.

In addition to an emphasis on the nature of leadership, this book focuses on placing theory into practice. We do not wish to diminish the value of theory. Without theory we have no valid way of analyzing and correcting failed practice. However, knowledge of theory without the ability to place it into reflective practice is not characteristic of effective leadership.

It has been my experience that graduate students in educational administration oftentimes complain that they are taught only theory and are left to their own devices to apply it. This approach is not the worst instructional method in that educators should be trained to be reflective practitioners who constantly strive to connect theory to practice. However, a truly effective instructional technique is to help students along in making those connections. Thus, at the end of each chapter, there are activities and exercises that are specifically aimed at placing theory into practice. This book also uses the case study approach to place theory into practice. Each chapter contains an extensive case study that readers are asked to analyze in light of the topic explored in that chapter. Appendix I contains information regarding this diagnostic approach and its implications.

Another assumption that is generally held by administrators is that if dramatic changes are not made during the first year of one's tenure, the so-called honeymoon period, changes may never be made. Once again, I challenge this assumption. I believe that change is far more effective when it is made in a culture of trust and of participation.

Therefore, I believe that a leader should spend the first several months in a new position establishing a sense of trust and setting the groundwork for participatory decision making. That is not to say that the leader need not have an educational vision. The fact is, without one, he or she will never get a job. However, the vision needs to be shaped and honed according to local needs, and the entire school community must "own" the vision if it is to reach fruition. Every salesperson is trained to "know the territory." Likewise, school administrators need to know the territory if they are to be successful leaders. Knowing the organizational structure and culture is imperative if an administrator hopes to be effective.

This book takes an organizational development approach to producing effective leadership. Picture yourself standing in the middle of a dense forest. Suppose you were asked to describe the characteristics of the forest: What types of trees are growing in the forest; how many acres of trees are there; where are the trees thriving; where are they not?

Faced with this proposition, most people would not know where to start and "would not be able to see the forest for the trees."

Newly appointed school administrators often have these same feelings of confusion when faced with the prospect of having to assume a leadership role in a complex organization like a school or school system. Where does one start? An effective way to start would be to systematically examine the components that make up an organization. Such a system of organizational diagnosis and prescription will lead to a comprehensive and integrated analysis of the organization's strengths and weaknesses and point the way toward possible improvement. This book suggests such a sequential and systematic approach. Using it effectively can produce dramatic and useful results.

In addition to "knowing the territory," engendering trust, and having an educational vision, successful school administrators must be able to communicate effectively; be able to motivate and manage their staffs properly; think of creative ways of continuously improving their programs; and be able and willing to adapt their leadership style to the situation they encounter.

This leads me to what I presumptuously refer to as my Seven Principles of Effective Leadership. Effective leaders:

- must be keenly aware of the organizational structure and culture of the school;
- must be able to engender a sense of trust in the faculty and staff;
- need to continuously improve the school program and, therefore, must be able to be agents for change;
- need to be able to adapt their leadership style to the situation;
- need to be well-organized and creative and have a clearly articulated educational vision;
- must be able to communicate effectively;
- must know how to motivate their faculty and staff and to be able to manage the conflicts that arise.

In my view, which is supported by a prodigious amount of empirical research, if an administrator can master the knowledge and skills encompassed in these seven principles, and do it with heart, he or she will be highly successful. This book addresses each of these principles in detail.

Finally, the Council of Chief State School Officers has published a document entitled *Interstate School Leaders Licensure Consortium: Standards for School Leaders*. The contents of this document were used in determining many of the topics in this book. A copy of this document is included as appendix III. And for professors interested in designing an online version of this text in the form of a graduate course in educational administration, a detailed course outline is supplied in appendix II. Last, this text utilizes a case study approach to diagnosing and prescribing remedies to an organization's flaws. There is a case study at the end of each chapter for this purpose. Appendix I contains a guide to using the case study approach.

1

ORGANIZATIONAL STRUCTURE IN SCHOOLS

The master in the art of living makes little distinction between his work and his play, his labor and his leisure, his mind and his body, his education and his recreation, his love and his religion. He hardly knows which is which. He simply pursues his vision of excellence in whatever he does, leaving others to decide whether he is working or playing. To him, he is always doing both.

—Zen Buddhist text

Being aware of the organizational structure and behavior in a school or school system is the first step in effective school administration. It is the administrator's means of "knowing the territory." In this chapter, we first address the various schools of organizational structure and, later, we discuss the components that comprise an organization's behavior or culture.

A HISTORICAL PERSPECTIVE

Tracing the history of organizational behavior and effective management provides a context for understanding its evolution and its current practice. By using these historical perspectives concurrently, we can enrich our understanding of organizational situations because they both provide a backdrop for the development of current organizational thought and remain current and relevant to organizational analysis today (table1.1).

STRUCTURAL PERSPECTIVES

The earliest theorists focused on the structuring and design of work and organizations. Organizational theory prior to 1900, scientific management, classical theory, bureaucracy, and decision-making theory each addressed issues of structure in the organization.

Prior to 1900, very little formal management or organizational theorizing occurred. In addition, few industrial organizations of the types we know today existed; the basic organizational models were the military and the Catholic Church. But the factory system had developed and was creating strong demands for theories of management. School systems, as we know them today, had not yet begun to be developed, so the need for organizational models and management principles was not yet evident.

SCIENTIFIC MANAGEMENT

In the early twentieth century, management emerged as a field of study with the theorizing of Frederick W. Taylor, a foreman at the Bethlehem Steel Works in Pennsylvania. Taylor's observations at the turn of the century about industrial efficiency and scientific management focused management theory on manufacturing organizations, which had become more common after 1900, and offered prescriptions for the effective structure of organizations and design of management activities. He described management as a science with managers and employees having clearly specified, yet different, responsibilities.[1]

In his report of his classic experiment, Taylor showed that a pig-iron handler, who formerly loaded twelve tons per day, loaded forty-seven tons after application of the principles of scientific management. Think of someone shoveling iron ore into a furnace. An observer, the equivalent of a modern-day industrial engineer, times on a stopwatch how long it takes a worker to pick up a shovel, move it and the ore into a car, drop off the ore, and then prime the shovel for the next load. At the same time, another observer records the precise physical movements the

Table 1.1 Historical schools of thought and their components

School	Decade	Perspective	Description
Organizational theory prior to 1900	Before 1900	Structural	Emphasized the division of labor and the importance of machinery to facilitate labor
Scientific management	1910s	Structural	Described management as a science, with employees having specific but different responsibilities; encouraged the scientific selection, training, and development of workers and the equal division of work between workers and management
Classical school	1920s	Structural	Listed the duties of a manager as planning, organizing, commanding employees, coordinating activities, and controlling performance; basic principles called for specialization of work, unity of command, chain of command, and coordination of activities
Bureaucracy	1920s	Structural	Emphasized order, system, rationality, uniformity, and consistency in management; these attributes led to equitable treatment for all employees by management
Human relations	1920s	Behavioral	Focused on the importance of the attitudes and feelings of workers; informal roles and norms influenced performance
Classical school revisited	1930s	Structural	Reemphasis on the classical principles described above
Group dynamics	1940s	Behavioral	Encouraged individual participation in decision-making; noted the impact of the work group on performance
Leadership	1950s	Behavioral	Stressed the importance of groups having both social and task leaders; differentiated between Theory X and Theory Y management
Decision-making	1950s	Behavioral	Suggested that individuals "satisfice" when they make decisions
Sociotechnical school	1960s	Integrative	Called for considering technology and work groups when understanding a work system
Systems theory	1960s	Integrative	Represented an organization as an open system with inputs, transformations, output, and feedback; systems strive for equilibrium and experience equifinality
Contingency theory	1980s	Integrative	Emphasized the fit between organizational processes and characteristics of the situation; called for fitting the organization's structure to various contingencies
Transformational leadership	Current	Integrative	Situational influence with emphasis on a vision and the personal charism to effect positive change in the organization.

worker made, such as whether he picked up the shovel with his right or left hand, whether he switched hands before moving it, how far apart he placed his feet, and so on. With these data, Taylor determined the physical positions that led to the fastest time for shoveling ore and developed the "science" of shoveling. Taylor's principles had the greatest impact when applied to increasing productivity on a relatively simple task.[2]

CLASSICAL SCHOOL

Henri Fayol, was a Frenchman who wrote at about the same time as Taylor, although his works did not have a widely read English translation until 1949.[3] Here we see the influence of management thinking abroad on the view of organizational behavior in the United States because, once translated, the principles described by Fayol became very popular in the United States. His comments typified the classical approach to administration. He listed the duties of a manager as planning, organizing, commanding employees, coordinating activities, and controlling performance, and he specified the fourteen principles of management shown in table 1.2.

Table 1.2 Fayol's principles of management.

1. Division of work—the specialization of work	9. Scalar chain (line of authority)—"the chain of superiors ranging from the ultimate authority to the lower ranks"
2. Authority—"the right to give orders, and power to exact obedience"	10. Order—all materials and people should be in an appointed place
3. Discipline—"obedience, application, energy, behavior, and outward marks of respect"	11. Equity—equality of (although not necessarily identical) treatment
4. Unity of command—"an employee should receive orders from one superior only"	12. Stability of tenure of personnel—limited turnover of personnel
5. Unity of direction—"one head and one plan for a group of activities having the same objective"	13. Initiative—"thinking out a plan and ensuring its success"
6. Subordination of individual interests to the general interest—the interest of an individual or group should not supersede the organization's concerns	14. Esprit de corps—"harmony, union among the personnel of a concern"
7. Remuneration—fair payment for services	
8. Centralization—degree of consolidation of management functions	

BUREAUCRACY

Max Weber, a German sociologist, addressed the issue of organizational administration in a somewhat different way. Here, too, a global influence on management permeates early thought. In the first part of the twentieth century, Weber studied European organizations and described what he considered to be a prototype form of organization, the bureaucracy. For many people, bureaucracy conjures up an image of massive red tape and endless unneeded details. For Weber, however, the major asset of bureaucracy was its emphasis on order, system, rationality, uniformity and consistency. These primary attributes in his view led to equitable treatment for all employees by management.[4]

In bureaucracies, each employee has specified and official areas of responsibility that are assigned on the basis of competence and expertise. Managers use written documents extensively in managing employees. Rules and regulations are translated into detailed employment manuals.

Managers also receive extensive training in their job requirements. Finally, office and plant management must use rules that are consistent, complete, and that can be learned.

BEHAVIORAL PERSPECTIVES

Although the scientific management, classical, and bureaucratic perspectives emphasize issues related to the structure and design of organizations, they do not address worker dissatisfaction, leadership, and dysfunctional interpersonal communication. Other researchers, including the human relations, group dynamics, decision-making, and leadership schools have explicitly considered the human side of organizations.

HUMAN RELATIONS SCHOOL

Beginning in 1924, the Western Electric Company, in conjunction with the National Academy of Sciences, performed five studies of various work groups at Western Electric's Hawthorne plant. The first study looked at the effects of lighting on the productivity of workers in different departments of the company. In the tradition of scientific management, it considered whether certain illumination levels affected output. Essentially, the researchers first increased the lighting to an extreme brightness and then decreased the light until the work area was so dim that assembly material could hardly be seen. Surprisingly, the workers maintained or even exceeded their normal output whether researchers increased or decreased illumination.[5] Subsequent studies attempted to explain these results by introducing a variety of changes in the workplace. The researchers examined the impact on output of rest pauses, shorter working days and weeks, wage incentives, and the nature of supervision. They also suggested that something other than the physical work environment or the organizational structure resulted in improved productivity among workers. In observing and interviewing the employees, the researchers discovered that during the experiments, the employees felt that someone paid attention to them, so their morale improved and they produced more. This so-called Hawthorne effect offered the first dramatic indication that the attitudes and feelings of workers could significantly influence productivity. In the final experiments of the Hawthorne series, the researchers identified another human feature of organizations, that is, that the informal groups that workers develop among themselves have a significant effect on productivity. This leads us to the next school of organizational behavior, group dynamics.

GROUP DYNAMICS

Later in the century, Kurt Lewin, a social psychologist at the University of Iowa, was asked to study methods of changing housewives' food habits away from meat consumption because there was a shortage of meat during the World War II years. He believed families expected housewives to serve meat and these expectations would present a significant barrier to change. He conducted experiments that showed that participation in decision making broke down the barrier. Housewives who joined in group discussions on the topic of meat consumption were ten times more likely to change their food habits than were housewives who received lectures on the subject. Studies such as this led to a greatly expanded awareness of the impact of the work group and spawned research on the relationship between organizational effectiveness and group dynamics.[6]

DECISION-MAKING THEORY

In the 1950s, Herbert Simon and James March introduced a different decision-making framework for understanding organizational behavior. Although they elaborated on the bureaucratic model by emphasizing that individuals work in rational organizations and thus behave rationally, their model, which eventually won them a Noble Prize in economics, added a new dimension, that is, the idea that a human being's rationality is limited. By offering a more realistic alternative to classical assumptions of rationality in decision making, this model supported the behavioral view of individual and organizational functioning. The model suggested that when individuals make decisions, they examine a limited set of possible alternatives rather than all available options. Individuals "satisfice," that is, they accept satisfactory or "good enough" choices, rather than insist on optimal choices. They make choices that are good enough because they do not search until they find perfect solutions to problems. Thus, purely scientific or structural views of management are inappropriate.[7]

LEADERSHIP

The 1950s saw the beginning of concentrated research in the area of leadership. Researchers and theorists in that era discussed the roles of managers and leaders in organizations and initiated a body of research on leadership. One classification described groups as having both task and social leaders. The task leader helps the group achieve its goals by clarifying and summarizing member comments and focusing on the group's tasks; the social leader maintains the group and helps it develop cohesiveness and collaboration by encouraging group members' involvement. A second classification distinguished between Theory X and Theory Y managers. Those who believe Theory X assume that workers have an inherent dislike of work, that they must be controlled and threatened with punishment if they are to be productive, and that they prefer to avoid responsibility. Managers who believe Theory Y, on the other hand, assume that people feel work is as natural as play or rest, that people will exercise self-direction toward the objectives to which they are committed, and that the average human being can learn to seek responsibility. These assumptions that managers hold, then, affect the way they treat their employees and also affect the employees' productivity.[8]

INTEGRATIVE PERSPECTIVES

In contrast to an emphasis primarily on structure or on the human side of organizations, organizational thought in the past few decades has emphasized the integration of these two perspectives, along with more specific consideration of environmental and other external influences. More recently, contingency theory has added an emphasis on fitting managerial and organizational features to the specific work situation.

SOCIOTECHNICAL SCHOOL

In the 1950s, several theorists moved away from an emphasis on structure or behavior. Instead, they studied technology, which they viewed as a significant influence on structure, and emphasized its interaction with functioning work groups, an element of the human perspective. As members of the sociotechnical school, which studied organizations in England, India, and Norway, Trist and Bamforth described a change in technology in a British coal mine. In the mine, workers were used to working independently in small, self-contained units in which they organized the work themselves. But the technology for mining coal improved in a way that required management to increase job specialization and decrease the workers' participation in job assignments. This greater job specialization followed from the scientific management and classical management traditions and was expected to increase productivity. But the coal miners hated the specialization. They preferred working with each other and performing a variety or tasks.[9]

Trish and Bamforth compared the performance of work groups whose jobs had become specialized when the new technology was introduced, causing a different social interaction, to that of work groups that retained the old pattern of social interactions. They found that absenteeism in the specialized groups was several times greater and productivity much lower than in the groups that had maintained their original relationships. After a number of studies such as these, the sociotechnical systems researchers concluded that technological changes must be made in conjunction with a strong social system and that both social and technical/structural aspects of jobs must be considered simultaneously.

SYSTEMS THEORY

The general systems model, with roots in both the behavioral and natural sciences, represents an organization as an open system, one that interacts with environmental forces and factors, in a way similar to physical systems, such as the human body, a microscopic organism, or a cell. First, this system comprises a number of interrelated, interdependent, and interacting subsystems. Second, the organization is open and dynamic. Third, it strives for equilibrium. And fourth, it has multiple purposes, objectives, and functions, some of which are in conflict.[10]

An organization is open and dynamic in that it continually receives new energy. This energy may be added in the form of new resources, goals, or information from the environment. These new energies are called "inputs." The new energy can also affect the transformation of the inputs into new "outputs." The organization itself, composed of task characteristics, characteristics of individuals, the formal organizational arrangements, and informal organization, transfers inputs into outputs. Task characteristics include the degree of specialization, amount of feedback, and extent of autonomy involved in performing work activities. Individual characteristics include the needs, knowledge, expectations, and experiences of organizational members. Formal organizational processes encompass the organization's structure, job design, reward system, performance evaluation system, and other human resources management practices. Among the organizational arrangements are the rules and procedures of a company. The informal elements refer to leader behavior, group and intergroup relations, and power behavior outside the formal hierarchy. As a result of such transformation of inputs, changes in outputs, such as performance, satisfaction, morale, turnover, and absenteeism may occur.

When organizations receive new inputs or experience certain transformations, they simultaneously seek stability, balance, and equilibrium. When organizations become unbalanced or experience disequilibrium, such as when changes in the environment or organizational practices make current resources inadequate, the organizations attempt to return to a steady state, which may mirror or significantly differ from the original state of equilibrium. They use information about their outputs, called feedback, or exchange, to modify their inputs or transformations to result in more desirable outcomes and equilibrium.

Feedback may also indicate which subsystems have similar goals and which have different or even conflicting goals. Various parts of organizations, individuals, managers, work groups, departments, or divisions, have multiple purposes, functions, and objectives, some of which may conflict.

Finally, organizations as open systems demonstrate equifinality, which suggests that organizations may employ a variety of means to achieve their desired objectives. For example, McDonald's achieves its objectives of growth and profitability by employing a highly specialized system for producing its hamburgers. Harvard University, on the other hand, employs a more flexible and adaptive operation to achieve its goals of providing a high-quality education to its students. No single structure or other transformation processes result in a predetermined set of inputs, outputs, and transformations. Thus, to survive, organizations must adapt to changes with appropriate changes in the system. This, then, brings us to a consideration of contingency theory.

CONTINGENCY THEORY

Like systems theory, contingency theory provides a more comprehensive view that calls for a fit between organizational processes and characteristics of the situation. Early contingency research looked at the fit between an organization's structure and its environment.[11] One early study prescribed mechanistic and organic systems for stable and change environments, respectively. Other research found that the type of structure the organization develops is influenced by the organization's technology. A mechanistic type of organization fits best with a mass production technology; a more organic form of organization, like a school, responds best to a unit technology or a continuous-process technology. Recent thinking in organization design has reemphasized the importance for organizational effectiveness of fitting organizational structure to various contingencies. Contingency theory has also extended to leadership, group dynamics, power relations, and work design. Its basic premise of fitting behavior to the situation underlies much of today's thought on organization structure and behavior.

SCHOOL ORGANIZATION

For ease of operation, the various schools of organizational thought can be grouped into three types of organizational theory, namely, classical organization theory, social systems theory, and open system theory.

CLASSICAL ORGANIZATION THEORY

As figure 1.1 illustrates, all three bodies of theory are presented in contemporary management thinking, although they entered the main-

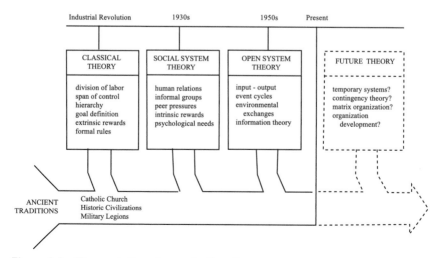

Figure 1.1   The evolution of organization theory

stream of thought at different historical periods. As mentioned earlier, the pioneer writers obviously did not originate the phenomena that they wrote about. When Weber (1864–1920) began writing at the turn of the century about bureaucracy, elements of bureaucracy had been present in descriptions of organized life dating back to ancient Rome and China.[12]

Most classical thinkers, such as Weber, Fayol, and Taylor, lived through the industrial revolution as it went through its most fervent stages around the turn of the twentieth century. As they watched the rapidly growing technology of mass production collide with the traditional patterns of management, they clearly saw the resulting inefficiency was wasteful and appalling.

As the classical theorist began to examine the problems of management erupting in the production centers of society, they shaped notions about organizations that were intended to resolve many of the administrative ills within them. Many of the classical theorists' ideas on work and management were defined as universal scientific principles. If these principles were applied to almost any organizational setting, it was argued, the result would be the efficient use of time, materials, and personnel.

The classical theorists believed that an application of the bureaucratic structure and processes or organizational control would promote rational, efficient, and disciplined behavior, making possible the achievement of well-defined goals. Efficiency, then, is achieved by arranging positions within an organization according to hierarchy and jurisdiction and by placing power at the top of a clear chain of command. Scientific procedures are used to determine the best way of performing a task, and then rules are written that require workers to perform in a prescribed manner. Experts are hired for defined roles and are grouped according to task specialization. Using rationally defined structures and processes such as these, a scientifically ordered flow of work can be carried out with maximum efficiency.

The conceptual model distilled from classical theory had a great impact on the practice and study of organizational life. It quickly spilled over the boundaries of industry and was incorporated into the practice of management in all sectors of society, including the schools.

SOCIAL SYSTEMS THEORY

Within the classical theory framework, the individual worker was conceived of as an object, a part of the bureaucratic machine. Preparing the work environment for maximizing labor efficiency was not unlike applying precepts from the physical sciences to the human domain of work. As Elton Mayo found in the Hawthorne Works' studies, the impact of social-psychological variables within a worker group was significant. The discovery that workers could control the production process to a considerable degree, independent of the demands of management, shattered many of the precepts central to classical theory. A new era of organization theory was upon us. This domain of thought is sometimes referred to as *social systems theory*.

Classical management theory taught that the needs of the organization and the needs of the worker coincided because if the company prospered, the worker would also prosper. However, as an awareness of the basic differences between the needs of the individual and the needs of the organization grew, and as worker groups became more sophisticated in the subrosa skills of manipulating the production process, management technology gave birth to the social systems theory and its approaches as a means of reducing conflict. The argument went that by being considerate, using democratic procedures whenever possible, and maintaining open lines of communication, management and workers could talk over their respective problems and resolve them in a friendly, congenial way.

Not unlike the classical theory of the previous generation, the human relations orientation to the problems of managerial control spread quickly to other sectors of society, including the schools. The social upheaval caused by the Depression and turmoil of World War II created a receptive climate for this new administrative theory. The enthusiasm for the human relations orientation dampened considerably after the 1950s because many worker organizations came to view it as only another management tactic designed to exploit workers.

However, the study of behavior in social system settings intensified, and a greater sophistication developed about how and why group members behave as they do under given conditions. In time, a natural social systems orientation to the analysis of behavior evolved in the literature as an alternative to the rational systems approach. The natural social systems orientation attempts to take into account how people do behave in organizations rather than how they should behave. The conceptual perspective of the natural social systems model suggests that an organization consists of a collection of groups (social systems) that collaborate to achieve system goals on some occasions and, on other occasions, that cooperate to accomplish the goals of their own groups. Coalitions among subgroups within an organization (e.g., English teachers, history teachers, and social studies teachers) form to provide power bases upon which action can be taken (e.g., "Let's all vote to reject writing behavioral objectives"). Within the social systems framework, the study of formal and informal power is one of several critical variables utilized to identify and analyze the processes of organizational governance.

OPEN SYSTEM THEORY

During the 1960s, another strand of thought developed, which originated in the new technostructure of society. The earlier two traditions of classical and social systems theory tend to view organizational life as a closed system, that is, as isolated from the surrounding environment. Open system theory conceives of an organization as a set of interrelated parts that interact with the environment. It receives inputs, such as human and material resources, values, community expectations, and societal demands; transforms them through a production process (e.g., classroom activities); and exports the product (e.g., graduates, new knowledge, revised value sets) into the environment (e.g., business, military, home, college) with value added. The organization receives a return (e.g., community financial support) for its efforts so it can survive and prosper. The cycle then begins once again (figure 1.2).

Within the systems theory context, the organization is perceived as consisting of cycles of events, which interlock through exporting and importing with other organizations, which are also made up of cycles of events. Management is very complex because the leadership has almost no control over the shifting conditions in the environment (e.g., new laws, demographic shifts, political climate, the market for graduates) on the input or the output side of the equation. Control of the production process is also complex because the various subsystems of the organiza-

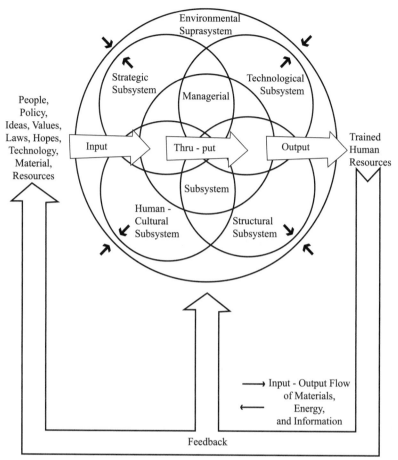

Figure 1.2. Open system model

tion (e.g., athletic department or minority group students) also are shaped by event cycles that are programmed by values, expectations, traditions, and vested interests. Changing these internal subgroups and their event cycles is a difficult task. The manager attempts to stream the cycles together so that minimum conflict and waste is generated.

Through the perspective of open system theory, a new logic on issues of organizational governance has emerged. It emphasizes the relationship of the organization with its surrounding environment, and thus places a premium on planning and programming for events that cannot be controlled directly. The key to making an open system work effectively and efficiently is its ability to gather, process, and utilize information. In a school, then, the facility with which a need is discovered, a goal is established, and resources are coalesced to meet that need will determine the effectiveness and efficiency of that school.

CONTINGENCY THEORY

In recent years, a view of organization development has surfaced that treats each organization, and even the entities within the organization, as relatively unique. For centuries, this orientation has been at the core of practitioner behavior, but has been seen basically as an anomaly, reflective of inefficiency or unpreparedness, and thus overlooked by management scientists. Currently, the changing situational character of management is now coming to be understood as a key to the management process itself.

Many management scholars and practitioners would now agree with the observation that contingency theory is perhaps the most powerful current and future trend in the organization field. At this stage of development, however, contingency theory is not really a theory. Rather, it is a conceptual tool that facilitates our understanding of the situational flow of events and alternate organizational and individual responses to that flow. Thus, as a conceptual tool, contingency theory does not possess the holistic character of the three major models discussed earlier. In many ways, contingency theory can be thought of as a subset of open system theory because it is through open system theory that we come to understand the dynamic flows of events, personnel, and resources that take place in organizations. We incorporate contingency theory techniques in our discussion of leadership, employee motivation, and communication.

CASE STUDY 1.1:
THE BURRELL CITY SCHOOL DISTRICT

Molly Sholly, being a new teacher to the Burrell City School District, did not understand the impact a "NO" vote toward the school budget would have on the school district's future. She had been teaching for four years in a large city school district where she was just a number and the budget was never an issue that was addressed at their level. After wanting to get out of the large urban school situation for several years, a teaching opportunity became available in the Burrell City School District. She was reluctant in taking the job for fear she would find herself in the same situation. The last thing Molly wanted was to leave the tenure status in her school for another school that was going to put her in the same situation and at the bottom of the seniority list. After going on the interview and inspecting the school and area, she decided this opportunity was one she should not pass up.

Now, after her first year with the Burrell City School District, Molly felt very comfortable with the staff and students and felt like she'd found her niche. It wasn't until the budget was defeated that she began to worry about the security of her job.

THE BURRELL CITY SCHOOL DISTRICT

Burrell, New Jersey, is a small urban city with a population of 11,000. The Burrell City School District is made up of three elementary schools (K–3), one intermediate school (4–6), and one high school that houses seventh through twelfth grades. The seventh and eighth grades have a separate wing of the building where their classes are held. The city is divided between a more-affluent side of the city and a less-affluent side. Two of the elementary schools get students from the affluent side of the city and the other elementary school receives most of the students from the less-affluent side of the city. This causes much competition between the schools and the less-affluent school always seems to have most of the behavior problems out of the three.

The board of education consists of nine members, who serve a term of three years with a turnover of two to three people per year. For many years, the school district did not have a good reputation. The students were known to be unruly and there was low teacher morale. It was not until a few years ago, when the district hired a superintendent from outside the district, that the reputation began to improve.

DR. EDWARD GOLDEN

Dr. Edward Golden, who had a reputation for being a strict by-the-book superintendent, came from a small suburban district. He was also chosen for his ability to follow through on the goals he set for a district. When he came to the Burrell City School District, the national test scores were below average and the graduation rate was below 60%. These statistics were taken seriously and goals were immediately developed to raise the test scores and the graduation rate in the next three years. Golden is well-respected by the teachers and the community for the way he has re-shaped the reputation of the district. He has a very strong personality and runs the district in an authoritarian manner. Since his arrival, the district has more structure and an improved management system. Dr. Golden has a good relationship with board of education. He seems to understand the way they operate and uses this knowledge to his advantage. The board re-spects Dr. Golden's input in certain situations, but they also make deci-sions on what is best for the district as a whole. He is an advocate for children and portrays the image of a salesman selling his best product.

THE BUDGET

Even before the budget was defeated, Burrell School District was not able to hire a full-time administrator for each school building. Edward Golden not only was responsible for his duties as superintendent, but also was the principal for the smallest elementary school in the district. In his absence, a head teacher was appointed to make decisions or deal with problems that may occur. The assistant superintendent, Donald Struge, also had several responsibilities within the district. Struge had been assistant superintendent for five years when the school district needed an intermediate school principal. No money was allocated in the budget to hire a new principal. Struge and Golden had become good friends over the years working together. Golden knew the effort Struge put into being an excellent assistant superintendent and felt he could handle the extra responsibilities as the intermediate school principal. The other two elementary schools were fortunate enough to have their own principal.

Patricia Glenn was the principal of the largest and less-affluent ele-mentary school. Robert McGee was the principal for the most-affluent el-ementary school in the district. Robert has served fifteen years in the school district and was retiring at the end of the school year. This had been the administrative situation for several years, and it had been working productively, until last year when the budget was defeated.

Edward Golden had a vision for the next school year. This would be the year each of the school buildings would have its own administrator. The schools would run more smoothly because the administration would not be stretched so thinly. Edward did not worry about the budget passing. It had passed in the prior years; it would not fail because of a small tax increase.

The plan for the next school year was to hire a new administrator to relieve Edward Golden of his duties as the principal of the elementary school. Dr. Struge, the assistant superintendent, would have his load lightened by moving from principal of the intermediate school to principal of the retiring Robert McGee's elementary school. The district would only need to hire a principal for one elementary school and the intermediate school. The board approved this proposal in May and was waiting for the budget to pass in order to start interviewing.

THE COMMUNITY

To Dr. Golden's disbelief, many rumors were circulating about the school tax increase and the uneasiness the community was feeling. The night of the vote was the first Molly Sholly saw of the anxiety so many teachers and administrators were feeling. Molly was signing out for the day and overheard her principal, Patricia Glenn, talking to a group of teachers. She was saying how nervous she and Dr. Golden were about the passing of the budget. She did not think much of it and went home for the day. The next day at school, she heard the news of the defeat. An article taped to the sign-in desk featured the budget defeat, along with other school districts where the budgets did not pass. School taxes were rising and the communities felt that they were high enough. Many people that were asked to comment said they voted no because they did not have children in the schools or that their children were grown and out of school. The community did not feel it necessary to take on the extra tax burdens if they did not have children in public schools. Another reason for the budget not passing could also have been the recurring low voter turnout. The people who felt strongly enough about the extra tax got out to vote, but the parents of the children in the schools in favor of the budget failed to do so. This relates back to the division of the community and the problems that are rising because of it.

THE AFTERMATH

Edward Golden took full responsibility for the defeated budget. He did not put the blame on the community or the parents of the school children. He sent letters home to all community members regretting the defeat and asking for suggestions on how to improve for the next school year's budget.

As a result of the budget defeat, Dr. Golden's request for restructuring was denied. He remained principal of the smallest elementary school and kept his superintendent duties. Donald Struge's responsibilities did not change. He remained principal of the intermediate school as well assistant superintendent. Patricia Glenn, the principal of the largest elementary school, was assigned to take over as principal of Robert McGee's elementary school because he was retired. Her duties, therefore, doubled. Patricia was reluctant to take on such a large responsibility. She had only been a principal in the Burrell School District for a year. Her first year was very successful. She took the largest elementary school, which had an unproductive previous year, increased teacher morale, and created wonderful relations with the community. Dr. Golden reassured her that she was capable of handling the two schools, as he has done in handling his double role.

The last repercussion that took place because of the budget defeat was the elimination of two elementary teaching positions. Six nontenured elementary teachers' jobs were being reviewed. At this point, Molly Sholly then realized how important the passing of a budget was, not only for a school district, but also for individuals employed by it.

Programs were also being reviewed to be cut. The elementary schools had a developmental first grade. This class was developed for children who were not ready for first grade but who were also not candidates for retention in kindergarten. This was a pilot program that could not be funded for another year. The extracurricular sports' teams were also being reviewed. Many teams with low participation were in jeopardy of being cut.

NOTES

1. F. W. Taylor, *The Principles of Scientific Management* (New York: Harper and Brothers, 1911), 36–37.

2. E. A. Locke, The Ideas of Frederick Taylor: An Evaluation, *Academy of Management Review* 7 (1982): 14–24.

3. H. Fayol, *General and Industrial Management*, trans. C. Storrs (London: Pitman, 1949).

4. M. Weber, *The Theory of Social and Economic Organization*, trans. and ed. A. M. Henderson and T. Parsons (New York: Oxford University Press, 1947).

5. C. E. Snow, A discussion of the relation of illumination intensity to productive efficiency, *The Tech Engineering News*, November 1927. Cited in E. J. Roethlisberger and W. J. Dickson, *Management and the Worker* (Cambridge, Mass.: Harvard University Press, 1939).

6. M. Radke and D. Klisurich, Experiments in Changing Food Habits, *Journal of the American Dietetics Association* 23 (1947): 403–409.

7. See C. S. Bartlem and E. A. Locke, The Coch and French Study: A Critique and Reinterpretation, *Human Relations* 34 (1981): 555–566, for another view of the significance of research on participation.

8. D. McGregor, *The Human Side of Enterprise* (New York: McGraw-Hill, 1961); E. H. Schein, The Hawthorne Group Studies Revisited: A Defense of Theory Y, Sloan School of Management Working Paper #756-74 (Cambridge: Massachusetts Institute of Technology, 1974).

9. E. K. Trist and K. W. Bamforth, Some Social and Psychological Consequences of the Long-Wall Method of Coal Getting, *Human Relations* 4 (1951): 3–38; other studies included A. K. Rice, *The Enterprise and Its Environment* (London: Tavistock, 1963), and F. E. Emery and I. L. Trist, *Sociotechnical Systems, Management Science: Models and Techniques*, vol. 2 (London: Pergamon, 1960).

10. D. Katz and R. L. Kahn, *The Social Psychology of Organizations*, 2nd ed. (New York: John Wiley & Sons, 1978).

11. J. Woodward, *Industrial Organization: Theory and Practice* (London: Oxford University Press, 1965); P. Lawrence and J. Lorsch, *Organization and Environment* (Boston: Harvard Business School Division of Research, 1967).

12. E. Mark Hanson, *Educational Administration and Organizational Behavior* (Boston: Allyn and Bacon, 1991).

2

SCHOOL CULTURE

Culture consists of the unwritten laws impressed on the souls of
those living under the same constitution.

—Philo

In addition to organizational structure, the other component of "knowing the territory" for the school administrator is to be aware of the organizational behavior or culture of a school. I have visited schools where
principals argue that the only things that tie their school systems together are the marching band, the athletic program, and a common concern for parking. The truth, however, is that the school behavior or culture is the tie that binds.

Organizational culture is composed of the shared beliefs, expectations, values, and norms of conduct of its members. In any organization,
the informal culture interacts with the formal organizational structure
and control system to produce a generally clear understanding of the
"way things are done around here." Even more than the forces of bureaucracy, the organization's culture is the glue that binds people together. It is through this culture that our images of reality are shaped,
often in an unconscious manner.

COMPONENTS OF CULTURE

In determining the nature of organizational culture, we can analyze its components, which include beliefs, expectations, and shared values; heroes and heroines; myths and stories; rituals and ceremonies; and the physical arrangements in the school.

Beliefs, Expectations, and Shared Values

Basic organizational philosophy reflects the beliefs, expectations, and shared values of its leaders. Together, these drive the organization toward its goals. Basic beliefs, which influence employee behavior and attitudes, define success for employees, and establish standards of achievement, may be a function of the requirements of the milieu in which the organization functions, as well as its national culture.

Heroes and Heroines

Heroes and heroines transmit culture by personifying its corporate values. Leaders viewed in this way reinforce the basic values of an organization's culture by providing role models, symbolizing their organization to the outside world, preserving the organization's special qualities, setting a standard of performance, motivating employees, and making success attainable and human. Managers who create heroes or heroines foster a set of corporate values that may stabilize the current organization or expedite change. We are all familiar with the long-time respected faculty member who oftentimes fulfills this role in schools.[1]

Myths and Stories

Myths, in this context, are stories about institutional heroes and heroines that facilitate the transmission and embedding of culture. What does the repeated telling of a story about the spectacular rise in standardized test scores under a certain principal tell you about a school's culture? Does a story about a school's success in sports under a certain principal give the same impression and reflect the same culture? The themes of such stories provide clues to an organization's culture.

Rituals and Ceremonies

Ceremonies, such as retirement dinners or employee-of-the-month awards, contribute to organizational culture by dramatizing the organization's basic values; for example, the award of a pin for twenty-five years of service reflects a school that values loyalty. Often-linked with a corresponding organizational story, such an event can provide an explanation of new behavior patterns. Such ceremonies can also act as rites of passage, delineating entry into an organization's inner circle. They can also expedite transitions in leadership, such as that experienced in the inauguration of a new college president.

Physical Arrangement

· The selection and arrangement of offices and furnishings often reveal significant insight into a school's culture. Compare the school that provides only a mail slot for its teachers to one that offers shared office space and telephones to its faculty. How might the cultures of these two schools differ? How could the physical arrangements in an organization cultivate teamwork? The way a school addresses these issues helps define its culture.

THE PROCESSES OF ORGANIZATIONAL BEHAVIOR

We now explore areas of organizational behavior that deal with the way we perceive events or other people, the way we understand the events and people we perceive, the way our past experiences and acquisition of knowledge and information influence this description and diagnosis, and the way we form attitudes about the situations based on our perceptions, understanding, and experience. These four processes are referred to as perception, attribution, learning, and attitude formation. Understanding them greatly enhances an administrator's ability to influence the school's culture.

PERCEPTION

Perception is the process by which each person senses reality and comes to a particular understanding or view. It is an active process that results in different people having somewhat different, even contradictory, views or understandings of the same event or person. Rarely do different observers describe events or persons in exactly the same way. Often, administrators and their subordinates, coworkers, or supervisors see and describe the same situation differently.

PERCEPTUAL DISTORTIONS

Perceptions sometimes suffer from inaccuracies or distortions. Although such biases are normal and human, they can have significant consequences when administrators or other members of the institution base action upon potentially invalid distortions. We discuss stereotyping, the halo effect, projection, and the self-fulfilling prophecy as examples. Additional distortions include suppression, repression, denial, displacement and rationalization.[2]

Stereotyping

Stereotyping occurs when an individual attributes behaviors or attitudes to a person on the basis of the group or category to which that person belongs. "Women teachers can't control a class" and "Principals are all dictators" illustrate stereotyping. We frequently stereotype members of ethnic groups, women, administrators, faculty, and nonprofessional personnel.

Why does stereotyping occur? Often individuals do not gather sufficient data about others to describe their behaviors or attitudes accurately. They may look for shortcuts to describe certain phenomenon without spending the time to analyze them completely. Alternatively, some individuals have personal biases against certain groups of individuals. Historical attitudes toward certain cultural groups may result in stereotypes. Americans may have certain views of Europeans and different views of Japanese, based on their historical experiences with the two groups. Using stereotypes reduces the accuracy of our perceptions about these groups.

Halo Effect

The halo effect refers to an individual's letting one salient feature of a person dominate the evaluation of that individual. Being willing to volunteer for extra projects, for example, can cause an administrator to evaluate a teacher as highly competent in the classroom. A neat personal appearance can cause a person to be judged as precise in his or her work and very well organized.

The halo effect frequently occurs in assessments of teacher performance. Individuals may be judged on the basis of one trait, for example, promptness, neatness, or enthusiasm, rather than on a composite of traits and skills over a period of time.[3]

Projection

Have you ever heard someone say, "My principal is prejudiced; my supervisor doesn't like women" or "my superintendent doesn't like minorities"? These observations about these administrators may be accurate, but they may also be a reflection of the teachers' prejudices. Or consider the principal who hesitantly approaches a prospective student's parent, feeling that the parent will not think that the school will offer a quality education to the child. The principal may be seeing his or her own attitudes or feelings about the school in the parent's response, whether or not the parent really feels that way.

Projection refers to an individual's attributing his or her own attitudes or feelings to another person. Individuals use projection as a defense mechanism, to transfer blame to another person, or to provide protection from their own unacceptable feelings. Individuals frequently attribute their own prejudices against minorities, supervisors, or employees, for example, to the other party. Hence, projection and its dysfunctional consequences can increase as the work force becomes more diverse; individuals who lack understanding or mistrust people who are different from themselves may project these insecurities onto others.

Projection involves an emotional biasing of perceptions. Fear, hatred, uncertainty, anger, love, deceit, or distrust may influence an individual's perceptions. In union–management relations, for example, each side attributes feelings of mistrust to the other side. Management might state that the union mistrusts them, when, in fact, it is management that mistrusts the union. They project their own feelings onto the other group, representing them as that group's feelings.

Self-Fulfilling Prophecy

In many situations, the participants expect certain behaviors from other participants. They then see these behaviors as occurring whether or not they actually do. Their expectations become self-fulfilling prophecies. They may expect workers to be lazy, bossy, or tardy; then they perceive they actually are lazy, bossy, or tardy. These expectations may be associated with stereotyping, the halo effect, or projection.

Our expectations influence and bias our perceptions of others, reducing their accuracy; they also have been shown to influence the performance of those of whom we have expectations. We are all familiar with the many studies that have linked teacher expectations and student achievement. If a teacher expects a minority student to fail, oftentimes the student does fail. Whereas, if a teacher expects all children to achieve, the children usually achieve.

DEALING WITH DISTORTIONS

How can we reduce dysfunctional perceptual distortions in organizations? First, individuals must gather sufficient information about other people's behavior and attitudes to encourage more realistic perceptions. Administrators, for example, must judge an individual's performance on his or her observed behavior, rather than on the behavior of a group to which the person belongs. Second, administrators must check conclusions they draw to ensure their validity. Third, they must differentiate between facts and assumptions in determining the basis of their perceptions. Fourth, they must distinguish among various aspects of an individual's behavior, rather than grouping even superficially related aspects. They must separate appearance from performance, productivity from attendance, personality from creativity. Fifth, to eliminate or reduce projection, individuals must first identify their true feelings. Do they feel anger, uncertainty, and mistrust? After recognizing these feelings, administrators must repeatedly assess whether and how they are influencing their perceptions of others.

PERCEPTION IN A MULTICULTURAL ENVIRONMENT

Cultural differences exist in how individuals process information; they affect the cognitive map, or the content and structure of the schemata used to understand the environment and influence behavior. They affect the stimuli we select to perceive, the way we organize them, and how we interpret them. Our cultural background may cause us to distort our perceptions in predictable or unpredictable ways.[4]

Cross-cultural misperceptions occur for at least four reasons. First, we have subconscious cultural blinders that cause us to interpret events in other countries and other cultures as if they were occurring in our own. Second, we lack a complete understanding of our own culture and its influence on our behavior. Third, we assume people are more similar to us than they are. Finally, and in general, our parochialism and general lack of knowledge about other cultures contribute to our misperceptions. An awareness of these differences can help us consider and represent the perspectives of several different observers when we describe events or people. If we can incorporate many people's perceptions into an account of a person or event, our description should be more accurate than if we attend only to our own perceptions.

THE ATTRIBUTION PROCESS

The need to determine why events occur is common and is inherent in the diagnostic approach that good administrators often take toward problem solving. Many of us, whether consciously or not, first ponder the reasons for many events and then decide why the events occurred. In this way, we attribute causes to the events. We move from description to diagnosis. As might be expected, different people often attribute a different cause to the same event.

Attribution theorists and researchers have studied the process of determining the causes of specific events, the responsibility for particular outcomes, and the personal qualities of individuals participating in the situation. One researcher has suggested that this process occurs in three stages. First, a person observes or is told about another person's action. Second, having identified the action, we determine whether the observed behavior was intended or accidental. Did the change in performance occur on purpose, or did it just happen by accident? If we assume that a decline in test scores, for example, occurred accidentally, we attribute its causes to fate, luck, accident, or a similar uncontrollable phenomenon. If, however, we assume that the decline was intended or controllable, we then move to stage 3. We question whether situational causes or personal characteristics explain the behavior. We might consider, for example, that the new curriculum was the major explanation of the change in performance; if so, we will attribute the decline to situational factors. If, on the other hand, we feel that laziness or ineptitude influenced performance, then we are likely to conclude that personal dispositions motivated the change. Although both situational and personal factors may have influenced the change in performance, we often simplify our understanding and attend primarily to only one cause.

ATTRIBUTIONAL BIASES

Attributions and attributional errors occur in predictable ways, based on a variety of factors. An individual can participate in a situation as an actor or an observer. Research about such attributions indicates that an actor in a situation emphasizes the situational causes of a behavior and deemphasizes the personal factors to protect his or her self-image and ego; the observer does the reverse. For example, a student who does poorly in a test might attribute his or her poor performance to the teacher's inability to get the subject across. Whereas, the teacher, being the observer in this situation, might attribute the student's poor performance to poor study habits.

Research has suggested that in performance appraisals in general, subordinates attribute performance more to situational causes, while administrators attributed subordinate behavior to personal causes. In addition, actors are less likely to assume moral responsibility for an action because they attribute it to external causes. Recognizing this bias should alert administrators to possible inaccuracies in their attributions and diagnoses. These misattributions become particularly significant in the conduct of performance reviews.[5]

ATTRIBUTION AND LOCUS OF CONTROL

Attribution and the concept of locus of control are closely related. Locus of control is the feeling an individual has about whether he or she is in control of his or her own destiny. Whether one believes that internal or external factors affect future events determines whether one has an internal or external locus of control. Those with an internal locus of control believe that future events are determined by their own individual abilities and personal qualities, while those with an external locus of control attribute future outcomes to factors outside of their control. Thus, the student who attributes a poor performance in a test to the teacher's inability to get the subject across can be said have an external locus of control, while the student who attributes the poor performance to his or her own lack of preparation would tend to have an internal locus of control. The objective, then, for school administrators would be to develop a strong internal locus of control in both themselves and their staffs.[6]

THE LEARNING PROCESS

In addition to perception and attribution, learning, which refers to the acquisition of skills, knowledge, ability, or attitudes, influences both description and diagnoses of organizational behavior. In this section, we focus on the way individuals learn, beginning with three models of learning and concluding with the administrative implications of learning.

THE BEHAVIORIST APPROACH

Behaviorists emphasize external influences and the power of rewards in learning. They emphasize the link between a given stimulus and response. Recall Pavlov's ground-breaking work with dogs. He noted that, upon presentation of powdered meat blown through a tube (unconditioned stimulus) to a dog, the dog salivated (unconditioned response). The ringing of a bell (neutral stimulus) yielded no salivation responses. After pairing the ringing bell with the piece of meat several times, Pavlov then rang the bell without the meat, and the dog salivated (conditioned response). In classical conditioning, after repeated pairing of neutral and unconditioned stimuli, solitary presentation of the neutral stimulus led to a conditioned response.[7]

Operant conditioning extends classical conditioning to focus on the consequences of a behavior. While a stimulus can still cue a response behavior, the desired or undesired consequence that follows the behavior determines whether the behavior will recur. For example, an individual who receives a bonus (a positive consequence) after creative performance (behavior) on a work assignment (stimulus) is more likely to repeat the creative behavior than if his or her performance is ignored (a negative consequence).

THE COGNITIVE APPROACH

In contrast to the behavior-reinforcement links that are central to behaviorist theories, cognitive theorists emphasize the internal mental processes involved in gaining new insights. They view learning as occurring from the joining of various cues in the environment into a mental map. In early cognitive experiments, rats learned to run through a maze to reach a goal of food. Repeated trials would cause a rat to develop and strengthen cognitive connections that identified the correct path to the goal.[8]

Employees, too, can develop a cognitive map that shows the path to a specific goal. In this case, the cognitive processes join the stimulus to result in a given behavior. On-the-job training, like a new teacher induction process, should result in a new cognitive map of job performance for junior teachers.

SOCIAL LEARNING APPROACH

Extending beyond both behavioral and cognitive learning theories, social learning theory integrates the behaviorist and cognitive approaches with the idea of modeling or imitating behaviors. Learners first watch others who act as models, next develop a mental picture of the behavior and its consequences, and finally try the behavior. If positive consequences result, the learner repeats the behavior; if negative consequences occur, no repetition occurs. The learning impact occurs when the subject tries the behavior and experiences a favorable result, as in the behaviorist approach. At the same time, the learner's development of a cognitive image of the situation incorporates a basic aspect of cognitive learning. The existence of social learning makes it important that teachers take their responsibility of acting as exemplars for the students very seriously. In addition, administrators need to model the behavior that they expect of the faculty.[9]

MANAGERIAL IMPLICATIONS OF LEARNING

How can school administrators encourage their own and others' learning in the workplace? They can ensure that appropriate conditions for learning exist; providing appropriate stimuli (e.g., professional development materials) should facilitate acquisition of the skills or attitudes desired. Administrators should reinforce desired learned behaviors. They should also provide environmental cues that encourage learning; structuring a context that supports learning is essential. In effect, just as we advise teachers to adapt their teaching styles to the variety of learning styles of their students, administrators must adapt their management styles to the variety of learning styles that are present on their faculties.

Administrators can use the following modeling strategy, for example. First, the administrator should identify the goal or target behaviors that will lead to improved performance. For example, a more extensive use of cooperative learning activities will lead to improving students' social skills. Second, the administrator must select the appropriate model and determine whether to present the model through a live demonstration, videotape, other media, or a combination of all of these. Third, the administrator must be sure the teachers are capable of meeting the technical skill requirements of the target behavior. For example, further training might be necessary. Fourth, the administrator must structure a favorable and positive learning environment to increase the likelihood that the teachers will learn the new behavior and act in the desired way. Starting cooperative learning with a particularly skilled teacher and a cooperative group of students will ensure success. Fifth, administrators must model the target behavior and carry out supporting activities, such as role playing. Conducting a faculty meeting using cooperative learning techniques would be an example of such a strategy. Sixth, they should positively reinforce reproduction of the target behaviors both in training and in the workplace. Teacher-of-month awards are an example of this strategy. Once the target behaviors are reproduced, administrators must maintain and strengthen them through a system of rewards until the behavior is institutionalized; that is, it becomes part of the school culture.

DEVELOPING PRODUCTIVE ATTITUDES

Another aspect of organizational behavior and culture is attitude formation. An attitude is a consistent predisposition to respond to various aspects of people, situations, or objects that we infer from a person's behavior or expressed attitude, as well as from other cognitive, affective, or connotative responses. Attitudes are pervasive and predict behavior toward their objects. We might, for example, determine an individuals' job satisfaction by inferring it from his or her general demeanor on the job or by asking the person to describe this attitude. We often use attitude surveys or other collections of attitude scales to assess individuals' attitudes toward their job, coworkers, supervisor, or the school or school system at large.[10]

COMPONENTS OF ATTITUDES

Research has suggested that attitudes have three components: cognitive, affective, and behavioral. The cognitive component includes the beliefs an individual has about a certain person object or situation. These learned beliefs, such as "All students can learn," serve as an antecedent to specific attitudes. Although we have many beliefs, only some are important enough to lead to significant attitudes. The affective component refers to the person's feeling that results from his or her beliefs about a person, object, or situation. A person may feel anger or frustration because he or she feels hard work deserves promotion and recognition and the person has worked hard but not been recognized in some way. The affective component becomes stronger as an individual has more often and directly experienced a focal object, person, or situation and as the feeling is expressed more often. The behavioral component is the individual's behavior that occurs as a result of his or her feeling about the focal person, object, or situation. A teacher may complain, request a transfer, or lower productivity because he or she feels dissatisfied with the work.[11]

A more recent way of looking at attitudes takes a sociocognitive approach. It considers an attitude as a representation of an individual's interaction with his or her social environment. The object of an attitude is represented as a member of a category in a person's memory. Then an individual uses the attitude to help evaluate an object, deciding, for example, whether it is good or bad, positive or negative, favored or not and then determining the strategy to take toward it.

ATTITUDES IN A MULTICULTURAL WORKPLACE

The more diverse the work force, the more likely it is that individuals will have an array of attitudes. Their beliefs, formed in large part from their socioeconomic backgrounds and other experiences, could vary significantly. Recent research suggests significant changes in attitudes toward various national and racial groups, as well a various gender roles.

As the work force becomes multinational, diagnosing the basis of attitudes and predicting their consequent behaviors becomes more problematic. According to one researcher, national cultures have been described as differing, for example, on four dimensions, which he labels *power distance, uncertainty avoidance, individualism*, and *masculinity*. Power distance is the extent to which a society accepts the fact that power in institutions and organizations is distributed unequally. Uncertainty avoidance refers to the extent to which a society responds to the potential occurrence of uncertain and ambiguous situations by providing career stability, establishing formal rules, not tolerating deviant ideas and behaviors, and believing in absolute truths and the attainment of expertise. Individualism implies a loosely knit social framework in which people are supposed to take care of themselves and their immediate families only. The opposite, collectivism, is characterized by a tight social framework in which people distinguish between in-groups and out-groups. Masculinity is the extent to which the dominant values in society reflect traditionally masculine behaviors, such as assertiveness and the acquisition of money and things, and a lesser concern for relationships. As a result of variations on these dimensions, interpersonal processes, group behavior, and organizational structure vary in different cultures.[12]

IMPLICATIONS OF SCHOOL CULTURE

Anyone who has visited numerous schools develops a sense of their different personalities, a concept frequently used to describe an organization's particular culture. Walking through a school, an observer can see physical manifestations of an underlying set of values; perhaps a huge trophy case immediately facing the visitors entrance, classroom desks bolted to the floor, a clean campus, football and basketball programs that overshadow math and science programs, faculty and staff constantly patrolling the halls, and so forth.

All of these mentioned here are tangible aspects of the school's culture. The intangible aspects of a school's culture can and often do parallel those values cited by Peters and Waterman in their influential book *In Search of Excellence*. In America's most successful companies, they found a number of consistent values to be held, such as: There is no substitute for superior quality and service; be the best; pay attention to detail; stay close to the client; do what you do best; work through people; facilitate innovation; and be tolerant of failed attempts.

Schools attempting to develop shared values are often illustrated by signs frequently found around buildings: "Knowledge Is Power"; "Wildcat Pride"; "Education Is About Alternatives"; "Just Say No"; and "All Children Can Achieve."

Administrators can influence the school's culture in a positive way. First, however, they must be aware of the importance of the school's culture and the components of it. If the administrator has a thorough knowledge of the school's culture, he or she can set about influencing it. Administrators can do so by exercising their leadership abilities and by developing a clear and appropriate educational vision. By employing some of the leadership strategies that we explore later in this book, a skilled administrator can positively influence the school's culture and bring about changes that can result in greater productivity, which, in educational terms, translates into all children reaching their academic potential.

SUMMARY

One of the administrator's first steps in effectively leading a school toward fulfilling its potential is to "know the territory." In more technical terms, knowing the territory means knowing how the school and the school system is structured (organizational structure) and how it behaves (organizational culture).

Over time, various theories of organizational structure have evolved. Schools have adopted different aspects of these theories. Today, schools are organized around classical organization theory, social systems theory, and open system theory. A few more-enlightened school districts use aspects of all three theories, adopting appropriate pieces of each approach depending on their individual and local needs. These school systems can be said to be structured according to the contingency theory of organization.

Organizational behaviors, like the shared beliefs, expectations, values, and norms of conduct, make up the school's culture. A school's culture also includes the myths and stories and the rituals and ceremonies that characterize the school.

If an administrator is to impact the school's culture in a positive manner, he or she must be keenly aware of the processes of organizational behavior, such as perception, attribution, learning, and attitude formation. Perceptual distortions, such as stereotyping, the halo effect, projection, and the self-fulfilling prophecy, need to be understood.

Attributional biases, the various learning styles prevalent among the faculty and staff, and how attitudes are formed are all important aspects of how the school culture develops. Understanding these processes can go a long way in enabling a school administrator to become an effective and successful leader. If administrators strive to lead rather than merely manage a school, the administrator needs to continually improve his or her school. Improvement requires change and effecting change requires a thorough knowledge of the school culture and insight into how to influence it for the better. Next, we take another step toward understanding the requirements of effective school leadership as we examine the concepts of leadership and leadership styles.

CASE STUDY 2.1: LINCOLN ELEMENTARY SCHOOL

Lincoln Elementary School is located in a large urban school district. Currently the school serves 400 students from K–5. The school's student body is predominantly African American. The school is divided into upper and lower schools; the upper school is identified as fourth and fifth grade. The lower school has kindergarten through third grade.

Lincoln has five Montessori classrooms. These classes comprise two Head Start preschool classrooms, one kindergarten, and two classes of first, second, and third grades that are combined. All of these classes are equipped with Montessori materials and certified Montessori teachers.

THE PROBLEM

At issue this year at Lincoln Elementary School has been a concern that the school may be taken over by the state because of low literacy skills scores, as measured by the state's standardized testing program and by the president's No Child Left Behind standards. The teachers seem to be working diligently with a new district-imposed curriculum aimed at improving learning and, in turn, improving the test scores. In fact, the scores have been improving slightly throughout the current school year. Supplies, however, have been scarce and the principal has been so anxious regarding the test scores that she has become more autocratic in her leadership style. The combination of limited resources and the principal's leadership approach have caused a frustration among the faculty and staff.

THE CULTURE

The culture of Lincoln Elementary School is a rather complex combination of stress, denial, enthusiasm, and a strong work ethic. The overwhelming stressors are the implementation of a new curriculum and the specter of being immersed in the high-stakes testing environment created, in part, by No Child Left Behind. As a result, the teaching staff has had the highest staff illness rate in the past five years.

Another influence of the school's culture is the implementation of a new truancy policy. Now, parents who allow their child to stay home for more than three consecutive days are called and notified that someone will arrive at their door step the following day if the child does not report to school. This approach has decreased the instances of truancy, but has alienated some parents. It is important that the entire school community cooperate and collaborate in addressing the educational deficiencies of the school and the school district. It is important that the school culture is trusting and respectful if improvement is to be had. It is also important that the culture be tolerant of change because it will only be through such reform that significant improvements can be made. The principal is aware that the school culture is not ideal for what lies ahead. What to do; what to do?

NOTES

1. Judith R. Gordan, *A Diagnostic Approach to Organizational Behavior* (Boston: Allyn and Bacon, 1993).

2. S. L. Brodsky, *The Psychology of Adjustment and Well-being* (New York: Holt, Rinehart and Winston, 1988).

3. M. E. Heilman and M. H. Stopeck, Being Attractive, Advantage or Disadvantage? Performance Evaluations and Recommended Personnel Actions as a Function of Appearance, Sex, and Job Type, *Organizational Behavior and Human Decision Processes* 35 (1985): 202–215.

4. S. G. Redding, Cognition as an Aspect of Culture and in Relation to Management Processes: An Exploratory View of the Chinese Case, *Journal of Management Studies* 17, no. 2 (1990): 127–148; J. B. Shaw, A Cognitive Categorization Model for the Study of Intercultural Management, *Academy of Management Review* 15, no. 4 (1990): 626–645.

5. E. K. Shaver, *An Introduction to Attribution Processes* (Cambridge, Mass.: Winthrop, 1975).

6. H. H. Kelley, Attribution Theory in Social Psychology, *Nebraska Symposium on Motivation* 14 (1967): 192–241.

7. I. Pavlov, *Conditioned Reflexes: An Investigation of the Physiological Activity of the Cerebral Cortex*, trans. and ed. G. V. Anrep (London: Oxford University Press, 1927). Comparable work done in the United States by J. B. Watson is described in *Behaviorism* (New York: Norton, 1924).

8. E. C. Tolman, *Purposive Behavior in Animals and Men* (New York: Appleton-Century-Crofts, 1932).

9. A. Bandura, *Social Learning Theory* (Englewood Cliffs, N.J.: Prentice-Hall, 1978).

10. G. Greenwald, Why Are Attitudes Important?, in *Attitude Structure and Function*, ed. A. R. Pratkanis, S. J. Breckler, and A. G. Greenwald (Hillsdale, N.J.: Erlbaum, 1989), 1–10.

11. S. Oskamp, *Attitudes and Opinions*, 2nd ed. (Englewood Cliffs, N.J.: Prentice Hall, 1991) offers a good overview of the measurement of attitudes.

12. G. Hofstede, Motivation, Leadership, and Organization: Do American Theories Apply Abroad? *Organizational Dynamics* 9 (Summer 1980): 45–46.

⚫3

ORGANIZATIONAL LEADERSHIP

The effective functioning of social systems from the local PTA to the United States of America is assumed to be dependent on the quality of their leadership.

—Victor H. Vroom

Leadership is offered as a solution for most of the problems of organizations everywhere. Schools will work, we are told, if principals provide strong instructional leadership. Around the world, administrators and managers say that their organizations would thrive if only senior management provided strategy, vision, and real leadership. Though the call for leadership is universal, there is much less clarity about what the term means.

Historically, researchers in this field have searched for the one best leadership style that would be most effective. Current thought is that there is no one best style. Rather, a combination of styles depending on the situation the leader finds himself or herself in has been found to be more appropriate. To understand the evolution of leadership theory thought, we take an historical approach and trace the progress of leadership theory, beginning with the trait perspective of leadership and moving to the more current contingency theories of leadership.

THE TRAIT THEORY

Trait theory suggests that we can evaluate leadership and propose ways of leading effectively by considering whether an individual possesses certain personality traits, social traits, and physical characteristics. Popular in the 1940s and 1950s, trait theory attempted to predict which individuals successfully became leaders and then whether they were effective. Leaders differ from nonleaders in their drive, desire to lead, honesty and integrity, self-confidence, cognitive ability, and knowledge of the business that they are in. Even the traits judged necessary for top-, middle-, and low-level management differed among leaders of different countries; for example, U.S. and British leaders valued resourcefulness, the Japanese intuition, and the Dutch imagination, but for lower and middle managers only.[1]

The obvious question is, can you think of any individuals who are effective leaders, but who lack one or more of these characteristics? Chances are that you can. Skills and ability to implement the vision are necessary to transform traits into leadership behavior. Individual capability, which is a function of background predispositions, preferences, cognitive complexity, and technical, human relations, and conceptual skills, also contribute.

The trait approach has more historical than practical interest to managers and administrators, even though recent research has once again tied leadership effectiveness to leader traits. One study of senior management jobs suggests that effective leadership requires a broad knowledge of and solid relations within the industry and the company, an excellent reputation, a strong track record, a keen mind, strong interpersonal skills, high integrity, high energy, and a strong drive to lead. In addition, some view the transformational perspective described later in this chapter as a natural evolution of the earlier trait perspective.

THE BEHAVIORAL PERSPECTIVE

The limitations in the ability of traits to predict effective leadership caused researchers during the 1950s to view a person's behavior rather than that individual's personal traits as a way of increasing leadership effectiveness. This view also paved the way for later situational theories.

The types of leadership behaviors investigated typically fell into two categories: production oriented and employee oriented. Production-oriented
leadership, also called *concern for production, initiating structure*, or
task-focused leadership, involves acting primarily to get the task done.
An administrator who tells his or her department chair to do "everything
he or she needs to do to get the curriculum developed on time for the
start of school" demonstrates production-oriented leadership. So does
an administrator who uses an autocratic style or fails to involve workers
in any aspect of decision making. Employee-oriented leadership, also
called *concern for people or consideration*, focuses on supporting the individual workers in their activities and involving the workers in decision
making. A principal who demonstrates great concern for his or her
teachers' satisfaction with their duties and commitment to their work
has an employee-oriented leadership style.[2]

Studies in leadership at Ohio State University, which classified individuals' style as initiating structure or consideration, examined the link
between style and grievance rate, performance, and turnover. Initiating
structure reflects the degree to which the leader structures his or her
own role and subordinates' roles toward accomplishing the group's goal
through scheduling work, assigning employees to tasks, and maintaining
standards of performance. *Consideration* refers to the degree to which
the leader emphasizes individuals' needs through two-way communication, respect for subordinates' ideas, mutual trust between leader and
subordinates, and consideration of subordinates' feelings. Although leaders can choose the style to fit the outcomes they desire, in fact, to achieve
desirable outcomes on all three dimensions of performance, grievance
rate, and turnover, the research suggested that managers should strive to
demonstrate both initiating structure and consideration.[3]

A series of leadership studies at the University of Michigan, which
looked at managers with an employee orientation and a production orientation, yielded similar results. In these studies, which related differences in high-productivity and low-productivity work groups to differences in supervisors, highly productive supervisors spent more time in
planning departmental work and in supervising their employees; they
spent less time in working alongside and performing the same tasks as
subordinates, accorded their subordinates more freedom in specific task
performance, and tended to be employee oriented.

A thirty-year research study in Japan examined performance and maintenance leadership behaviors. Performance here refers specifically to forming and reaching group goals through fast work speed; outcomes of high quality, accuracy, and quantity; and observation of rules. Maintenance behaviors preserve the group's social stability by dealing with subordinates' feelings, reducing stress, providing comfort, and showing appreciation. The Japanese, according to this and other studies, prefer leadership high on both dimensions over performance-dominated behavior except when work is done in short-term project groups, subordinates are prone to anxiety, or effective performance calls for very low effort.

MANAGERIAL ROLES THEORY

A study of chief executive officers by Henry Mintzberg suggested a different way of looking at leadership. He observed that managerial work encompasses ten roles: three that focus on interpersonal contact—(1) figurehead, (2) leader, (3) liaison; three that involve mainly information processing—(4) monitor, (5) disseminator, (6) spokesman; and four related to decision making—(7) entrepreneur, (8) disturbance handler, (9) resource allocator, and (10) negotiator. Note that almost all roles would include activities that could be construed as leadership—influencing others toward a particular goal. In addition, most of these roles can apply to nonmanagerial positions as well as managerial ones. The role approach resembles the behavioral and trait perspectives because all three call for specific types of behavior independent of the situation; however, the role approach is more compatible with the situation approach and has been shown to be more valid than either the behavioral or trait perspective.[4]

Though not all managers will perform every role, some diversity of role performance must occur. Managers can diagnose their own and others' role performance and then offer strategies for altering it. The choice roles will depend to some extent on the manager's specific job description and the situation in question. For example, managing individual performance and instructing subordinates are less important for middle managers than for first-line supervisors, and less important for executives than for either lower level of manager.

EARLY SITUATIONAL THEORIES

Contingency or situational models differ from the earlier trait and behavioral models in asserting that no single way of leading works in all situations. Rather, appropriate behavior depends on the circumstances at a given time. Effective managers diagnose the situation, identify the leadership style that will be most effective, and then determine whether they can implement the required style. Early situational research suggested that subordinate, supervisor, and task considerations affect the appropriate leadership style in a given situation. The precise aspects of each dimension that influence the most effective leadership style vary.

THEORY X AND THEORY Y

One of the older situational theories, McGregor's Theory X/Theory Y formulation, calls for a leadership style based on individuals' assumptions about other individuals, together with characteristics of the individual, the task, the organization, and the environment. Although managers have many styles, Theories X and Y have received the greatest attention. Theory X managers assume that people are lazy, extrinsically motivated, and incapable of self-discipline or self-control, and that they want security and no responsibility in their jobs. Theory Y managers assume people do not inherently dislike work, are intrinsically motivated, exert self-control, and seek responsibility. A Theory X manager, because of his or her limited view of the world, has only one leadership style available, that is, autocratic. A Theory Y manager has a wide range of styles in his or her repertoire. This theory illustrates the way assumptions influence action tendencies, which together with internal and external modifiers should prescribe effective leadership behavior.[5]

How can an administrator use McGregor's theory for ensuring leadership effectiveness? What prescription would McGregor offer for improving the situation? If an administrator had Theory X assumptions, he would suggest that the administrator change them and would facilitate this change by sending the administrator to a management development program. If a manager had Theory Y assumptions, McGregor would advise a diagnosis of the situation to ensure that the selected style matched the administrator's assumptions and action tendencies, as well as the internal and external influences on the situation.

FREDERICK FIEDLER'S THEORY

While McGregor's theory provided a transition from behavioral to situational theories, Frederick Fiedler developed and tested the first leadership theory explicitly called a *contingency* or *situational model*. He argued that changing an individual's leadership style is quite difficult, but that organizations should put individuals in situations that fit with their style. Fiedler's theory suggests that managers can choose between two styles: task oriented and relationship oriented. Then the nature of leader–member relations, task structure, and position power of the leader influences whether a task-oriented or a relationship-oriented leadership style is more likely to be effective. *Leader–member relations* refer to the extent to which the group trusts and respects the leader and will follow the leader's directions. *Task structure* describes the degree to which the task is clearly specified and defined or structured, as opposed to ambiguous or unstructured. *Position power* means the extent to which the leader has official power, that is, the potential or actual ability to influence others in a desired direction owing to the position he or she holds in the organization.[6]

The style recommended as most effective for each combination of these three situational factors is based on the degree of control or influence the leader can exert in his or her leadership position. In general, high-control situations (I, II, and III) call for task-oriented leadership because they allow the leader to take charge. Low-control situations (VII and VIII) also call for task-oriented leadership because they require, rather than allow, the leader to take charge. Moderate-control situations (IV, V, VI, and VII), in contrast, call for relationship-oriented leadership because the situations challenge leaders to get the cooperation of their subordinates. Despite extensive research to support the theory, critics have questioned the reliability of the measurement of leadership style and the range and appropriateness of the three situational components. This theory, however, is particularly applicable for those who believe that individuals are born with a certain management style, rather than the management style being learned or flexible.[7]

CONTEMPORARY SITUATIONAL LEADERSHIP

Current research suggests that the effect of leader behaviors on performance is altered by such intervening variables as the effort of subordinates, their ability to perform their jobs, the clarity of their job responsibilities, the organization of the work, the cooperation and cohesiveness of the group, the sufficiency of resources and support provided to the group, and the coordination of work group activities with those of other subunits. Thus, leaders must respond to these and broader cultural differences in choosing an appropriate style. A leader-environment-follower interaction theory of leadership notes that effective leaders first analyze deficiencies in the follower's ability, motivation, role perception, and work environment that inhibit performance and then act to eliminate these deficiencies.[8]

PATH-GOAL THEORY

According to path-goal theory, the leader attempts to influence subordinates' perceptions of goals and the path to achieve them. Leaders can then choose among four styles of leadership: directive, supportive, participative, and achievement oriented. In selecting a style, the leader acts to strengthen the expectancy, instrumentality, and valence of a situation, respectively, by providing better technology or training for the employees; reinforcing desired behaviors with pay, praise, or promotion; and ensuring that the employees value the rewards they receive.[9]

Choosing a style requires a quality diagnosis of the situation to decide what leadership behaviors would be most effective in attaining the desired outcomes. The appropriate leadership style is influenced first by subordinates' characteristics, particularly the subordinates' abilities and the likelihood that the leader's behavior will cause subordinates' satisfaction now or in the future; and second by the environment, including the subordinates' tasks, the formal authority system, the primary work group, and organizational culture. According to this theory, the appropriate style for an administrator depends on his or her subordinates' skills, knowledge, and abilities, as well as their attitudes toward the administrator. It also depends on the nature of the activities, the lines of authority in the organization, the integrity of their work group, and the task technology involved. The most desirable leadership style helps the individual achieve satisfaction, meet personal needs, and accomplish goals, while complementing the subordinates' abilities and the characteristics of the situation.

Application of the path-goal theory, then, requires first an assessment of the situation, particularly its participants and environment, and second, a determination of the most congruent leadership style. Even though the research about path-goal theory has yielded mixed results, it can provide a leader with help in selecting an effective leadership style.

THE VROOM–YETTON MODEL

The Vroom-Yetton theory involves a procedure for determining the extent to which leaders should involve subordinates in the decision-making process. The manager can choose one of five approaches that range from individual problem solving with available information to joint problem solving to delegation of problem-solving responsibility. Table 3.1 summarizes the possibilities.

Selection of the appropriate decision process involves assessing six factors: (1) the problem's quality requirement, (2) the location of information about the problem (3) the structure of the problem, (4) the likely acceptance of the decision by those affected, (5) the commonality of organizational goals, and (6) the likely conflict regarding possible problem solutions. Figure 3.1 illustrates the original normative model, expressed as a decision tree. To make a decision, the leader asks each question, A through H, corresponding to each box encountered, from left to right, unless questions may be skipped because the response to the previous question leads to a later one. For example, a no response to question A allows questions B and C to be skipped; a yes response to question B after a yes response to question A allows question C to be skipped. Reaching the end of one branch of the tree results in identification of a problem type (numbered 1 through 18) with an accompanying set of feasible decision processes. When the set of feasible processes for group problems includes more than one process (e.g., a "no response" to each question results in problem type 1, for which every decision style is feasible), final selection of the single approach can use either a minimum number of hours (group processes AI, AII, CI, CII, and GII are preferred in that order), as secondary criteria. A manager who wishes to make the decision in the shortest time possible, and for whom all processes are appropriate, will choose AI (solving the problem himself or herself using available information) over any other process. A manager who wishes to maximize subordinate involvement in the decision making as a training and development tool, for example, will choose DI or GII (delegating the problem to the subordinate, or together with subordinates reaching a decision) if all processes are feasible and if time is not limited. Similar choices can be made when analyzing individual problems. Research has shown that decisions made using processes from the feasible set result in more effective outcomes than those not included.[11]

Suppose, for example, the teacher evaluation instrument in your institution was in need of revision. Using the decision tree, we would ask the first question: Is there a quality requirement such that one solution is likely to be more rational than another? Our answer would have to be yes. Do I have sufficient information to make a high-quality decision? The answer is no. Is the problem structured? Yes. Is acceptance of the decision by subordinates crucial to effective implementation? Yes. If I were to make the decision myself, is it reasonably certain that it would be accepted by my subordinates? No. Do subordinates share the organizational goals to be attained in solving this problem? Yes. Is conflict among subordinates likely in preferred solutions? Yes. Do subordinates have sufficient information to make a high-quality decision? Yes.

Following this procedure, the decision tree indicates that GII would be the proper approach to revising the teacher evaluation form. GII indicates that the leader should share the problem with his or her faculty. Together, they generate and evaluate alternatives and attempt to reach agreement on a solution. The leader's role is much like that of a chairperson coordinating the discussion, keeping it focused on the problem, and ensuring that the crucial issues are discussed. You do not try to influence the group to adopt "your" solution, and you are willing to accept and implement any solution that has the support of the entire faculty. We take a further look at the Vroom–Yetton model when we discuss decision making later in this book.

The recent reformulation of this model uses the same decision processes, AI, AII, CI, CII, GII, GI, DI, as the original model, as well as the criteria of decision quality, decision commitment, time, and sub-

Table 3.1 Decision-Making Processes

For Individual Problems	For Group Problems
AI You solve the problem or make the decision yourself, using information available to you at that time.	**AI** You solve the problem or make the decision yourself, using information available to you at the time.
AII You obtain any necessary information from the subordinate, then decide on the solution to the problem yourself. You may or may not tell the subordinate what the problem is, in getting the information from him. The role played by your subordinate in making the decision is clearly one of providing specific information that you request, rather then generating or evaluating alternative solutions.	**AII** You obtain any necessary information from subordinates, then decide on the solution to the problem yourself. You may or may not tell subordinates what the problem is, in getting the information from them. The role played by your subordinates in making the decision is clearly one of providing specific information that you request, rather than generating or evaluating solutions.
CI You share the problem with the relevant subordinate, getting his ideas and suggestions. Then, you make the decision. This decision may or may not reflect your subordinate's influence.	**CI** You share the problem with the relevant subordinates individually, getting their ideas and suggestions without bringing them together as a group. They you make the decision. This decision may or may not reflect your subordinates' influence.
GI You share the problem with one of your subordinates, and together you analyze the problem and arrive at a mutually satisfactory solution in an atmosphere of free and open exchange of information and ideas. You both contribute to the resolution of the problem with the relative contribution of each being dependent on knowledge rather than formal authority.	**CII** You share the problem with your subordinates in a group meeting. In this meeting you obtain their ideas and suggestions. Then, you make the decision, which may or may not reflect your subordinates' influence.
DI You delegate the problem to one of your subordinates, providing him or her with any relevant information that you possess, but giving responsibility for solving the problem independently. Any solution that the person reaches will receive your support.	**GII** You share the problem with your subordinates as a group. Together you generate and evaluate alternatives and attempt to reach agreement (consensus) on a solution. Your role is much like that of chairman, coordinating the discussion, keeping it focused on the problem, and making sure that the crucial issues are discussed. You do not try to influence the group to adopt "your" solution and are willing to accept and implement any solution that has the support of the entire group.

ordinate development. It differs by expanding the range of possible responses to include probabilities, rather than yes or no answers to each diagnostic question, and it uses a computer to process the data. Although both formulations of this model provide a set of diagnostic questions for analyzing a problem, they tend to oversimplify the process.

A. Is there a quality requirement such that one solution is likely to be more rational than another?
B. Do I have sufficient info to make a high quality decision?
C. Is the problem structured?
D. Is acceptance of decision by subordinates critical to effective implementation?
E. If I were to make the decision by myself, is it reasonably certain that it would be accepted by my subordinates?
F. Do subordinates share the organizational goals to be attained in solving this problem?
G. Is conflict among subordinates likely in preferred solutions? (This question is irrelevant to individual problems.)
H. Do subordinates have sufficient info to make a high quality decision?

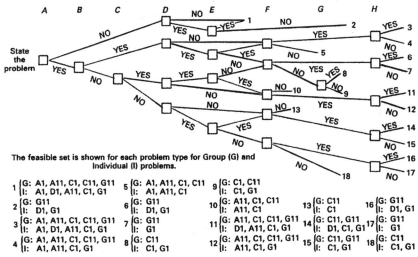

The feasible set is shown for each problem type for Group (G) and Individual (I) problems.

1 {G: A1, A11, C1, C11, G11 / I: A1, D1, A11, C1, G1}
2 {G: G11 / I: D1, G1}
3 {G: A1, A11, C1, C11, G11 / I: A1, D1, A11, C1, G1}
4 {G: A1, A11, C1, C11, G11 / I: A1, A11, C1, G1}
5 {G: A1, A11, C1, C11 / I: A1, A11, C1}
6 {G: G11 / I: D1, G1}
7 {G: G11 / I: G1}
8 {G: C11 / I: C1, G1}
9 {G: C1, C11 / I: C1, G1}
10 {G: A11, C1, C11 / I: A11, C1}
11 {G: A11, C1, C11, G11 / I: D1, A11, C1, G1}
12 {G: A11, C1, C11, G11 / I: A11, C1, G1}
13 {G: C11 / I: C1}
14 {G: C11, G11 / I: D1, C1, G1}
15 {G: C11, G11 / I: C1, G1}
16 {G: G11 / I: D1, G1}
17 {G: G11 / I: G1}
18 {G: C11 / I: C1, G1}

Figure 3.1.   Decision process flow chart for both individual and group problems.

Their narrow focus on the extent of subordinate involvement in decision making also limits their usefulness.

THE HERSEY–BLANCHARD MODEL

In an attempt to integrate previous knowledge about leadership into a prescriptive model of leadership style, this theory cites the "readiness of followers," defined as their ability and willingness to accomplish a specific task, as the major contingency that influences appropriate leadership style.[12] Follower readiness incorporates the follower's level of achievement motivation, ability, and willingness to assume responsibility for his or her own behavior in accomplishing specific tasks, and education and experience relevant to the task. The model combines task and relationship behavior to yield four possible styles, as shown in figure 3.2. Leaders should use a telling style, and provide specific instructions and closely supervise performance, when followers are unable and un-willing or insecure. Leaders should use a selling style, and explain decisions and provide opportunity for clarification, when followers have moderate-to-low readiness. Using a participating style, where the leader shares ideas and helps facilitate decision making, should occur when followers have moderate-to-high readiness. Finally, leaders should use a delegating style, and give responsibility for decisions and implementation to followers, when followers are able, willing, and confident.

Although some researchers have questioned the conceptual clarity, validity, robustness, and utility of the model, as well as the instruments used to measure leadership style, others have supported the utility of the theory. For example, the Leadership Effectiveness and Description (LEAD) Scale and related instruments, developed to measure leadership style by the life-cycle researchers, are widely used in industrial training programs. This model can easily be adapted to educational administration and be used analytically to understand leadership deficiencies and combine it with the path-goal model to prescribe the appropriate style for a variety of situations.

REFRAMING LEADERSHIP

Bolman and Deal have developed a unique situational leadership theory that analyzes leadership behavior through four frames of reference: structural, human resource, political, and symbolic. Each of the frames offers a different perspective on what leadership is and how it operates in organizations. Each can result in either effective or ineffective conceptions of leadership.[13]

Structural leaders develop a new model of the relationship of structure, strategy, and environment for their organizations. They focus on implementation. The right answer helps only if it can be implemented. Structural leaders sometimes fail because they miscalculate the difficulty of putting their design in place. They often underestimate the resistance that it will generate, and they take few steps to build a base of support for their innovations. In short, they are often undone by human resource, political, and symbolic considerations. Structural leaders do continually experiment, evaluate, and adapt, but because they fail to consider the entire environment in which they are situated, they sometimes are ineffective.

Human resource leaders believe in people and communicate that belief. They are passionate about "productivity through people." They demonstrate this faith in their words and actions and often build it into a philosophy or credo that is central to their vision of their organizations. Human resource leaders are visible and accessible. Peters and Waterman popularized the notion of "management wandering around," the idea that managers need to get out of their offices and interact with workers and customers. Many educational administrators have adopted this aspect of management.

Effective human resource leaders empower; that is, they increase participation, provide support, share information, and move decision mak-

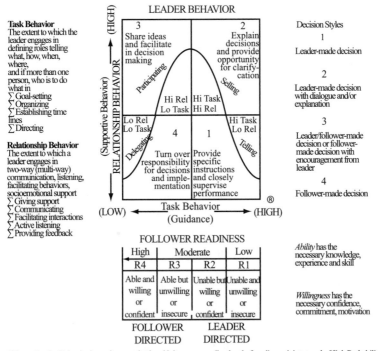

Figure 3.2. Model of Situational Leadership

ing as far down the organization as possible. Human resource leaders often like to refer to their employees as "partners" or "colleagues." They want to make it clear that employees have a stake in the organization's success and a right to be involved in making decisions. When they are ineffective, however, they are seen as naive or as weaklings and wimps.

Political leaders clarify what they want and what they can get. Political leaders are realists above all. They never let what they want cloud their judgment about what is possible. They assess the distribution of power and interests. The political leader needs to think carefully about the players, their interests, and their power; in other words, he or she must map the political terrain. Political leaders ask such questions as whose support do I need? How do I go about getting it? Who are my opponents? How much power do they have? What can I do to reduce the opposition? Is the battle winnable? However, if ineffective, these leaders are perceived as being untrustworthy and manipulative.

The symbolic frame provides still a fourth turn of the kaleidoscope of leadership. In this frame, the organization is seen as a stage, a theater in which every actor plays certain roles and attempts to communicate the right impressions to the right audiences. The main premise of this frame is that whenever reason and analysis fail to contain the dark forces of ambiguity, human beings erect symbols, myths, rituals, and ceremonies to bring order, meaning, and predictability out of chaos and confusion. Transforming leaders are visionary leaders, and visionary leadership is invariably symbolic. Examination of symbolic leaders reveals that they follow a consistent set of practices and rules.

Transforming leaders use symbols to capture attention. When Diana Lam became principal of the Mackey Middle School in Boston in 1985, she knew that she faced a substantial challenge. Mackey had all the usual problems of urban public schools: decaying physical plant, lack of student discipline, racial tension, troubles with the teaching staff, low morale, and limited resources. The only good news was that the situation was so bad that almost any change would be an improvement. In such a situation, symbolic leaders will try to do something visible, even dramatic, to let people know that changes are on the way. During the summer before she assumed her duties, Lam wrote a letter to every teacher to set up an individual meeting. She traveled to meet teachers wherever they wanted, driving two hours in one case.

She asked teachers how they felt about the school and what chances they wanted.

She also felt that something needed to be done about the school building because nobody likes to work in a dumpy place. She decided that the front door and some of the worst classrooms had to be painted. She had few illusions about getting the bureaucracy of the Boston public school to provide painters, so she persuaded some of her family members to help her do the painting. When school opened, students and staff members immediately saw that things were going to be different, if only symbolically. Perhaps even more important, staff members received a subtle challenge to make a contribution themselves.

Each of the frames captures significant possibilities for leadership, but each is incomplete. In the early part of the century, leadership as a concept was rarely applied to management, and the implicit models of leadership were narrowly rational. In the 1960s and 1970s, human resource leadership became fashionable. The literature on organizational leadership stressed openness, sensitivity, and participation. In recent years, symbolic leadership had moved to center stage, and the literature now offers advice on how to become a visionary leader with the power to transform organizational cultures. Organizations do need vision, but it is not their only need and not always their most important one. Leaders need to understand their own frame and its limits. Ideally, they will also learn to combine multiple frames into a more comprehensive and powerful style.

TRANSFORMATIONAL LEADERSHIP

A charismatic or transformational leader uses charisma to inspire his or her followers. He or she talks to the followers about how essential their performance is, how confident he or she is in the followers, how exceptional the followers are, and how he or she expects the group's performance to exceed expectations. Lee Iacocca, in industry, and the late Marcus Foster and Notre Dame's Reverend Theodore Hesburgh, in education, are examples of this type of leader. Such leaders use dominance, self-confidence, a need for influence, and conviction of moral righteousness to increase their charisma and consequently their leadership effectiveness.[14]

A transformational leader changes an organization by recognizing an opportunity and developing a vision, communicating that vision to organizational members, building trust in the vision, and achieving the vision by motivating organizational members. The leader helps subordinates recognize the need for revitalizing the organization by developing a felt need for change, overcoming resistance to change, and avoiding quick-fix solutions to problems. Encouraging subordinates to act as devil's advocates with regard to the leader, building networks outside the organization, visiting other organizations, and changing management processes to reward progress against competition also helps them recognize a need for revitalization. Individuals must disengage from and disidentify with the past, as well as view change as a way of dealing with their disenchantments with the past or the status quo. The transformational leader creates a new vision and mobilizes commitment to it by planning or educating others. He or she builds trust through demonstrating personal expertise, self-confidence, and personnel integrity. The charismatic leader can also change the composition of the team, alter management processes, and help organizational members reframe the way they perceive an organizational situation. The charismatic leader must empower others to help achieve the vision. Finally, the transformational leader must institutionalize the change by replacing old technical, political, cultural, and social networks with new ones. For example, the leader can identify key individuals and groups, develop a plan for obtaining their commitment, and institute a monitoring system for following the changes. If an administrator wishes to make an innovative program acceptable to the faculty and the school community, for example, he or she should follow the above plan and identify influential individuals who would agree to champion the new program, develop a plan to gain support of others in the community through personnel contact or other means, and develop a monitoring system to assess the progress of the effort.[15]

A transformational leader motivates subordinates to achieve beyond their original expectations by increasing their awareness about the importance of designated outcomes and ways of attaining them; by getting workers to go beyond their self-interest to that of the team, the school, the school system, and the larger society; and by changing or expanding the individual's needs. Subordinates report that they work harder for such leaders. In addition, such leaders are judged higher in leadership potential by their subordinates, as compared to the more common transactional leader.

One should be cognizant, however, to the negative side of charismatic leadership that can exist if the leader overemphasizes devotion to himself or herself, makes personal needs paramount, or uses highly effective communication skills to mislead or manipulate others. Such leaders can be so driven to achieve a vision that they ignore the costly implications of their goals. The superintendent who overexpands his or her jurisdiction in an effort to form an "empire," only to have the massive system turn into a bureaucratic nightmare, is an example of transformational leadership gone sour. Nevertheless, recent research has verified the overall effectiveness of transformational leadership style.

DEVELOPING AN EDUCATIONAL VISION

A requisite for transformational leadership is an educational vision. Although there seems to be a sense of mystery on the part of some educators regarding what an educational vision is, the process for developing one is not at all complex. The first step is to develop a list of broad goals. "All Children Achieving" is an example of such a goal. These goals should be developed in conjunction with representatives of all segments of the school community, otherwise there will be no sense of "ownership," the absence of which will preclude successful implementation.

The next step in the process is to merge and prioritize the goals and to summarize them in the form of a short and concise vision statement. The following is an example of a typical vision statement:

> Our vision for the Exeter School System is that all of our graduating students, regardless of ability, will say that "I have received an excellent education that has prepared me to be an informed citizen and leader in my community." Our students will have a worldview, and as a result of their experience in the Exeter School System, will be committed to a process of lifelong learning and the making of a better world by living the ideals of fairness and justice through service to others.

The key concepts in the above vision are all students achieving, excellence, leadership, multiculturalism, lifelong learning, values, and community service. It is these concepts that the transformational leader stresses in all forms of communication and in all interactions with the school community.

The final step in the process is the institutionalizing of the educational vision. This step ensures that the vision endures when the leadership changes. Operationalizing and placing the important concepts of the vision into the official policies and procedures of the school system is one way of helping to institutionalize the educational vision and incorporating into the school culture.

IMPLICATIONS FOR EDUCATION

The implications of leadership theory for educational administrators are rather clear. The successful administrator needs to have a sound grasp of leadership theory and the skills to implement it. The principles of situational and transformational leadership theory are guides to effective administrative behavior. The leadership behavior applied to an inexperienced faculty member may be significantly different than that applied to a more experienced and tested one. Task behavior may be appropriate in dealing with a new teacher, while relationship behavior may be more appropriate when dealing with a seasoned teacher.

The four frames of leadership discussed by Bolman and Deal can be particularly helpful to school administrators. Consideration of the structural, human relations, political, and symbolic implications of leadership behavior can keep an administrator attuned to the various dimensions affecting appropriate leadership behavior. With the need to deal with collective bargaining entities, school boards, and a variety of other power issues, the political frame considerations may be particularly helpful in understanding the complexity of relationships that exist between administrators and these groups. Asking oneself the questions posed earlier under the political frame can be an effective guide to the appropriate leadership behavior in dealing with these groups.

SUMMARY

Recently, a plethora of research studies have been conducted on leadership and leadership styles. The overwhelming evidence indicates that no one singular leadership style is most appropriate in all situations. Rather, an administrator's leadership style should be adapted to

the situation so that at various times task behavior or relationship behavior might be appropriate. At other times and in other situations, various degrees of both task and relationship behavior may be most effective.

The emergence of transformational leadership has seen leadership
theory come full circle. Transformational leadership theory combines aspects of the early trait theory perspective with the more current situational or contingency models. The personal charisma of the leader along
with his or her ability to formulate an educational vision and to communicate it to others determine the transformational leader's effectiveness.

Because the effective leader is expected to adapt his or her leadership
style to an ever-changing environment, administration becomes an even
more complex and challenging task. However, a thorough knowledge of
leadership theory can make some sense of the apparent chaos that the
administrator faces on almost a daily basis.

CASE STUDY 3.1:
BERKS COUNTY INTERMEDIATE UNIT

The Berks County Intermediate Unit (BCIU) is an educational service
agency serving the eighteen school districts of Berks County, Pennsylvania. It provides numerous programs for school district staff on many levels, from the board rooms and administrative offices into the classroom.
In addition, the IU works with teachers and other staff to coordinate student activities, such as spelling bees and student leadership programs, on
county and regional levels.

Since its founding in 1971 by the legislators, the education environment
has changed dramatically. BCIU's strength as an institution is the result of
its being able to adapt to these changes—in funding, technology, educational
research, and other areas—and, in many ways, anticipating changes, preparing school district leaders and staffs for the challenges ahead.

BCIU's school districts and other clients may call upon a staff experienced in many areas of education, from services to students with special
needs to training and development programs for teachers and administrative staff. BCIU adapts to meet the particular need of a school, school
district, nonpublic school, or other organization.

GOVERNANCE STRUCTURE

The IU's Board of Directors consists of eighteen members, one from each of its constituent school districts and meets twice a month. There is also a Chiefs' Council made up of the eighteen district superintendents who "advise" the Executive Director on matters relative to programs and budgets impacting school districts.

BUDGET

Of its 35 million dollar total budget (85 separate program budgets), only 3.3 million is subject to approval by the school districts. The remaining 31.7 million dollars relates to programs with which the districts have little or minimal financial say. For example, Head Start, which is federally funded, the Community Child Care Program, funded by clients, United Way, and the Administrative Budget financed by indirect cost that each IU program is assessed for services such as human resources department or payroll services, and so on. The revenue source breakdown is as follows:

Local	6.6%
State	19.3%
Federal	31.7%
Entrepreneurial	42.4%

ORGANIZATIONAL STRUCTURE

This Organization Chart shows the top management of the BCIU. The employee breakdown is as follows:

Management	32 employees
Technical/Support	78
Bargaining Units	1
AFSCME/clerical	52
BCIUA/(teachers)	84

PSSU (Day Care)	50
Head Start	48
Transportation	116
Other	40
Total	500

LEADERSHIP

KRH, executive director of the Intermediate Unit, has been at BCIU since 1970, the year IUs were born. Prior to that, he was employed by the County Schools Office, the precursor to IUs. Starting as an IMS (Instructional Materials Service) program specialist, he advanced up the management ladder through supervisor and assistant executive director, and in 1992 he became executive director. His contract was renewed by the board in 2002 for another four years. He plans to retire in the year 2006. KRH currently has a harmonious relationship with the board and has had one since his appointment in 1992. His relationship with the superintendents is not always so harmonious. In fact, a faction of the superintendents' group actively campaigned against his appointment in 1992. His predecessor had been a gentle manager, keeping peace at all costs among the eighteen superintendents. In contrast, KRH is a very aggressive, task-oriented leader, more akin to a business man, as attested to the excellent financial status of BCIU, in times when other IUs were floundering and their very existence is questioned. He has an entrepreneurial approach and this vision has led the IU into diversified services, including computer repair, Internet installation, tax-billing, Management Information Services, to name just a few. He views the IU as a business. Once monthly, the cabinet (executive director, assistant executive director, management services director, and human resources director) meet in an R&D (Research and Development) session to explore new avenues of products and services. The assistant executive director, JLL, has responsibility for the educational and social services programs. In contrast, she is a relational leader, although when needed, she can be a task-oriented leader. She is well respected by the Board and the superintendents for her knowledge of curriculum, strategic planning, and current trends in education. KRH depends on her greatly to be on the "cutting edge" of educational developments. JRK, the Director of Management Services (Business Manager), and EAW, the Human Resources Director, serve as "gatekeepers," keeping the finances and legal, contractual houses in order. JRK and EAW serve the districts by keeping them up to date on financial and legal issues, respectively. KRH gives his top management team much leeway in their areas of expertise.

To employees lower down the organization chart, KRH is somewhat feared. He is a very direct, bottom-line manager and, in the past, as assistant executive director under a kinder, gentler executive director, often had to be the hatchet man.

THE CURRENT ISSUE

The present governor's agenda includes, along with vouchers, another hot topic—charter schools. Although the legislature has not even passed a bill (yet) authorizing charter schools, $1 million in seed money (grants of $25,000) is available from the Pennsylvania Department of Education to school districts, community agencies, parents, institutions of higher learning, and others to pilot charter schools. KRH, unlike his superintendent counterparts, did not merely dismiss vouchers or charter schools as the agenda of an anti–public education governor, but sees these as a business opportunity for the IU. A voucher system would need a middleman—a broker—to implement such a system. A perfect fit for IUs who already serve as an "intermediary" between the Pennsylvania Department of Education and 501 public school districts and numerous diocesan/private schools.

At the last superintendents' meeting, he proposed that the districts and BCIU form a consortium, apply for the planning grants, pool their seed money, and plot an alternative education charter school for elementary students. Although alternative education programs for secondary students are common, such programs for elementary students are not. Reaching troubled youth in the third, fourth, fifth, and sixth grades with alternative education programs may "catch" them before more serious trouble occurs and more drastic actions are necessary. Although many of the superintendents agree with the concept, they are absolutely against BCIU spearheading such a charter school program. For the IU to do so would be cooperating with a governor whom the superintendents believe wishes to destroy public education. At the last Chief's Council meeting, the superintendents told KRH that if he pursued a grant for BCIU to start a charter school, he would be setting up the IU in an adversarial role with the school districts and they would not send any students to the pilot charter school.

KRH was angry with the superintendents. He believed that some of the governor's criticism of public educators is deserved. They "don't see the handwriting on the wall," KRH told the BCIU Board (made up of one member from each district) how the superintendents feel. Several board members are angry that the superintendents squelched the idea without consulting their boards. Some board members feel that each district Board, not the superintendents, should evaluate what ventures the district goes into with BCIU.

NOTES

1. S. A. Kirkpatrick and E. A. Locke, *Leadership: Do Traits Matter?* Academy of Management Executive 5, no. 2 (1991): 49.

2. R. M. Stogdill and A. E. Coons, eds., *Leader Behavior: Its Description and Measurement* (Columbus: Ohio State University Bureau of Business Research, 1957).

3. E. Fleishman, E. F. Harris, and R. D. Buret, *Leadership and Supervision in Industry* (Columbus: Ohio State University Press, 1955); E. Fleishman and E. F. Harris, Patterns of Leadership Behavior Related to Employee Grievances and Turnover, *Personnel Psychology* 1 (1959): 45–53.

4. H. Mintzberg, *The Nature of Managerial Work*, 2nd ed. (Englewood Cliffs, N.J.: Prentice-Hall, 1979).

5. D. McGregor, *The Human Side of Enterprise* (New York: McGraw-Hill, 1961); E. H. Schein, The Hawthorne Studies Revisited: A Defense of Theory Y, Sloan School of Management Working Paper #756–74 (Cambridge: Massachusetts Institute of Technology, 1974), p. 3.

6. F. E. Fiedler and M. M. Chemers, *Improving Leadership Effectiveness: The Leader Match Concept*, 2nd ed. (New York: Wiley, 1984).

7. F. E. Fiedler and J. E. Garcia, *New Approaches to Effective Leadership* (New York: Wiley, 1987).

8. N. W. Biggart and G. G. Hamilton, An Institutional Theory of Leadership, *Journal of Applied Behavioral Sciences* 234 (1987): 429–441.

9. R. J. House, A Path-Goal Theory of Leader Effectiveness, *Administrative Science Quarterly* 16 (1971): 321–338; and R. J. House and T. R. Mitchell, Path-Goal Theory of Leadership, *Journal of Contemporary Business* (Autumn 1974): 81–97.

10. V. H. Vroom and P. W. Yetton, *Leadership and Decision Making* (Pittsburgh: University of Pittsburgh Press, 1973) is the original version; V. H. Vroom and A. G. Jago, *The New Leadership: Managing Participation in Organizations* (Englewood Cliffs, N.J.: Prentice-Hall, 1988) is the most recent version.

11. R. H. G. Field, A Test of the Vroom-Yetton Normative Model of Leadership, *Journal of Applied Psychology* 67 (1982): 523–532.

12. P. Hersey and K. H. Blanchard, *Management of Organizational Behavior*, 5th ed. (Englewood Cliffs, N.J.: Prentice-Hall, 1988).

13. Lee B Bolman and Terrance E. Deal, *Reframing Organizations* (San Francisco, Jossey-Bass, 1991).

14. R. J. House, A 1976 Theory of Charismatic Leadership, in *Leadership: The Cutting Edge*, ed. J. G. Hunt and Larson (Carbondale: Southern Illinois University Press, 1977), 36–59.

15. A. R. Willner, *The Spellbinders: Charismatic Political Leadership* (New Haven, Conn.: Yale University Press, 1984); A. Conger and R. N. Kanungo, Toward a Behavioral Theory of Charismatic Leadership in Organizational Settings, *Academy of Management Review* 12 (1987): 637–647.

4

MOTIVATING AND
REWARDING INDIVIDUALS

Neither regulations nor resources, neither technical innovations nor
program reorganizations, can significantly alter school performance
if the teacher motivation system fails to energize and shape teacher
behavior in ways that link educational program requirements to student learning needs.

—Douglas E. Mitchell, Flora Ida Ortiz, and Tedi K. Mitchell

The next step in preparing oneself to be an effective administrator is
to adopt an approach to motivate one's colleagues to attain the educational vision that you have jointly developed. To begin the process, you
might ask yourself: What motivates individuals to behave, think, or feel
in certain ways? What factors make you or others more willing to work,
to be creative, to achieve, to produce? Theory and research in the area
of motivation provide a systematic way of diagnosing the degree of motivation and of prescribing ways of increasing it. There are basically two
views of motivation. One view posits that individuals are motivated by
inherited, conflicting, and unconscious drives. This view was popularized by Freud and Jung, and more recently by Skinner, Maslow, and
Glasser. This view is operationalized through the so-called content theories of motivation. In this chapter, we examine such content theories

as Maslow's need theory, McClelland's Trichotomy, ERG theory, Herzberg's Two-Factor theory, and Glasser's control theory.

The other view of motivation says that an individual is basically rational and is normally conscious of his or her pursuit of goals. Plato and Aristotle, and more recently Jerome Bruner, are associated with this view. This perspective has spawned the so-called process theories of motivation, including the equity theory, expectancy theory, and goal-setting theory.

In the first half of this chapter, we examine five motivation perspectives: need theories, equity theory, reinforcement theory, expectancy theory, and goal-setting theory. In the second half, we consider compensation alternatives and reward systems in educational institutions.

NEED THEORIES

Suppose the president of a college makes $100,000 a year and a faculty member earns $50,000. And suppose this college decided to base part of its annual salary increases on whether the college met its recruitment quota. Why would such a college think this policy might motivate its employees? Early motivation theorists would explain such a situation by saying that the college expects the new policy to meet the employees' needs—their basic requirements for living and working productively. As the work force in organizations becomes more diverse, recognizing the individuality of needs becomes paramount; identifying and responding to them becomes a crucial issue in effective management.

How do we identify employees' needs? To do a good job of identifying them, we probably would need to spend a great deal of time talking with the employees and observing their behavior both in and out of the work environment. Many times, determining employees' needs outside of the work environment is conjecture. In the example given earlier, we might conjecture that such a policy might meet the employees' achievement motive.

In this section, we present, in brief, four of the most popular needs theories: Maslow's hierarchy-of-needs theory, Alderfer's ERG theory, McClelland's need-for-achievement theory, and Herzberg's two-factor theory. Each of these theories describes a specific set of needs the researchers believe individuals have, and each differs somewhat in the number and kinds of needs identified. They also differ as to how unfulfilled needs influence motivation. Finally, in this section, we discuss one of the newer needs theories, control theory, which is the brainchild of William Glasser.

Maslow's Hierarchy of Needs

In 1935, Abraham Maslow developed the first needs theory, and it is still one of the most popular and well-known motivation theories. Maslow stated that individuals have five needs, arranged in a hierarchy from the most basic to the highest level, as shown in figure 4.1: physiological, safety and security, belongingness and love, esteem, and self-actualization.[1]

Physiological needs are the most basic needs an individual has. These include, at a minimum, a person's requirement for food, water, shelter, sex, the ability to care for his or her children, and medical and dental coverage. Safety needs include a person's desire for security or protection. This translates most directly into concerns for short-term and long-term job security, as well as physical safety at work. Belongingness and love needs focus on the social aspects of work and nonwork situations. Virtually all individuals desire affectionate relationships or regular interaction with others, which can become a key facet of job design. Esteem needs relate to a person's de-

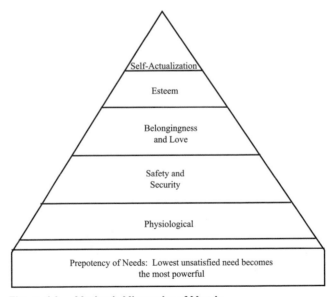

Figure 4.1. Maslow's Hierarchy of Needs

sire to master his or her work, demonstrate competence and accomplishments, build a reputation as an outstanding performer, hold a position of prestige, receive public recognition, and feel self-esteem. Self-actualization needs reflect an individual's desire to grow and develop to his or her fullest potential. An individual often wants the opportunity to be creative on the job or desires autonomy, responsibility, and challenge.

According to needs theory, organizations must meet unsatisfied needs. In Maslow's scheme, the lowest unsatisfied need, starting with the basic physiological needs and continuing through safety, belonging and love, esteem, and self-actualization needs, becomes the prepotent or most powerful and significant need. Although the order may vary in certain special circumstances, generally the prepotent need motivates an individual to act to fulfill it; satisfied needs do not motivate. If, for example, a person lacks sufficient food and clothing, he or she will act to satisfy those basic physiological needs; hence, this person would most likely work to receive pay or other benefits to satisfy those needs. On the other hand, a person whose physiological, safety, and belongingness needs are satisfied will be motivated to satisfy needs at the next level, the esteem needs. For this person, pay will not motivate performance unless it increases esteem, but a promotion or other changes in a job's title or status, which satisfy esteem needs, are likely to motivate.

Administrators should understand that the popularity of this theory of motivation stems primarily from its simplicity and logic, not from strong current research support. In general, research indicates that two or three categories of needs, rather than five, exist, and that the relationships, relative importance, and sequences are not consistent from one individual to another. In addition, the ordering of needs may vary in different cultures, and thus Maslow's theory may not be generalized across cultures.

Consider again the example of the college that attached some of the salary increases to whether the college reached its recruitment goals. To use Maslow's theory to diagnose the likely effectiveness of the new policy, we can ask three questions: (1) Which needs have already been satisfied? (2) Which unsatisfied need is lowest in the hierarchy? (3) Can those needs be satisfied with the new policy? If, for example, the physiological and safety needs have been satisfied, then the social needs become prepotent; if the new policy can satisfy those needs, which is unlikely, then, according to Maslow's theory, it would be motivating.

Alderfer's ERG Theory

Alderfer's ERG theory addresses one criticism of Maslow's theory by collapsing the hierarchy into three needs: existence, relatedness, and growth (ERG). Existence includes both physiological and safety needs and corresponds to Maslow's lower-order needs; relatedness comprises both love and belongingness needs. Growth incorporates both esteem and self-actualization needs.[2]

Individual differences in various needs may be associated with differences in an individual's developmental level, as well as differences in group experiences. For example, while an elementary school teacher is attaining certification, his or her existence needs might predominate; as the teacher attains financial security, the needs might shift to primarily relationship ones; later, when the teacher has added financial responsibilities, such as a family or an aged parent, satisfying his or her existence needs may again become important.

The ERG theory also states that unsatisfied needs motivate individuals, and that individuals generally move up the hierarchy in satisfying their needs. For example, individuals with unsatisfied relatedness needs would be motivated to produce if their performance resulted in their satisfying these needs. As lower-order needs are satisfied, they become less important, but according to ERG theory, higher-order needs become more important as they are satisfied. For example, increased opportunity for autonomy, which satisfies growth needs, has also increased the requirements for satisfying those needs in the future. If an employee is frustrated in satisfying higher-order needs, such as growth needs, for example, he or she might try instead to satisfy lower-level needs by seeking work situations with social interaction.

Consider, for example, the employee who earns a good salary, has a reasonably high standard of living, and has made many friends at work. According to Maslow and Alderfer, this person probably would be motivated to satisfy his or her growth needs. What if, in trying to satisfy these needs, the individual finds that he or she is continually frustrated in attempts to get more autonomy and responsibility, features of the job that generally encourage individual growth? When asked, the employee now reports that having friends at work and getting together with them outside of work is most important. Frustration in satisfying a higher need has resulted in a regression to a lower level of needs.

In using Alderfer's theory to diagnose motivation situations, such as finding ways to motivate a poorly performing employee to improve his or her productivity or efficiency or to motivate a highly productive employee to continue at or surpass his or her present performance level, we can ask questions similar to those we asked for Maslow, with the addition of three more. First, what needs are the individuals involved in the situation experiencing? Second, what needs have been satisfied, and how have they been met? Third, which unsatisfied need is the lowest in the hierarchy? Fourth, have some higher-order needs been frustrated? Fifth, has the person refocused on a lower-level need? Sixth, how can the unsatisfied needs be satisfied?

McClelland's Needs-for-Achievement Theory (or Trichotomy of Needs)

McClelland's needs for achievement, affiliation, and power resemble the higher-order needs we have described so far. Need for achievement is a need to accomplish and demonstrate competence or mastery; a person who continuously asks for and masters increasingly difficult tasks demonstrates a need for achievement. Early and recent research linked this need to effective managerial performance in the United States and abroad. Based on his assumption that he can teach an individual the need for achievement, McClelland and his associates designed and conducted training sessions that teach managers how to act like a person high in need for achievement as a way of increasing performance.[3]

Need for affiliation is need for love, belonging, and relatedness; a person who seeks jobs high in social interaction shows this need. Need for power is a need for control over one's own work or the work of others; a person who insists on autonomy in his or her work or who seeks supervisory responsibility likely has need for power. Other early research showed that male managers with a high need for power tended to run more productive departments than did managers with a high need for affiliation. A person may demonstrate each need overtly or covertly; a teacher, for example, might seek a position with more autonomy or may work harder when given it. He or she may visibly delight in social activities or complain about always working alone. Although each person has all three needs to some extent, only one of them tends to motivate an individual at any given time.

The projective Thematic Apperception Test (TAT) also measures these needs. The respondent describes what he or she sees as occurring in a series of pictures. The respondent projects his or her needs into the description of the picture. For example, if you viewed the picture as a problem-solving meeting, then you would receive a positive score on need for achievement. If you viewed the picture as being a social gathering, then you would receive a positive score on need for affiliation. If you viewed the picture as being a situation dominated by a single person, then you would receive a positive score on need for power. Professional test administrators have detailed protocols for scoring the pictures included in the TAT and similar tests. Because of the time and skill required in the administration and scoring of the test, its cost is relatively high and only a trained professional can administer and score it.

Herzberg's Two-Factor Theory

Frederick Herzberg and his associates described features of a job's content, including responsibility, autonomy, self-esteem, and self-actualization opportunities, known as *motivators*, which motivate a person to exert more effort and ultimately perform better. Early job redesign efforts focused on increasing these motivators. Because serious criticisms of the theory's rigor and validity have existed, its major contribution is a historical one.

Herzberg also described hygiene factors, aspects of a job that can meet physiological, security, or social needs, including physical working conditions, salary, company or institutional policies and practices, and benefits, that satisfy the lower-order needs and prevent dissatisfaction. Although hygiene factors per se do not encourage individuals to exert more effort, they must be at an acceptable level before motivators can have a positive effect. For example, offering autonomy and responsibility to a teacher when working conditions and salary levels are on a poverty level will result in dissatisfaction and limits the occurrence of motivation. [4]

This theory has been subjected to significant criticism. This criticism focuses on the research method used to collect data as well as the classification of some factors, especially pay, as both a motivator and a hygiene factor. His theory also ignores individual differences and may overemphasize the importance of pleasure as a desired outcome.

Control Theory

William Glasser suggests that individuals strive to gain control over their emotions and behavior so that they will have healthier and more productive lives. His control theory posits that individuals are born with five basic human needs: survival, love, power, fun, and freedom. These needs must be satisfied in order for individuals to be productive in their work and private lives. According to Glasser, people need to control their own behavior so as to make the most need-satisfying choices possible, his definition of a quality school, for example, and its attainment of excellence through his axioms.

The survival need is the innate desire of individuals to be safe and secure. Love and belonging refer to the need for affiliation and affirmation. Power is the need to obtain knowledge and expertise. To Glasser, knowledge is power. Our inalienable right to the pursuit of happiness is our effort to fulfill the need for fun. And the opportunity to make free choices is what Glasser believes satisfies our need for freedom.[5]

According to Glasser, effective managers will see that these five needs are satisfied if his or her employees are expected to be productive. Coercion and competition are counterproductive. Quality performance, therefore, cannot be achieved in an adversarial setting. Workers will perform if coerced, but they will not perform in a quality manner. Competition enables one person to succeed while others fail. Cooperation, on the other hand, allows many winners.

Although Glasser's control theory has not been verified by empirical research, it has been demonstrated to be successful in a school system setting in the Johnson City, New York, school district, where standardized achievement test scores increased dramatically while Glasser's techniques were being used. The faculty was also judged to be more productive when programs were implemented that satisfied the five basic needs.

UTILIZATION OF NEEDS THEORIES

The extent to which current needs theories explain motivation in organizations has been questioned by some researchers who maintain that the concept is difficult to prove or disprove for several reasons. First, needs are difficult to specify and measure. Second, relating needs to various job characteristics, such as an institution's benefit plan, can be problematic. Third, need-satisfaction models fail to account for variances in individuals' behaviors and attitudes. Fourth, attributing needs to individuals may stem from a lack of awareness of external causes that influence behavior. Finally, applying needs may result in stereotyping individuals and ignore the dynamic quality of individual behavior.

Despite these caveats, however, needs theory can be utilized effectively in educational settings. When an administrator is developing or refining the overall school program and organizational goals, he or she should analyze each component with the various needs in mind to be certain that some aspect of the activity or policy addresses one or more of our common needs. For example, if a teacher is preparing a lesson, he or she should go through Glasser's or another theorist's needs, to see if the lesson addresses the learner's needs for survival, love, power, fun, and freedom. In the same way, if an administrator is implementing a Total Quality Management program at his or her institution, the administrator must incorporate facets that would satisfy each of the faculty and staff's needs in some way.

EQUITY THEORY

The second major type of motivation theory evolved from social comparison theory. Lacking objective measures of performance or appropriate attitudes, individuals assess and compare their performance and attitudes to that of others. Equity theory assumes that people assess their job performance and attitudes by comparing both their contribution to work and the benefits they derive from work to the contributions and benefits of a comparison other, an individual whom the person selects and who, in reality, may be like or unlike the person. A high school teacher, for example, might compare his or her effort and rewards to another teacher, but may compare his or her effort to that of the principal, or even the superintendent.

Equity theory further states that a person is motivated in proportion to the perceived fairness of the rewards received for a certain amount of effort. You might have heard a student complain that "I'm going to stop studying so hard. Scott is no brighter than I am and he never seems to study and still gets A's." This student has compared his effort with that of Scott's and perceived an inequity in this school situation. In fact, no actual inequity may exist, but the perception of inequity influences the student's subsequent actions.[6]

Specifically, this student compared his perceptions of two ratios. (1) the ratio of his outcomes to his inputs to (2) the ratio of another's outcomes to inputs. Outcomes might include pay, status, and job complexity; inputs include effort, productivity, age, sex, or experience. Thus, he or she might compare his pay-to-experience ratio to another's ratio, or their status-to-age ratio to another's. For example, employee A might feel that he or she receives $25 for each hour of effort he or she contributes to the job; in contrast, he or she might assess that employee B receives $50 for each hour of effort contributed to the job. Employee A perceives that his or her ratio of outcomes to inputs (25 to 1) is less than employee B's (50 to 1). In fact, employee B might only receive $25 for each hour of effort. But, according to equity theory, the facts do not influence motivation; perceptions of the situation do. Recent research suggests, however, that equity calculations can be difficult because of cognitive differences in assessment and performance. Instead, individuals look for long-term rather than short-term parity in work situations; they compare their rank order on merit and rank order on a scales of reward outcomes, and see equity as a goal to work for over time.[7]

According to equity theory, individuals are motivated to reduce any perceived inequity. They strive to make these ratios equal by changing either the outcomes or the inputs. The student referred to earlier, for example, might reduce his inputs (his effort) to make the ratio the same as Scott's. If he cannot change his own inputs or outcomes, he might adjust either his perception of Scott's outcomes or inputs or his attitude toward the situation by reevaluating his effort or obtaining more accurate information about Scott's grades and study habits and adjusting the ratio accordingly.

In theory, the same adjustment process occurs when a person perceives he or she receives too much reward for the input or has too complex a job in comparison to others. Thus, if a person believes that he or she is overpaid, the individual should either increase his or her effort or ask that his or her pay be decreased. Although early studies suggested that this would happen, recent research has questioned whether this overjustification effect really occurs.

While equity theory basically makes strong intuitive sense, the empirical evidence has been mixed. The concept of equity sensitivity in part explains these findings by suggesting that individuals have different preferences for equity (e.g., a preference for higher, lower, or equal ratios) that cause them to react consistently but differently to perceived equity and inequity.

In a sense, equity theory oversimplifies the motivational issues by not explicitly considering individual needs, values, or personalities. This oversimplification becomes particularly important as the work force becomes more diverse. Cross-cultural differences may also occur in preferences for equity, as well as the preferred responses to inequitable situations.

To determine whether equity exists in the workplace, we can use a questionnaire, such as the Organizational Fairness Questionnaire.

REINFORCEMENT THEORY

This theory applies behaviorist learning theories to motivation. It emphasizes the importance of feedback and rewards in motivating behavior through diverse reinforcement techniques, including positive reinforcement, punishment, negative reinforcement, or extinction.[8]

First, reinforcement techniques can either encourage or eliminate the desired behavior; second, they can be actively applied or passively used.

Positive reinforcement involves actively encouraging a desired behavior by repeatedly pairing desired behaviors or outcome with rewards or feedback. For example, a development officer at a private school may be given a bonus if he or she performs beyond expectations. The desired behavior, performing beyond expectations, is paired with the financial reward. This feedback shapes behavior by encouraging the reinforced or rewarded behavior to recur. If the behavior is not precisely what is desired by a superior or client, repeated reinforcements, resulting in successive approximations to the desired behavior, can move the actual behavior closer to the desired behavior. For example, if a teacher's use of a variety of instructional techniques is desired, the principal might compliment the teacher when a new technique is used, and when more new techniques are used, additional praise may be given. This and other incentives are used until the best performance occurs. This behavior would then be reinforced with praise and other rewards until it became more or less permanent.

Punishment actively eliminates undesirable behaviors by applying an undesirable reinforcer to an undesirable behavior. In this way it differs from negative reinforcement, which rewards the cessation or withdrawal of an undesirable behavior. Using punishment, a superintendent might assign a principal who has challenged the superintendent's view on site-based management to an undesirable school in the district.

How will the principal react to the punishment? Most likely, the principal will feel bitterness or anger toward the superintendent. This attitude, which results from the use of punishment, could have long-term negative consequences for the principal's performance. Punishment often creates secondary consequences of tension and stress and could result in unpredictable and unobservable outcomes, and so it should be used only as a last-resort motivator.

In negative reinforcement, an individual passively encourages a desired behavior by withholding punishment. The term *negative* stems from the removal of the individual from a punitive situation when the desired behavior occurs, for example, the person who is convicted of a crime and refuses to cooperate with police regarding others who were involved, is sent to prison (punished), and is then released (removing the punishment) upon naming his or her accomplices. Releasing (removing) the prisoner from his or her punishment encourages or reinforces the desired behavior (naming the accomplices).

Extinction passively eliminates an undesired behavior by withholding positive reinforcement. Typically, the failure to apply positive reinforcements causes the desired behaviors to cease. A teacher who repeatedly volunteers her services for advisory committees but receives neither compensation, status, nor praise for this added effort likely will stop volunteering. By withholding reinforcement, an administrator may also cause desired behaviors, such as greater productivity, creativity, and attendance, to stop.

The timing and frequency of reinforcement significantly influence its impact. Fixed and variable schedules reflect the extent to which reinforcement is regular and known in advance or not. A paycheck is officially administered according to a fixed schedule: The employee receives a paycheck after completing his or her last desired behavior in the time period. Often, this type of reinforcer loses the power to motivate good performance because it is received regardless of the individual's behavior. Merit increases, bonuses, and praise are often given on variable schedules. Education is a profession where it is particularly difficult to utilize the principle of variable schedules reinforcement because merit pay is so infrequently allowed.

Interval and ratio schedules describe the extent to which reinforcement corresponds with a specific time interval (a week, month, or year) or a given number of responses or outputs, such as fifty units of a particular product. Holiday bonuses illustrate reinforcements given according to an interval schedule. They are given once a year at a predetermined time. Piecework rates illustrate reinforcement according to a ratio schedule. Piecework pay is given after a specific number of articles are produced.

In general, continuous reinforcement along fixed and interval schedules more effectively encourages desired behaviors in the short term; a weekly paycheck motivates workers immediately to perform as desired. Intermittent reinforcement according to variable and ratio schedules more effectively sustains desired behaviors over the long run; not knowing when or whether a merit increase will be given tends to motivate workers to continue performing at a high level in hopes such reinforcement will occur. Ensuring performance in the medium run might require adding a fixed-ratio component, such as an incentive program.

EXPECTANCY THEORY

Expectancy theory has dominated research about motivation since the early 1970s, principally because it has strong empirical support, integrates diverse perspectives on motivation, and provides explicit ways to increase employee motivation. Perhaps more than the preceding theories, expectancy theory offers a comprehensive view of motivation that integrates many of the elements of the needs, equity, and reinforcement theories. The research done in education regarding teacher expectations and students of all ages fulfilling these expectations is a compelling example of expectancy theory in action.

Victor Vroom popularized the expectancy theory in the 1960s with his model that stated that motivation is a function of expectancy, valence, and instrumentality:

$$Motivation = Expectancy \times Valence \times Instrumentality$$

This simple formulation identifies the three basic components of expectancy theory. Expectancy refers to a person's perception of the probability that effort will lead to performance. For example, a person who perceives that if he or she works harder, then he or she will produce more has a high expectancy. A person who perceives that if he or she works harder, then he or she will be ostracized by other employees and will not receive the cooperation necessary for performing has a lower expectancy. If expectancy is zero, then motivation will be lower than if expectancy is positive.

Instrumentality refers to a person's perception of the probability that certain outcomes, positive or negative, will be attached to that performance. For example, a person who perceives that he or she will receive greater pay or benefits if he or she produces has high instrumentality. Motivation is a function of the degree of instrumentality, in addition to expectancy and valence.

Valence refers to a person's perception of the value of specific outcomes, that is, how much the person likes or dislikes receiving these outcomes. An individual with high esteem needs generally will attach a high valence to a new job title or a promotion. When valence is high, motivation is likely to be higher than when valence is less positive or negative.

Vroom's simplified introduction of expectancy theory was followed in the 1970s by a more complex formulation:

$$Motivation = E_P (P_O) (V)$$

Here, E_P refers to the employee's perception of whether effort leads to performance; this is analogous to expectancy. The relation P_O refers to the employee's perception of whether performance leads to outcomes, including fatigue, pay, benefits, job challenge, among others. The variable V refers to the valence, or value attached to the outcome.

We can examine the case of a college professor using this formulation of motivation. If the college professor perceives that devoting more time to scholarly research will result in his or her performing better, the E_P will be positive. If the professor perceives that he or she receives a promotion and a pay raise if he or she performs the job well, then P_O will be positive. If the professor likes receiving a promotion and a raise, then V will be positive. We can operationalize this equation by arbitrarily assigning values to each variable. Because performance can lead to multiple outcomes, each with different valences or values, each performance-to-outcome expectancy is multiplied by the corresponding valence. For example, consider a new teacher who knows that if he or she demonstrates that much effort is being exerted to be productive in the classroom, he or she will have a contract renewal, this results in a positive performance-to-outcome expectancy. But teachers also know that if they put in too much time and effort, they will be ostracized by their coworkers for being a "pawn of the administration," so the performance-to-outcome expectancy is much less positive, and probably approaches zero. These products are then summed before being multiplied by the effort-to-performance expectancy.

A revised expectancy theory, which was developed in the late 1970s, incorporates the intrinsic and extrinsic outcomes of performing a task. In this model, motivation is reduced if an individual does not value either intrinsic or extrinsic outcomes, or if the person perceives that either the intrinsic or extrinsic performance-to-outcome expectancies are low. For example, the teacher's motivation will be reduced either if he or she does not like doing her or his tasks (intrinsic) or if he or she does not receive desired rewards (extrinsic) for performing them.

Although evidence for the validity of the expectancy model is mixed, managers can still use it to diagnose motivational problems or to evaluate effective motivation. (1) Does the individual perceive that effort will lead to performance? (2) Does the individual perceive that certain behaviors will lead to specified outcomes? (3) What values do individuals attach to these outcomes? Answers to these questions should help administrators determine the level of an employee's work motivation, then identify any deficiencies in the job situation and prescribe remedies. The expectancy perspective implies the value of equity in the work situation, as well as the importance of consistent rewards; in fact, both equity and reinforcement theory have been viewed as special cases of expectancy theory. It also addresses the issue of individual differences and offers the opportunity for quantification of the various facets of motivation. Hence, expectancy theory, more than any other presented so far, offers a comprehensive diagnostic tool.

GOAL-SETTING THEORY

Although extensive research has been conducted on the goal-setting process and its relationship to performance, in this section we highlight only a sample of the findings. Goals, which any member of an organization can set, describe a desired future state, such as lower absenteeism, higher standardized test scores, higher teacher and staff satisfaction, or specified performance levels. Once established, they can focus behavior and motivate individuals to achieve the desired end state.[10]

Goals can vary in at least three ways: specificity, difficulty, and acceptance. The specificity or clarity of goals refers to the extent to which their accomplishment is observable and measurable. "Reducing absenteeism by 20 percent" is a highly specific goal for a school; "all children achieving" is a much less specific goal. Goal difficulty, or the level of performance desired, can also vary significantly. A superintendent of schools might set a goal to recruit 10 percent more of the children in his or her school district and to increase standardized test scores by 10 percent; the first goal might be relatively easy, the second extremely difficult. Although goal-setting research originally called for setting moderately difficult goals, now empirical studies indicate that a linear relationship exists between goal difficulty and performance. Empirical studies that combined the two characteristics of goal specificity and difficulty showed that better performance accompanied specific difficult goals than vague, nonquantitative ones. Individuals' acceptance of stated goals, or their commitment to accomplishing the goals, may vary. In general, a subordinate is less likely to accept a goal as his or her own and try to accomplish it if a manager assigns the goal rather than jointly sets it with the subordinate. Commitment is influenced not only by participation in goal setting, but also by the authority who sets the goals unilaterally or collaboratively; the existence of peer pressure to accomplish the goals; the values, incentives, and rewards associated with goal performance; the person's expectancy of success; and the existence of any self-administered rewards for goal accomplishment. High expectancy that effort will lead to performance plus high self-efficacy, or an individual's judgment of his or her ability to accomplish a specified course of action, here a specific goal, also influence commitment, and ultimately performance. Employees tend to increase their goals after success and reduce them after failure. In addition, the analytical strategies used in performing tasks are a key link between goals and performance on complex tasks.

Early research indicated that goal-setting programs improve performance at both managerial and nonmanagerial levels over an extended period of time in a variety of organizations. It also recognized the role of feedback as a necessary condition for goal setting; individuals required information about their effectiveness in meeting their goals as part of continuing to work toward them.[11]

Contemporary recent research has suggested that performance was a function of employees' ability, acceptance of goals, level of the goals, and the interaction of the goal with their ability. Characteristics of the participants in goal setting, such as their authority or education, can have an impact on its effectiveness; for example, workers are more likely to accept goals from individuals with legitimate authority. Acceptance of the goals also has consequences for how difficult the goals can be; workers are likely to perform a task if the goals are difficult and accepted, but not difficult and rejected. When joined with attempts to raise expectancies that effort leads to performance, setting difficult goals can boost productivity. But most research has looked at single goals. Studies of setting multiple goals suggest that accomplishment of one results in some sacrifices of a second, reflecting the limited cognitive capacity of some individuals. In very complex jobs, like teaching, however, goal setting might not be feasible because multiple goals might be necessary. Or goal setting could lead to bureaucratic behavior, where setting the goals becomes an end in itself.[12]

Individuals set goals in response to work-related demands placed on them, and the goals in turn lead to performance. The strength of the relationship between goals and performance is affected by the worker's ability, commitment to the task, and receipt of feedback about performance, as well as the complexity of the task and other situational constraints. Further, performance increases when workers pay attention to a task, exert effort on it, and persist over time in doing it. In diagnosing a situation where employees lack motivation to perform the job correctly and effectively, we can analyze the goal-setting behavior in terms of the research just described. We can evaluate each of the factors and offer ways of improving them. In particular, we can focus on goals and make three assessments. First, we ask whether the individual has goals. Second, we determine whether the individual accepts his or her goals; such acceptance depends on whether the individuals perceive the goals as reasonable, are themselves self-assured, and have previous successes in accomplishing goals. Third and finally, we must assess whether feedback has been provided on route to goal accomplishment.

REDESIGN OF WORK

Work redesign modifies specific jobs to increase both the quality of the employees' work experience and the performance. *Jobs*, as a central concern in work design, are defined simply as a set of tasks grouped together under one job title; for example, teacher, principal, and custodian are designed to be performed by a single individual. Moreover, jobs are bureaucratic, they are part of the organization, they exist independently of job incumbents, and they are relatively static. Jobs do change, but not on a day-to-day basis. As a strategy for motivation and change, then, work-redesign programs alter the content and process of jobs to match the work motivation of individuals. That is, work-redesign efforts modify the school organization to enhance educator and student motivation.[13]

From a motivational perspective, work design makes assumptions about the needs, values, expectations, and goals of individuals and uses the assumptions as guides to develop jobs. This approach tries to maximize individual work motivation by increasing intrinsic aspects of the job itself. The idea is to have task motivation stem from intrinsic properties of the task or job rather than from extrinsic incentives or rewards attached to holding the job or to job performance. As a consequence of using a motivational approach, proponents claim that work-redesign programs improve the lives of individuals in at least four ways:

1. The fit between individual motivation and job content is improved.
2. Behavior is altered directly and tends to stay changed.

3. Opportunities for starting other needed organizational changes arise.
4. The long-term result is an organization that humanizes rather than dehumanizes the people.

The approach to work redesign that will be considered here is career ladders.

CAREER LADDERS

As a redesign of educational work, career-ladder programs are seen by many policy makers as moving teaching careers closer to the professional end of the occupational continuum. Career ladders became one of the most touted and widely mandated reforms of teaching and schools during the l980s.

Three reasons are generally offered as rationale for creating career-ladder programs. The first is based on the research finding that many of the best teachers leave their instructional careers after a brief foray in the classroom. Historically, about 50 percent of a teacher cohort will leave teaching during the first six years. Moreover, a disproportionate percentage of those leaving teaching are the most academically talented. These data suggest that new teachers lack strong professional career orientations and that schools depend on new, transient college graduates to maintain the teaching force. The second reason given for redesign is based on the observation that teaching in the elementary and secondary schools has a flat career path. Teachers have limited opportunities for advancement in their instructional work. New and experienced teachers have the same role expectations. Teachers with motivations to advance or gain new responsibilities generally have two choices; they can remain frustrated in their self-contained classrooms or they can leave. A third reason supporting the need of career ladders is that, although teaching is demanding work requiring creativity and versatility, it is repetitive. Despite the variety of classroom challenges and achievements, one year can look a lot like the next and there is little prospect to change the year-to-year pattern. Hence, career-ladder programs were seen as ways to attract and retain highly talented individuals to education.[14]

A career-ladder program redesigns jobs to provide individuals with prospects for promotion, formalizes status ranks for teachers, matches teacher abilities with job tasks, and distributes the responsibilities for school and faculty improvements to the professional staff. In essence, the goal of career-ladder programs is to enrich work and enlarge teacher responsibilities. Career ladders, as job-enrichment models, generally include promotions to higher ranks with the assumption of additional duties at each higher step. For example, mentoring and supervising new teachers, developing curriculum materials, and evaluating programs are typical.

By using job-enrichment strategies, career-ladder programs can address some of the concerns about teaching jobs. Such programs can provide teachers with opportunities and incentives to grow professionally, to develop new skills, to increase task variety and responsibility, to accept new challenges, and to promote collegiality. The innovation also increases teacher involvement in the professional aspects of schooling, that is, authority over the decision-making process for their students. Career-ladder plans focus on recruitment, retention, and performance incentives to enhance the attractiveness of teaching. At its best, this approach to work redesign reflects the belief that intelligent and creative teachers can be attracted to teaching and that the overall quality of the teaching force can be improved by a staged career with differential staffing responsibilities and reward allocations.

Overall, the research findings indicate that career-ladder programs as examples of work redesign in schools are conceptualized and implemented with varying degrees of success. When designed and instituted appropriately, they can have positive effects on school programs, curricula, and instruction. Moreover, they can promote teacher and administrator satisfaction and motivation by making the work itself more interesting, increasing autonomy and responsibility, and raising expectations for psychological growth.

REWARD SYSTEMS

An effective reward system ties rewards to performance. Individuals who work harder, produce more, or produce better-quality outputs should receive more rewards than poorer performers. In education, however, it is difficult to assess productivity. Therefore, there has been a great resistance to reward systems based on merit and productivity. Reward systems should also offer a sufficient number and diversity of rewards. Some organizations lack the resources to offer sufficient extrinsic rewards to employees to motivate them to perform or to encourage their satisfaction; in these cases, organizations must consider job enrichment or quality of working life programs as ways of increasing intrinsic rewards instead. Nonpublic schools, for example, oftentimes lack the material resources to reward teachers and staff extrinsically, but offer better working conditions, thus fulfilling the faculty and staff's intrinsic needs.

The criteria for the allocation of rewards must be clear and complete. Individual organizational members should know whether they receive rewards for level or quality of performance, attendance, innovativeness, or effort, for example. The criteria for receipt of specific wages, benefits, or incentive must be clearly defined. This is why it is imperative that an accurate and fair employee assessment program be in effect. At the same time, management must ensure that workers perceive that an equitable distribution of rewards occurs. Finally, organizational rewards should compare favorably with rewards in similar organizations. For school districts to attract and retain qualified and competent teachers, administrators, and staff they must offer rewards comparable to their counterparts in other school districts.

MERIT PAY

Perhaps the most controversial use of rewards in school organizations is in merit pay plans. In its pure form, merit pay is a compensation system in which pay is based on an individual's performance with at least a portion of a person's financial compensation being a performance bonus. High performers receive more money; low performers receive less money. The underlying principle is that some teachers or administrators earn more for doing the same work as others, only better. As practiced in school settings, however, merit pay supplements the standard salary schedule and forms only a small part of the employee's salary.

The criteria for receiving merit pay typically include being assessed as an excellent teacher (e.g., displaying prescribed teaching behaviors, increasing student test scores) and doing extra work for extra pay (e.g., serving as a mentor, leading extracurricular activities, conducting in-service workshops). Two common types of merit rewards are salary bonuses and increased status through public recognition of superior performance.

Although merit pay policies have been enacted, removed, revived, and retried for decades, few endure. Merit pay does not appear to be a viable approach to redistribute economic or status rewards in school settings unless a mutually accepted performance assessment program can be established.[15]

CASE STUDY 4.1: WICKETT MIDDLE SCHOOL

It is eight AM as the young Sam Burger closes the door to his car and begins his walk to the graffiti-covered Wickett Middle School, his place of employment. There is a grim look on his face, and you can see distinctly the disgust and tiredness in Sam's eyes. As he walks up the concrete stairs leading to the entrance of Wickett Middle School, he kicks out of the way some of the usual garbage thrown in his path.

Sam opens the door and walks inside, where he is greeted by an NTA. "Good Morning, Mr. Burger." Sam puts on his friendliest face and acknowledges the NTA with a "Hello." As he stands there, a few school children come running by. Sam yells, "Slow Down!" The children ignore him and continue running. He walks into the mail room and then the main office. Sam signs in at the desk and says "Hello" to a few colleagues, who draggingly walk in. He then walks out of the office and begins the dreaded daily journey to his classroom.

On his way to the classroom, Sam stops to talk with a fellow colleague, Mrs. Bowens. Mrs. Bowens privately converses with Sam and informs him that she is putting in for a transfer from Wickett and cannot wait until the end of the year. Sam shakes his head and responds, "I don't blame you. I have to wait until the end of the year before I can get out of this zoo. I will not make it eight years here, like yourself. I would not wait another minute if I were you. Especially, after the way Mr. Notlieb, the school principal, rudely shrugged off your question yesterday at the staff meeting. That just shows he does not care about any of us. I don't know who he thinks he is. We are in the classroom, doing whatever it takes to try and teach these kids something and he is playing around in his office on the computer. We are trying our best with some of the toughest kids to teach in America and he rudely shrugs you off like that . . . This is not to mention the fact that we have few supplies, no books, not enough desks, burnt out lights hanging in the room, busted windows, and everything else that is wrong with this ridiculous building. I have no energy as it is, trying to deal with these kids, the last thing I need to see is the school principal shrugging off my colleagues. Yeah, he cares."

Mrs. Bowens listens and shakes her head up and down. "You're right, Sam. You're right. I use to have the will to put up with everything for the children, but not anymore. I just cannot fight the administration and the kids at the same time. Look around this place, everyone is so depressed it is ridiculous." Sam responds, "I know, it is very sad."

Sam continues down the hallway to his room and opens his classroom door, turns on the few lights that work and begins to prepare for another day at Wickett.

THE WICKETT MIDDLE SCHOOL

The Wickett Middle School is a part of a large city school district. It has approximately one thousand students coming through its doors every day. The students range from grade five to grade eight. It is a relatively new facility, built about thirty years ago. However, poor maintenance and vandalism has really left its toll on the interior and exterior of the building. Most of the students come from relatively poor families, with about 98 percent having an income below the poverty level.

In the past, the teachers hung together with the administration to keep the school together. However, resentment toward the acting principal, Mr. Notlieb, has really inhibited the staff's commitment, morale, and desire to continue teaching at Wickett. More and more teachers are continually transferring and the effectiveness of the school has gone out the door with those who already left.

MR. NOTLIEB

During the last eight years of Wickett Middle School history, Mr. Notlieb has been principal. In the past, it was sort of a privilege to be an administrator of such a relatively new facility that had a lot to offer. However, all of that has changed.

Mr. Notlieb is an excellent paper principal. He is very good at record keeping and running the logistics of the school. However, he is not a very good interpersonal principal. His voice is weak low and not very commanding. He spends most of his day at meetings or in his office. Very little of his time is spent around the school. A lot of staff personnel dislike him for the above-mentioned reasons. He is simply not an empowering leader. Things are done his way and that is it, no debate or discussion. No room is left for others to voice their opinion about anything.

MRS. BOWENS

Mrs. Bowens is a tenured teacher in her late thirties. She has spent the last eight years at Wickett Middle School. The reason she chose Wickett was because of the wonderful things she had heard about the previous principal. Little did she know that a new principal was coming to Wickett the same year as she.

Mrs. Bowens is known for voicing her opinion for the good of the school and for being very emotional. She is also known for being a dedicated teacher, who is often seen at the school very early and after school very late. Her will and energy has all but run out. After all of the years dealing with the often-difficult students and the unappreciative or unsupportive administration, she has just about given up on Wickett.

SAM BURGER

Sam Burger is new to Wickett Middle School. This is his second year in the school district and he is still untenured. He came to Wickett a short time ago full of energy and with high expectations. However, he has quickly lost both. Sam feels that he can no longer be called a teacher, but rather should be called a prison guard. The students' awful behavior was more than he expected in the beginning and Sam thought he could lean toward the administration for help. He mistakenly believed that they would be supportive and encouraging.

Sam spent the whole first quarter of school without books for his students. He was also given very few supplies and actually does not have enough desks for every student in his room. However, his spirits remained high until the last straw finally hit.

Mr. Notlieb decided it was time for his young teacher to be observed. Well, Sam taught his class and Mr. Notlieb observed him for two hours. At the end of the time, Sam was excited to actually be able to accomplish so much with the students. However, Mr. Notlieb was not so excited. A few days later, Mr. Notlieb finished Sam's write-up and put it in his mailbox. Sam found it and read the four-page report. He was graded unsatisfactorily for the first time in his life. There was a whole list of concerns, but not one explanation on how to improve his inadequacies. It was also the first time anyone had seen the observation form. Mr. Notlieb decided to use a new way to observe teachers, handed down from the district office, that he had not informed any of his staff about. These issues infuriated Sam and have basically taken away any desire Sam had to perform his job. The other teachers heard about what had occurred and rallied around him. They also informed Sam of Mr. Notlieb's tendency to rip apart his new teachers for whatever reason. This calmed Sam a bit, but it was still no excuse.

The morale at Wickett Middle School is very low and that it is directly linked to the poor administration of the school's principal. There are other administrators involved, who try to do what they can, however, they are on fairly tight leashes.

SUMMARY

Given the number of motivation theories available, which can be confusing to all of us, perhaps the best approach for the educator is to be situationally selective. Steers and Porter write: "In recent years . . . the notion of a multiple strategy using different approaches to motivation at one time or another depending upon the nature of the organization, its technology, its people, and its goals and priorities has come to be labeled a 'contingency approach' to management."

An interesting movement in this direction has been developed by Mitchell, Ortiz, and Mitchell in their case studies of the work orientations of fifteen teachers. The teachers fall into four national groups created by two overlapping distinctions: (1) differing views on the mission and goals of education and (2) the degree to which they identify with other adults in the school or their students.

The first group, called the *master teachers*, comprises the task-oriented instructional leaders who believe in academics discipline and rigor and getting to the so-called student at risk. The master teachers' rewards tend to be adult centered, and their major criticism is reserved for administrators who do not provide essential support when it is most needed.

Another group, called the *instructors*, is also dedicated to intellectual achievement, but they identify more with their students than with other adults. "They view teaching as a technically sophisticated, skilled craft, and they believe that students learn through active engagement in intellectually stimulating activities." The teachers referred to as *coaches* identify with students and place nurture and development goals ahead of measurable academic achievement. These teachers shift back and forth between stressing the rigorous demands of the curriculum and offering warmth, receptiveness, and encouragement to students. Primary goals are for students to get along with each other and be respectful.

Finally, helpers see their role as aiding students to deal with the demands of schooling so they can later meet the demands of life. These teachers tend to identify with other adults and do not feel they are personally responsible for the grade-level achievement of their students. If the students can cope with the academic curriculum, then the teachers have done their jobs. This group contained all the weakest teachers in the study.

The point is that teachers are not generic human beings. They differ in terms of what motivates and rewards productive and creative behavior. The important task for all educational administrators is to gain insight into the special motivational requirements and reward structures of specific teachers and staff and, if possible, match them with whatever the situation requires. As has been our constant theme in this book, therefore, instructional motivation becomes quite situational. Thus, the situation determines the theory of motivation that should be utilized, and because a variety of situations are in an educational setting, aspects of various motivational theories should be utilized at various times.

NOTES

1. A. H. Maslow, *Motivation and Personality*, 3rd ed. (New York: Harper & Row, 1987).

2. C. P. Alderfer, *Existence, Relatedness, and Growth: Human Needs in Organizational Settings* (New York: Free Press, 1972).

3. D. McClelland, *The Achieving Society* (Princeton, N.J.: D. Van Nostrand, 1961); D. C. McClelland, *Motives, Personality, and Society: Selected Papers* (New York: Praeger, 1984).

4. F. Herzberg, B. Mausner, and B. B. Snyderman, *The Motivation to Work* (New York: Wiley, 1959); F. Herzberg, *The Managerial Choice: To Be Efficient and to Be Human* (Salt Lake City: Olympus, 1982).

5. William Glasser, *Control Theory, A New Explanation of How We Control Our Lives* (New York, Harper and Row, 1984).

6. S. Adams, Inequity in Social Exchange, in *Advances in Experimental and Social Psychology*, vol. 2, ed. L. Berkowitz (New York: Academic Press, 1965), pp. 267–300. See also E. Walster, W. Walster, and E. Berscheid, *Equity: Theory and Research* (Boston: Allyn and Bacon, 1978).

7. B. A. Mellers, Equity Judgment, A revision of Aristotelian views, *Journal of Experimental Psychology: General* 111 (1982): 242–270; M. H. Birnbaum, Perceived Equity in Salary Policies, *Journal of Applied Psychology* 68 (1983): 49–59.

8. E. L. Thorndike, *Behaviorism* (New York: Norton, 1924); B. F. Skinner, *The Behavior of Organisms: An Experimental Approach* (New York: Appleton-Century, 1938).

9. M. G. Evans, Organizational Behavior: The Central Role of Motivation, in J. G. Hunt and J. D. Blair, eds., 1986 Yearly Review of Management of the Journal of Management (1986): 203–222, counters the overwhelming evidence in support of this theory by suggesting that the identification and assessment of an individual's valences over time remains a problem.

10. R. Vance and A. Colella, Effects of Two Types of Feedback on Goal Acceptance and Personal Goals, *Journal of Applied Psychology* 75 (1990): 68–76.

11. G. P. Latham and G. A. Yukl, A Review of Research on the Application of Goal Setting in Organizations, *Academy of Management Journal* 18 (1975): 824–845.

12. See B. D. Bannister and D. B. Balkin, Performance Evaluation and Compensation Feedback Messages: An Integrated Model, *Journal of Occupational Psychology* 63 (1990): 97–111, for a model of intervening variables between feedback and motivation; see also J. R. Larson, The Performance Feedback Process: A Preliminary Model, *Organizational Behavior and Human Performance* 33 (1984): 42–76; R. C. Liden and T. R. Mitchell, Reactions to Feedback: The Role of Attributions, *Academy of Management Journal* 28 (1985): 291–308.

13. Wayne K. Hoy and Cecil G. Miskel, *Educational Administration*, 5th ed. (New York, McGraw-Hill, 1997).

14. A. W. Hart, A Career Ladder's Effect on Teacher Career and Work Attitudes, *American Educational Research Journal* 24, no. 4 (1987): 479–503.

15. W. A. Firestone, Merit Pay and Job Enlargement as Reforms: Incentives, Implementation and Teacher Response, *Educational Evaluation and Policy Analysis* 13, no. 3 (1991): 269–288.

5

EFFECTIVE COMMUNICATION

It appears then that genuine friendship cannot exist where one of the parties is unwilling to hear the truth and the other is equally indisposed to speak it.

—Cicero

One of the perennial complaints of school personnel is a lack of communication between themselves and another segment of the school community. Oftentimes, the greatest perceived "communications gap" is between the faculty and the administration. If an administrator is to be effective, then he or she must master the skill of effective communication.

In this chapter, we examine the nature of effective communication, a central organizational process that can occur at the intrapersonal, interpersonal, intragroup, intergroup, institutional, and public levels. As a linking mechanism among the various organizational subsystems, communication is a central feature of the structure of groups and organizations. It builds and reinforces interdependence between and among the various parts of the institution.

The chapter first describes the communication process and then its five components: encoding, transmission, decoding and listening, noise, and feedback. Next it looks at downward, upward, and lateral communication.

Then it discusses how interpersonal relations and attitudes affect the quality of communication, as well as issues of informal communication. It continues by presenting a set of strategies for improving communication accuracy. The chapter concludes with a discussion of a special type of communication in education—interviewing.[1]

THE COMMUNICATION PROCESS

Perception, attribution, motivation, individual personality and personal development, group characteristics, and organizational factors all affect the way individuals transmit information and receive information transmitted by another. We begin with a simple example of the communication process. A teacher recently asked the principal how long the new ecology curriculum would be. The principal responded by stating, "Ten weeks." When the teacher asked that simple question and the principal replied, they both participated in a complex communication process.

In communication, an input is transformed by encoding and decoding, resulting in another meaning, or output, which is fed back to the sender. There are several steps of the process. Each of these steps should follow three principles of ethical communication:

1. Organization members should not intentionally deceive one another.
2. Organization members' communication should not purposely harm any other organization member or members of the organization's relevant environment.
3. Organization members should be treated justly.[2]

Encoding

Once a person has a meaning to convey, he or she needs to determine the means to convey that meaning, in other words, the way to encode it. The sender uses his or her own frame of reference as the background for encoding information. It included the individual's view of the organization or situation as a function of personal education, interpersonal relationships, attitudes, knowledge, and experience.

Going back to the teacher–principal example, first the teacher had a meaning he wished to convey. The principal later learned that he wanted to determine the content and comprehensiveness of the ecology curriculum. The teacher did not want to know its length but rather its scope. Notice that this meaning differs from the question he asked. Next, he had to decide how to encode this meaning. He had to decide, for example, an efficient way of getting the needed information. He considered, probably unconsciously, whom he should ask: the principal, a teacher colleague, the assistant principal. Should he ask the question by phone, in a letter, or directly? What specific question should he ask so that he would be understood? What nonverbal messages should accompany his question? How else might the teacher have encoded the message to make it clearer? He might have asked what tasks would be included in the ecology curriculum development? Or he might have asked the desired outcomes? In encoding the message, the teacher should have considered what was the most effective way to convey his desire for certain information? On the other hand, as we will see, the principal should have asked that the question be clarified so that she could respond accurately.

The choice of words or language in which a sender encodes a message will influence the quality of communication. Because language is a symbolic representation of a phenomenon, room for interpretation and distortion of the meaning exist. Consider the instructor who decides to present an entire class in a foreign language that few or none of the students understand. Think about the superintendent of schools whose directions are so ambiguous that the principals cannot determine the most appropriate way to act. In each of these cases, the inappropriate use of language can limit the quality of effective communication. People can use the same words but attribute different meanings to them; such bypassing can occur in cross-cultural situations or in stressful situations.[3]

A sender can create misunderstandings by using language in a number of ways. The sender might use words that are too abstract and have many mental images associated with them. Or the sender might overgeneralize messages and fail to recognize subtleties. The use of jargon frequently creates misunderstandings, as does the use of slang or colloquialisms in speech. Some senders consciously use messages to confuse the issue. Some politicians have been accused of this, not to mention principals, superintendents, and college presidents.

Misuses of language are especially common between superiors and their subordinates. For example, a subordinate can create misunderstandings by distorting information upward, for example, telling the administrator only good news, paying the principal compliments whenever possible, always agreeing with the principal and the superintendent, insulating the principal from information detrimental to him or her. The principal can create misunderstandings by withholding information or not conveying what he or she really thinks about the teacher.

The use of gestures, movements, material things, time, and space can clarify or confuse the meaning of verbal communication. For example, the kind of facial expressions that accompany a request for time off may indicate its importance or triviality.

Nonverbal cues serve five functions. They repeat the message the individual is making verbally; an individual who nods after he or she answers affirmatively confirms the verbal message with the nonverbal gesture. They can contradict a message the individual is trying to convey; a superintendent who pounds the desk while stating that he or she does not care about the situation being discussed uses verbal and nonverbal communication that disagree. The nonverbal communication can, in some cases, be more powerful or accurate than the verbal communication. Nonverbal cues might also substitute for a verbal message; a teacher with "fire in his eyes" conveys information without using verbal messages. They can add to or complement a verbal message; a college dean who beams while giving praise increases the impact of the compliment to the subordinate. Or, nonverbal communication might accent or underline a verbal message; for example, speaking very softly or stamping your feet shows the importance an individual attaches to a message. Senders must recognize, therefore, the significance of nonverbal communication and use it to increase the impact of their verbal communication.

The actual transmission of the message follows the encoding; the sender must convey the message to the receiver. Here, the teacher went to the principal's office. He walked in and asked how long the ecology curriculum would be. Thus the transmission of his message took place primarily by verbal channels. In determining the appropriateness of this medium, the teacher should consider among other factors the medium's richness, as determined by its speed of feedback, variety of communication channels, extent of personal interactions, and the richness of language. As tasks become more ambiguous, administrators should increase the richness of the media they use; for example, they should send nonroutine and difficult communications through a rich medium, such as face-to-face communication, and routine simple communications through a lean medium, such as a memorandum. They should also use rich media to increase personal visibility and implement institutional strategies.

Transmission

The widespread availability of electronic media for communication, including messaging and conferencing systems, has had a significant impact on the accessibility of information and the speed of transmission. Table 5.1 lists the features of various electronic media.

Table 5.1 Features of various electronic media

Type of Media	Brief Description	Type of Communication Supported	Timing and Geography	Typical s Feature
(1) Voice Messaging	Augmentation for telephone communication Ability to leave and retrieve voice or synthesized voice messages	One-to-one One-to-many	Asynchronous Time independent Geographic distribution	Message forwarding Distribution lists Message storage and retrieval Message editing
(2) Electronic Messaging (EMC)	Substitution for telephone or face-to-face User creates a written document using a computer terminal or the equivalent	One-to-one One-to-many	Asynchronous Time independent Geographic distribution	Message creating and editing User receives messages in an electronic in-basket; messages may be answered, filed and/or discarded Message storage and retrieval Distribution list Message forwarding
Conferencing Systems (1) Audio and Audiographic	Similar to telephone conference call	Group	Synchronous Geographic distribution	Ability to transmit graphic materials

Type of Media	Brief Description	Type of Communication Supported	Timing and Geography	Typical s Feature
Conferencing Systems (2) Video	Participants cannot see each other May have visual aids Substitution for face-to-face meeting, travel	Group	Synchronous Geographic distribution One-way in multiple locations Two-way in two locations only	accompanying a meeting Images of speaker and images of other participants displayed simultaneously Graphical materials also displayed
(3) Computer	Substitution for face-to-face meeting, travel Transmits voice and images of participants Can be one-way or two-way Substitution for face-to-face meeting, travel Meetings conducted using text (no audio, no video)	Group One-on-one	Synchronous or asynchronous Time independent Geographic distribution	Text editing, storage and retrieval Transcript of proceedings maintained Ability for private communication among participants Ability to poll conference participants and collect results of a vote Bulletin boards Preparation and editing of shared documents
(4) Integrated Systems	Substitution for telephone or face-to-face Augmentation of traditional written communication Provides support for messaging, word processing, data processing, and administrative activities using a single interface	One-to-one One-to-many	Asynchronous Time independent Geographic distribution	Same features as electronic messaging Ability to create, edit, store and retrieve, and transmit formal documents Electronic calendars and scheduling Ability to retrieve shared documents. Support for traditional data processing

Management information systems, now using computer-based software programs, also facilitate communication by making large quantities of information available and assisting in its analysis. Most school systems and other educational institutions have information specialists who make relevant information available to the various parts of the school community. Some school systems integrate the use of management information systems technologies into the regular performance of positions at all levels of the system.

The advent of the various communications technologies has influenced the amount of information transmitted in organizations. Ideally, individuals involved in the communication process receive an appropriate amount of information. Sometimes, they receive too little information, called *underload*, or too much information, called *overload*. Individuals who require limited coordination with others, experience great physical distance from others, have highly routine jobs with few time constraints and few decisions to be made, and have ability and desire to communicate typically experience underload. Those who require extensive coordination to do the job, experience close physical proximity to others, have unique job requirements with few time constraints and many decisions to be made, and have a high ability and desire to communicate are more likely to experience overload. Underload can result in alienation, lack of motivation, and apathy; overload can cause high stress, confusion, and mistakes.

Decoding and Listening

Not only does the sender influence the effectiveness of communication, but the quality of listening by the receiver also helps determine communication quality. The principal in our example performed the next step of the communication process. She needed to decode the message she had received to attach some meaning to it. An individual's decoding of a message, like encoding, depends on his or her frame of reference. She might have interpreted the teacher's question in several different ways, again based on her frame of reference. She might, for example, have viewed the teacher's question as a plea for an easy work load; or she might have felt that the teacher literally wanted the information he requested, the number of weeks the curriculum project would require. If there had been conflict between the teacher and the principal, the principal might have interpreted the question as something meant to annoy her or distract her from her work, or as something that would support the principal's view of the teacher as incompetent. If her usual perception was that the teacher was a hard worker, then she might have interpreted the question as another indication of his concern and industriousness.

The misunderstanding between the principal and the teacher in our example emphasized the importance of listening. Collecting data is the first step in quality communication. Receivers can listen in directing, judgmental, probing, smoothing, or active ways. In effective listening, the receiver practices active listening by trying to understand both the facts and the feelings being conveyed. It requires determining what the speaker is trying to say from his or her own viewpoint. Consider the example of the principal and the teacher. If the principal acknowledged the feelings and body language of the teacher, she might have asked a probing question that would have clarified the situation and brought about an accurate response. Listeners, then, must recognize the importance of nonverbal communication and look for nonverbal cues that support or contradict verbal information.[5]

Noise

Many decodings reflect some noise or interference in the communication process. They suggest some factors, such as conflict, between the principal and the teacher or the principal's understanding of the messages in such a way that she did not "hear" what the teacher intended. Noise can include physical noise that interferes with transmission, such as static on a telephone line or the noise created by office or school machinery. But noise might be inaudible. The presence of a silent third party during a conversation could act as noise that distracts the receiver from hearing what the speaker said. Or the frame of reference of the receiver may cause that person to hear the message in a way other than the one in which it was intended. Noise can also include characteristics of senders or receivers, such as their socioeconomic background, experience education, or value system.

What types of noise likely exist in communications described in the opening example? Differences in roles in the organization can create noise. Biases in their attributions for poor performance can create noise. So, too, can various perceptual predispositions, such as different personal and organizational goals, attitudes, and orientations.

Recent research suggests that men and women communicate differently. A classic story illustrates a basic difference between male and female communication. A man and a woman were driving to a meeting at a location that they had never before visited. After fifty minutes of driving around in circles, the woman was visibly upset. When asked why, she responded that she was not upset about being lost, but was furious that her male companion had repeatedly refused to stop and ask questions.[5] Women ask for information and men resist asking for it.

In one study, women sounded more polite but also were more uncertain, whereas men used more informal pronunciations, sounded more challenging, direct, and authoritative; the feminine style was more accommodating, intimate, collaborative, and facilitative, whereas the male style was more action oriented, informational, and controlling. Recognizing such differences should facilitate more accurate diagnoses of communication problems.[5]

Feedback

Feedback refers to an acknowledgment by the receiver that the message has been received; it provides the sender with information about the receiver's understanding of the message being sent. The principal's feedback to the teacher, in which she provided only the length of the project, indicated an inaccurate understanding. If the principal had told the teacher that the project will involve a detailed feasibility study and cost analysis, the principal would have conveyed a different understanding.[6]

Often, one-way communication occurs between administrators and their colleagues. Because of inherent power differences in their positions, administrators might give large quantities of information and directions to their faculty and staff without providing the opportunity for the faculty and staff to show their understanding or receipt of the information. These managers often experience conflict between their role as authorities and a desire to be liked by their colleagues. Other administrators have relied on the use of written memoranda as a way of communicating with faculty and staff. In addition to the inherent lack of feedback involved in this format, the use of a single channel of communication also limits the effectiveness of communication. The proliferation of the use of e-mail has alleviated this problem somewhat by providing a relatively facile feedback mechanism.

Why do administrators sometimes not involve their faculty and staff in two-way communication? In some instances, administrators do not trust their colleagues to contribute effectively. In other situations, lack of self-confidence by the administrator makes him or her appear uninterested in or unconcerned about others' opinions. Or administrators assume that their faculty and staff have the same goals as they do, and thus feel that input from colleagues is not required or would not add anything of significance to the process.

What is your attitude toward feedback? You can assess it by completing questionnaires designed to measure attitudes. The higher your score, the more discomfort you feel in giving feedback. Recognizing a discomfort about giving or receiving feedback is a key step in eliminating this barrier and improving the quality of managerial communication. Encouraging feedback from others helps show them that you are concerned about them as individuals, in ways that go beyond merely ensuring that they produce.

Subordinates also have responsibility for encouraging two-way communication. Although managers might attempt to protect their power positions, subordinates attempt to protect the image their supervisor holds of them. Frequently, for example, an assistant superintendent will withhold negative information about themselves or their activities. Or they might fail to inform the superintendent about his or her needs and values. Other subordinates mistrust their superiors and so withhold any information from them. Why do these situations arise? Some subordinates assume that they and their bosses have different goals. Others mistrust their bosses. Still others lack persistence in seeking responses from their supervisors. Impression of management, therefore, plays a key role in whether individuals send feedback. They might assess in what way asking for feedback will be interpreted and how the resulting information will affect each person's public image. In order for effective communication to take place, then, subordinates must show that they, too, are willing to build relationships with their superiors.

THE DIRECTION OF COMMUNICATION

The educational leader's ability to successfully communicate is a function of his or her capability to encourage subordinates to participate actively in the communication process. They must understand the significance of the direction of communication. Although structural factors facilitate and direct communication to a high degree in organizations, these hierarchical arrangements contribute to communication difficulties in organizations as well. Centralization of authority at the higher levels of the organization restricts the dissemination of information. Some organizational members might have access to more information than others. Some subsystems might have more access than other subsystems. Because some people either know much more or possess different information, centralization, which discourages shared information, increases the potential for misunderstandings among the various subsystems. The extent to which organizations have specialized work groups also influences the quality of communication. Where differences exist among departments in their goals and expertise, communication among peers may be limited. Administrators in high schools and colleges must be keenly aware of this phenomenon.[7]

Downward Communication

Administrators use this type of communication to disseminate information and directives to subordinates. Using downward communication to share both good news and bad news with teachers and staff should be followed by an opportunity for feedback. Encouraging face-to-face communication between all levels of employees and administrators through school and classroom visits or administration/staff discussion groups, publishing faculty and staff newsletters, and even introducing a communication hotline can facilitate accurate downward communication.

Too often, however, downward communication becomes one way, with no provision for feedback. Although most administrators intend to communicate accurately to their colleagues, some consciously or unconsciously distort downward communication. Administrators can withhold, screen or manipulate information. What results from this type of communication? Subordinates can become very distrustful of their managers and circumvent them to obtain accurate information. They might rely instead on rumors, obtaining equally distorted and potentially harmful information. In some organizations, downward communication between supervisors and immediate subordinates is relatively accurate, but information from top management fails to pass accurately through the hierarchy and reach the lower-level employees; managers might adjust or delay it along the way so it better fits their objectives. In addition, managers and subordinates may differ in their perceptions of the quality of downward communication. For example, if a superintendent delays the communication of poor standardized test scores for the school district until his or her contract is renewed, he or she would be thwarting the communication process and distorting downward communication.

Although open communication has been considered a panacea for many organizational problems, some researchers have argued that characteristics of the individuals involved, their relationships, and the organization and environment in which they function should influence how open communication should be. Disclosure and directness can backfire if, for example, the principal of a school indicates prematurely to a faculty that the school might be closing in a downsizing of the district. Letting out such information prematurely can have the effect of a self-fulfilling prophecy.

Upward Communication

Encouraging ongoing upward communication as part of the organization's culture can minimize such dysfunctional consequences. Primarily a feedback vehicle, upward communication refers to messages sent from subordinates to their supervisors. Top and middle management must create a culture that promotes honest upward communication as a way of counteracting employees' tendencies to hide potentially damaging information. Such a culture encourages employee participation in decision making, rewards openness, and limits inflexible policies and arbitrary procedures. It also promotes creativity and innovation. Acting constructively on information communicated upward reinforces its future occurrence and limits administrative isolation. If a culture of open communication and trust is established in a school, for example, teachers and staff will be more likely to be totally frank and bring new ideas to the administration.

Whereas, in a culture of coercion and vindictiveness, teachers and staff will withhold information and become defensive.

Lateral Communication

Sharing information, engaging in problem solving, and coordinating the work flow with employees at their same level in the organization complements both downward and upward communication. Although some messages need to go through formal channels, many can be handled through informal channels, or laterally. Teachers sharing classroom management techniques with each other, principals forming a support group with other principals, and custodians purchasing cleaning materials in conjunction with custodians in other institutions to save money on bulk purchases are examples of lateral communication. Communication directly between colleagues and counterparts typically has greater speed and accuracy, although distortions can still occur in encoding, transmission, and decoding. Although employees in different or distant departments might have historical problems communicating directly, the advent of electronic communication devices should remove some obstacles. Still, in some cases, managers insist that workers rely on the hierarchy for an exchange of information. This is especially true when communicating with the public. It is often necessary when communicating with parents, for example, that a uniform message be communicated. In these cases, the hierarchical approach is more appropriate.

Special roles in the organization can facilitate accurate lateral communication. Gatekeepers screen information and access to a group or individual. Situated at the crossroads of communication channels, these positions act as nerve centers, where they switch information among people and groups. Human resource professionals and external relations personnel are examples of individuals who can serve the gatekeeper role. Mid-level administrators can also serve this role.

INTERPERSONAL RELATIONS AND COMMUNICATION

The relationship between the individuals or groups communicating, as well as the type of climate they create during their communication, affects the accuracy with which messages are given and received. The sender's and receiver's trust of and influence over each other, the sender's aspirations regarding upward mobility in the organization, and norms and sanctions of the group to which the sender and receiver belong influence the quality of communication. When people trust each other, their communication tends to be more accurate and open; on the contrary, when they distrust each other, they are more likely to be secretive or hesitant to speak openly. This is why it is imperative for a school administrator to engender trust in their colleagues if they expect to be effective. Suppose, for example, a college dean establishes an elaborate induction program for new faculty. In a culture of trust, senior faculty will perceive the induction program as an appropriate way of assimilating the junior faculty into the school culture. In a culture of distrust, however, it is just as likely that such an elaborate induction program will be perceived as an attempt by the administration to co-opt the junior faculty to the detriment of the senior faculty.

MULTICULTURAL COMMUNICATION ISSUES

Cross-cultural issues can affect the quality of communication. For example, differences in norms for the appropriate amount of interpersonal space exist in different cultures. Effective communication requires deciphering basic values, motives, aspirations, and assumptions across geographical, functional, or social class lines. It also means seeing one's own culture as different, but not necessarily better. Cross-cultural miscommunication occurs when a receiver misunderstands the message transmitted by a sender of another culture. For example, if an African American faculty member describes the school's principal as an "operator" to an Hispanic faculty member, the Hispanic will most likely not understand the implication.[8]

The compatibility or incompatibility of the verbal and nonverbal styles used to communicate can also influence the effectiveness of intercultural communication. Verbal styles differ along a variety of dimensions. Japanese camouflage the speaker's true intent in an indirect style, use role-centered or contextual language, and are receiver oriented. The Arabs use an elaborate style or very expressive language in everyday communication. In contrast, North American communication can be described as direct, personal, instrumental, and succinct. Non-verbal communication also varies in cultures because individuals attach different meanings to interpersonal space, touch, and time. For example, interpersonal distance is low among South Americans, Southern and Eastern Europeans, and Arabs, and high among Asians, Northern Europeans, and North Americans.

To ensure quality communication, communicators should first assume that cultural differences exist, and they should try to view the situation from the perspective of their foreign colleagues. They can then adjust their encoding or decoding and their use of language or listening skills to respond to likely differences. Knowledge of the characteristics of diverse cultures facilitates such an adjustment. A cultural integrator, a person who understands differences in a society from the home country and the ways the organization can adapt to them, can also reduce the barrier of inadequate cross-cultural sensitivity. Until all individuals have cross-cultural sensitivity, such special arrangements might be necessary for quality multicultural communication. Multicultural considerations such as these are becoming increasingly important in educational institutions, especially those in higher education. It is not uncommon to have significant numbers of faculty, administration, and staff who are from cultures other than that of the majority.

IMPROVING COMMUNICATION

What can individuals do to improve their communication in both formal and informal settings? In this section, we examine three ways of increasing communication effectiveness: creating a supportive communication climate, using an assertive communication style, and using active listening techniques.

In communicating with their faculties and staffs, administrators know they must create a trusting and supportive environment. Creating such a climate has the objective of shifting from evaluation to problem solving and formation in communication. They must avoid making employees feel defensive, that is, threatened by the communication. They can create such an atmosphere in at least six ways:[9]

1. They use descriptive rather than valuative speech and do not imply that the receiver needs to change. An administrator could describe teacher traits in terms of strengths and areas in need of further development, rather than describing them as weaknesses.

2. They take a problem orientation, which implies a desire to collaborate in exploring a mutual problem, rather than trying to control or change the listener. An administrator can ask the teacher what he or she hopes to achieve in the lesson, or for the academic year, rather than setting out a list of goals for the teacher.

3. They are spontaneous and honest and reveal their goals, rather than appearing to use "strategy" that involves ambiguous and multiple motivations. A superintendent might share with the school community the need for restructuring and possible areas of downsizing rather than doing so surreptitiously.

4. They convey empathy for the feelings of their listener, rather than appearing unconcerned or neutral about the listener's welfare. They give reassurance that they are identifying with the listener's problems, rather than denying the legitimacy of the problems. When reviewing a union grievance with a teacher, the principal may indicate sensitivity to the teacher's position even though the decision could ultimately go against the teacher.

5. They indicate that they feel equal rather than superior to the listener. Thus, they suggest that they will enter a shared relationship, not simply dominate the interaction. A college dean might come out from behind his or her desk and sit next to a colleague to indicate a relationship of equality.

6. Finally, they communicate that they will experiment with their own behavior and ideas, rather than be dogmatic about them. They do not give the impression that they know all the answers and do not need help from anyone. An administrator can concede that he or she does not know if his or her suggestion will work, but ask that the employee in question "try it."

In addition, supportive communication emphasizes a congruence between thoughts and feelings and communication. An individual who feels unappreciated by a supervisor, for example, must communicate that feeling to the supervisor, rather than deny it or communicate it inaccurately. Communication must also validate an individual's importance, uniqueness, and worth. Nondefensive communication recognizes the other person's existence; recognizes the person's uniqueness as an individual, rather than treating him or her as a role or a job; acknowledges the worth of the other person; acknowledges the validity of the other person's perception of the world; and expresses willingness to be involved with the other person, at least during the communication.

Interpersonal communication can be improved by encouraging individuals to communicate using as complete knowledge of themselves and others as possible. The Johari window provides an analytical tool that individuals can use to identify information that is available for use in communication. Table 5.2 illustrates this model of interpersonal knowledge.[10] Notice that information about an individual is represented along two dimensions: (1) information known and unknown by the self and (2) information known and unknown by others.

Together, these dimensions form a four-category representation of the individual. The open self is information known by the self and known by others. The blind self is information unknown by the self and known by others, such as others' perceptions of your behavior or attitudes. The concealed self is information known by you and unknown by others; secrets we keep from others about ourselves fall into this category. Finally, the unconscious self is information that is unknown to the self and unknown to others. To ensure quality communication, in most cases, an individual should communicate from his or her open self to another's open self and limit the amount of information concealed or in the blind spot. Guarded communication might be appropriate, however, if one party has violated trust in the past, if the parties have an adversarial relationship, if power and status differentials characterize the culture, if the relationship is transitory, or if the corporate culture does not support openness.

Table 5.2 Johari window

	Known by Self	Unknown by Self
Known by Others	Open Self	Blind Self
Unknown by Others	Concealed Self	Unknown Self

THE ASSERTIVE COMMUNICATION STYLE

An assertive style, which is honest, direct, and firm, also improves communication. With this style, a person expresses personal needs, opinions, and feelings in honest and direct ways and stands up for his or her rights without violating the other person's. Assertive behavior is reflected in the content and the nonverbal style of the message. The assertive delegator, for example, "is clear and direct when explaining work to subordinates, doesn't hover, [and] . . . criticizes fairly, objectively, and constructively."[11]

Consider the situation of a superintendent whose assistant has missed two important deadlines in the past month. How would she respond assertively? She might say to her assistant: "I know you missed the last two deadlines. Is there an explanation I should know? It is important that you meet the next deadlines. You should have let me know the problems you were facing and explained the situation to me, rather than saying nothing." An assertive response can include the expression of anger, frustration, or disappointment, but it is couched in terms that would allow for feedback to obtain the employee's explanation for the behavior. This distinguishes it from an aggressive style, which is inappropriate behavior.

We can further contrast the assertive approach to nonassertive and aggressive styles. Nonassertive communication describes behavior where the sender does not stand up for personal rights and indicates that his or her feelings are unimportant; the person might be hesitant, apologetic, or fearful. In the situation of a missed deadline, nonassertive behavior might involve saying nothing to your assistant, hoping the situation would not recur. Individuals act nonassertively because they might mistake assertion for aggression, mistake nonassertion for politeness or being helpful, refuse to accept their personal rights, experience anxiety about negative consequences of assertiveness, or lack assertiveness skills.[12]

Aggressive communication stands up for an individual's rights without respecting the rights of the other person. Aggressive behavior attempts to dominate and control others by sounding accusing or superior. In the situation of the missed deadlines, an aggressive response might be "You always miss deadlines. You're taking advantage of me and the situation. If you miss another deadline, disciplinary action will be taken." Although such a response might result in the desired behavior in the short run, its long-term consequences likely will be dysfunctional, resulting in distrust

between the individuals involved. Ultimately, such behavior will negatively affect productivity and will especially affect the submission of creative and innovative solutions offered to management by the employee.

USING ACTIVE LISTENING TECHNIQUES

Active listening, which requires understanding both the content and the
intent of a message, can be facilitated by paraphrasing, perception
checking, and behavior description.

The receiver can paraphrase the message conveyed by the sender by
stating in his or her own way what the other person's remarks convey.
For example, if the sender states, "I don't like the work I am doing," the
receiver might paraphrase it as: "Are you saying that you are dissatisfied
with the profession of education?" or "Are you dissatisfied with the
grade that you teach?" or, "Do you wish to be reassigned to another
school?" Notice that these ways of paraphrasing the original message
suggest very different understandings of the original statement. The
sender, upon receiving this feedback from the receiver, can then clarify
his or her meaning.

Alternatively, the receiver might perception check, that is, describe
what he or she perceives as the sender's inner state at the time of communication to check his or her understanding of the message. For example, if the sender states, "I don't like the work I am doing," the receiver might check his or her perception of the statement by asking,
"Are you dissatisfied by the way you are being treated?" or, "Are you dissatisfied with me as a supervisor?" Answers to these two questions will
identify different feelings.

A third way of checking communication is through behavior description.
Here, the individual reports specific, observable actions of others without
making accusations or generalizations about their motives, personality, or
characteristics. Similarly, description of feelings, where the individual specifies or identifies feelings by name, analogy, or some other verbal representation, can increase active listening. For example, to help others understand you as a person, you should describe what others did that affects you
personally or as a group member. Then, you can let others know as clearly
and unambiguously as possible what you are feeling.

COMMUNICATION NETWORKS IN SCHOOLS

Communication is embedded in all school structures. In the traditional classical or bureaucratic model, formal communication channels, (networks) traverse the institution through the hierarchy of authority. Figure 5.1 illustrates a typical school district's formal communication network. Note that the chart delineates the formal communication channels and that every member reports to someone. The directors report to the assistant superintendent for instruction, who, with the assistant superintendent for finance, reports to the superintendent. The line of communication from the superintendent to the teachers goes through five hierarchical levels. This is reasonably short and direct for a large school district.

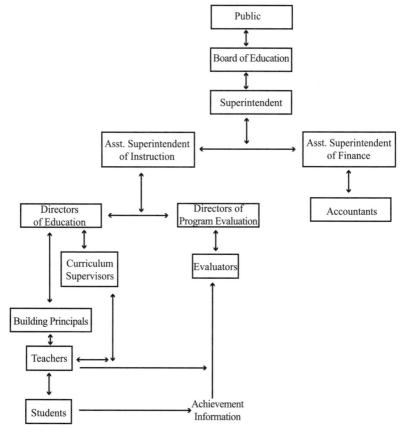

Figure 5.1   Formal communication channels for program implementation in a school district

With all organizations, formal restrictions on the communication process are apparent. "Making certain to go through proper channels" and "following the chain of command" are two common expressions that reflect a demand for control and structure of communication in organizations. Three characteristics of school bureaucracies seem particularly crucial to the formal system of communication. They are centralization in the hierarchy, the organization's shape or configuration, and the level of information technology.[13]

The degree that authority is not delegated but concentrated in a single source in the organization is important to the effectiveness of communication systems. In centralized schools, a few positions in the structure have most of the information-obtaining ability. For example, the superintendent and two assistant superintendents pictured in our illustration would gather most of the information for the formal system of communication. If the district is decentralized or loosely coupled, however, the information-obtaining potential is more or less spread across all of the positions. Research examining the different information-obtaining abilities supports the finding that centralized structures are more efficient communicators when the problems and tasks are relatively simple and straightforward. When the problems and tasks become more complex, however, decentralized hierarchies appear to be more efficient. We would argue that because the process of education is, by nature, complex, communication is an educational setting would be facilitated by a more decentralized structure (social systems or open systems models).

The number of hierarchical levels or tallness versus flatness of the school organization also affects the communication processes. Hierarchical levels and size are structural characteristics that are commonly associated with the shape of an organization. A school district with five levels, such as the one depicted here, differs from systems with more or fewer levels in its ability to communicate across levels and from top to bottom. The number of levels can be seen as the distance a message must travel. As the distance increases, the chance for message distortion increases and the satisfaction with the quality and quantity of communication decreases. Teachers will generally express less satisfaction with messages from superintendents than from principals. In addition, organizational size is negatively related to communication quality; as the district becomes larger, communication becomes more impersonal or formal and quality declines. This is part of the reason that the subdividing of large school districts into charter schools and "houses" within schools is proliferating. For communication and other purposes, "smaller is better."

Technology also appears to have a significant effect on organizational communication, though that effect remains somewhat speculative. As compared to other organizations, schools, and even colleges, have a relatively low level of technology. However, as communication technology becomes more sophisticated in schools, its use will dramatically alter the communication that takes place in both the formal and informal networks.

We are living in a creative and dynamic era that is producing fundamental changes, as is apparent in such advances as computer networks, electronic mail, computer conferences, communication satellites, data-handling devices, and the various forms of distance education. Until recently, electronic information exchange has largely been adapted to convey voice, vision, text, and graphics as distinct and separate types of communication. During the next few years, simultaneous and instantaneous transmission of voice, vision, text, and graphics to many locations will be common. Even imagining these technologies together with the geographic distribution of participants does not adequately capture the differences between these and traditional media. Consequently, the potential influence of such technologies on all aspects of communication in schools is probably underestimated.

EXTERNAL COMMUNICATION

The open system model of organizational structure highlights the vulnerability and interdependence of organizations and their environments. External environments are important because they affect the internal structures and processes of organizations; hence, one is forced to look both inside and outside the organization to explain behavior within school organizations. However, the growing necessity to interact with the outside environment placed added responsibilities and demands on the school district's communications processes. The need to communicate with parents, government officials, advocacy groups and the mass media cannot be denied. This necessity, however, is a relatively recent phenomenon and presents difficulties to administrators whose training does not normally include communicating with the public through the mass media.

Although the principles of effective communication still prevail when dealing with the outside community, some nuances need to be stressed. Perhaps the most important aspect of communication that needs to be considered when dealing with the public is the uniformity of the message. The message must be clear and consistent and be emanating from a singular source. In these cases, the "chain of command" and "channels of communication" need to be well defined and structured along the lines of the classical model. It is imperative that the school "speak with one voice." Someone in the school district should be designated as the clearinghouse for all external communication. This individual, or office, should review all external communication for clarity and accuracy and school personnel should be keenly aware of the school's policy with regard to external communication. Thus, although a more loosely structured communication system is very appropriate for internal communications, a more tightly structured one is necessary for effective external communications.

MATRIX DESIGN

To overcome some of the problems of the classical structure of most organizations, including schools, matrix or mixed designs have evolved to improve mechanisms of lateral communication and information flow across the organization.[14] An example of a matrix organization for a university is provided in figure 5.2.

The matrix organization, originally developed in the aerospace industry, is characterized by a dual authority system. There are usually functional and program or product line managers, both reporting to a common superior and both exercising authority over workers within the matrix. Typically, a matrix organization is particularly useful in highly specialized technological areas that focus on innovation. But that certainly does not preclude use in those educational settings where creativity and innovation needs to be fostered. The matrix design allows program managers to interact directly with the environment vis-à-vis new developments. Usually each program requires a multidisciplinary team approach; the matrix structure facilitates the coordination of the team and allows team members to contribute their special expertise.

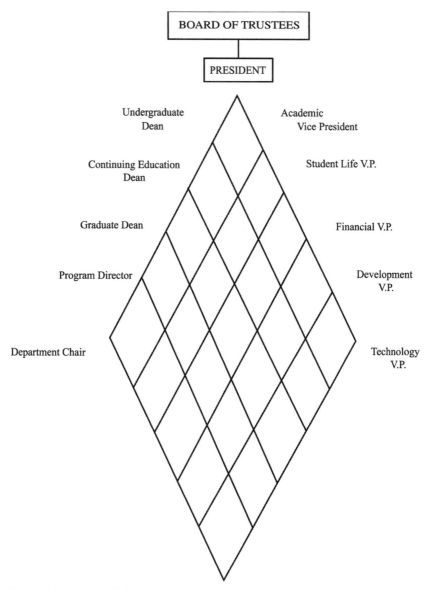

Figure 5.2   Matrix design

The matrix design has some disadvantages that stem from the dual authority lines. Individual workers might find having two supervisors to be untenable because it can create conflicting expectations and ambiguity. The matrix design can also be expensive in that both functional and program managers might spend a considerable amount of time in meetings attempting to keep everyone informed of program activities.

The use of matrix design in education is not very common, but it is a viable way of organizing when communication needs to occur outside the "proper channels." The popularity of interdisciplinary and multicultural courses and programs in education has caused an increased interest in matrix design. Many high schools and colleges are informally organized in a matrix design. It would most likely serve these institutions well to consider it as a formal organizational structure, especially in cases when communication problems are evident.

INTERVIEWS

Communication problems are most acute when administrators conduct some type of employee evaluation, such as an employment appraisal or an employment interview. In employment interviews, the communicators transmit information that allows them to make decisions about the fit between a job applicant and an available position. In performance appraisal, the administrator and employee share information about the employee's performance to date and future development.

The interviewer or assessor can ask open-ended questions or closed-ended questions. Open-ended questions allow the interviewee to structure the response to the question and present information that he or she feels is important.

Closed-ended questions, such as, "Tell me the first thing that you would do upon meeting your class for the first time" and "Who was the person who was most influential in your career choice?" allow the interviewer to focus a response more precisely. An interview can move from open-ended questions to closed-ended questions, alternate the two types of questions, or begin with closed-ended questions and end with open-ended ones.

The types of questions asked must also be geared to the nature of the position to be filled. In most interviews, the interviewer tries to make the interviewee feel at ease by beginning with questions that are relatively easy to answer and then moving on to questions that the interviewee might find more difficult.

Increasing the effectiveness of communication and the reliability of appraisals requires supervisors to obtain more complete descriptions of the employee's behavior. When we rely on a single source of information, persistent biases occur. One study indicated that raters who had a positive affect toward ratees were most lenient and those with a negative affect were least lenient. Another suggested that the raters who thought workers did well in one area, such as dependability, tended to think the employee did well in several areas (Halo Effect).[15]

Interviews can be conducted using a variety of different formats. Here is an interview agenda that can be effective:

1. Establish the atmosphere. Open the interview slowly and try to create a warm, pleasant, relaxed atmosphere that will reduce the candidate's anxiety.

2. Ask focused questions. Such questions will elicit the knowledge and information you need about the candidate. You want to learn of his or her perceptions of personal strengths and weaknesses, his or her understanding and philosophy of education, his or her verbal fluency, and his or her ability to project enthusiasm. The use of "what if" questions often works well to get the candidate indirectly to share these beliefs and attitudes with you.

3. Be an active listener. Ask open-ended questions, rather than yes or no questions. Support the candidate verbally with body language and "tell me mores." He or she should be contributing about 70 percent of the conversation to your 30 percent during the interview.

4. Share school information with the candidate. Remember the candidate also has a decision to make ("Do I want to come to work for you?"). Tell him or her about the specific job vacancy; with whom he or she may be working, particularly if those individuals met the candidate; the kinds of students enrolled in the school; particular programs that the school may have; and information about the school community if the candidate is not from the area.

5. Close the interview. Thank the individual for his or her time and openness. Share the next steps in the selection process including when he or she might expect to hear from you or how he or she might keep up with the decision process.

6. Write out your notes. Gather information from the others who participated in the interview process. Often, a team discussion works well. If several candidates are to be interviewed before a decision is made, the use of a checklist or some formatted method of recording your perceptions is wise so that later comparison can be more objective.

The interviewing process is particularly important in that if you make prudent and wise hiring decisions, they will preclude employee relations' problems in the future. Many a problematic teacher or staff member could have been screened out during the recruitment and selection process by a particularly astute interviewer.

CASE STUDY 5.1: THE CARSON SCHOOL SYSTEM

ORGANIZATIONAL STRUCTURE, BEHAVIOR, AND CULTURE

Carson School District is a large, diverse district located in suburban Philadelphia. Total enrollment for the year 1996 is 7,026 pupils with 418 members of the teaching faculty within the 9 buildings. The organizational structure of the district utilizes the classical theory as a means of organizing its administration, faculty, and staff.

Classical organization is necessary and accepted by all staff. The culture, however, of the school system and the behavior of the highest level administrators is clearly one that focuses on human relations. These administrators have a long history within the district as teachers and colleagues. They are well respected and genuinely liked. Yearly district social events are planned and attended enthusiastically by all levels of staff within the district.

The following chart illustrates the classical structure of the Carson School System:

9 Member School Board
Superintendent
Assistant Superintendent

Curriculum
Human Resources
Instructional Materials
Pupil Services
Principals
7 Elementary Schools
Junior High School
Senior High School
Assistant Principals
Faculty
Other Staff

Within each building, the contingency theory is evident. Building administrators generally have the power to employ various means of management depending upon the situation that is before them. The open system of management is clearly evidenced in the active PTO groups and various community involvements in the township. Social system components vary within each building, depending on the style of the principals and the needs of the staff. A classical approach is present on a daily basis if the situation calls for immediate and unquestioned authority.

THE JUNIOR HIGH SCHOOL

The junior high school includes seventh, eighth, and ninth grades with a total enrollment of 1,612. The following chart illustrates the hierarchy within this building:

Principal
Assistant Principal   Assistant Principal   Assistant Principal
7th Grade   8th Grade   9th Grade
            Department Chairpersons (7)   Aides
            Teachers (123)   Clerks
            Instructional Aides (5)   Secretaries
                                               Total (29)

PROBLEM

In August 1996, a new principal, Dr. Nancy Winters, was hired after an extensive search and intensive interviewing process. The former principal, John Evans, had worked in the district for a total of thirty-eight years, first as a teacher, second as an assistant principal, and last as a principal for eighteen years. John was well liked, but for years had become an ineffectual leader.

John's leadership style could best be described as laissez-faire. The number seasoned teachers had grown very comfortable with the status quo, but a growing number of new, inexperienced teachers who were in need of clearly defined structure and guidance set the stage for conflict when the new school year opened late in August.

LEADERSHIP

Dr. Winters is clearly a strong leader who sees the need for change. She brings a great deal of experience from a former job in which she institutionalized change, and she wants to have it happen again. The faculty, however, is not clear as to what needs to be changed, what her vision for them is, or how the institutionalization will affect them. Because she operates within a situational leadership style, she has confused and frustrated members of the faculty and is quickly setting up divisions within a faculty that had previously been united.

Her recent autocratic decisions regarding detentions have angered teachers, who in the past had been left alone to make those decisions. She has lengthened enormously and completely revamped the structure of monthly faculty meetings. Now staff are engaged in monthly in-servicing that seems to address Dr. Winters's perceived ineffectualness of the faculty.

Vroom-Yetton's model of the decision-making process describes a stage in which the leader gathers information from subordinates, does not necessarily tell them what the problem is, and then generates solutions. Dr. Winters has engaged in that mode of decision making most of the time.

Individual principal–teacher conferences have been held since the start of school. A forty-five-minute to one-hour conference with the principal, with an informal protocol, has been encouraged. It is here that she has gathered information and then acted upon it without teachers ever knowing the part they have played.

As of this date, there has been no forum for teachers to learn of her vision or for her to incorporate subordinates in the decision-making process. Many faculty members, if honest with themselves, would agree there is a need for change but are not being given a chance to use their abilities to advance that change. There are many strong, able, experienced "leaders" within the faculty who could initiate change in a positive manner. Dr. Winters, however, is quickly alienating the staff with her style of leadership in many areas.

MOTIVATION AND MANAGEMENT

Teachers in the past had experienced fulfillment of Glasser's five innate drives. John Evans, the former principal, provided faculty with the feeling of belonging, gave them power because he felt they had the knowledge and experience necessary, the freedom to make decisions, and they pursued "fun" together as a staff. The district provides the need for survival with a generous salary and benefits package. With those five innate needs in place, faculty could have effected change successfully. The problem with John Evans was, he did not have a vision for change.

Dr. Winters on the other hand, seems to have a vision, although the staff are unsure what it is, but the cost of her vision seems to be the loss of some of the staff's innate needs being met. She has taken away some of their power and freedom, which had provided them with an internal locus of control.

Her vision and the institutionalization of the same could be successfully met if the innate needs were in place and communication opened up for the staff to understand and share her vision. Her vision must become their vision in order for them to institutionalize change.

ORGANIZATIONAL COMMUNICATION

Communication, like all aspects of leadership should be contingent on the situation. Dr. Winters should certainly practice a classical chain of command in certain situations and does so. She is currently practicing a social system of communication at the macro level, by holding "Power Breakfasts" for parents on a monthly basis. These early morning meetings provide an opportunity for parents to discuss ideas, concerns, and questions.

A matrix organization of communication needs to be established for the staff. One in which lines of communication are multidirectional and will tap into the diversity, creativity, and strengths of all of the staff. It is open communication that will build trust. Dr. Winters must learn to trust us, and we must learn to trust her

SUMMARY

A foreign-born plumber in New York once wrote to the Bureau of Standards that he found hydrochloric acid fine for cleaning drains, and he asked if they agreed. Washington replied: "The efficacy of hydrochloric acid is indisputable, but the chlorine residue is incompatible with metallic permanence."

The plumber wrote back that he was mighty glad the Bureau agreed with him.

Considerably alarmed, the Bureau replied a second time: "We cannot assume responsibility for the production of toxic and noxious residues with hydrochloric acid, and suggest that you use an alternative procedure." The plumber was happy to learn that the Bureau still agreed with him.

Whereupon Washington wrote: "Don't use hydrochloric acid; it eats hell out of pipes."

Communication with ease and clarity is no simple task. There are, however, various orientations toward how it can be most effectively carried out. Classical theory, social system theory, and open system theory all incorporate a perspective toward the communication process; or, who should say what through which channel to whom and toward what effect. Classical theory stresses that the communication process exists to facilitate the manager's command and control over the employees in a formal, hierarchical, and downwardly directed manner. The purpose is to increase efficiency and productivity.

The social system orientation suggests that to be effective, communication has to be two way and that the meaning of the message is as much to be found in the psychological makeup of the receiver as it is the sender. The channels can be informal as well as formal and include anyone who has an interest in a particular subject.

The open system orientation emphasizes the communication process working toward drawing the various subsystems of an organization into a collaborating whole. Also, drawing the organization's actions into a close fit with the needs of its environment is an essential outcome of the process. This orientation emphasizes that between senders and receivers, the communication process must penetrate social class differences, cultural values, time orientations, and ethnocentrism of all types.

None of the conceptual frameworks, by itself, escapes the barriers to communication. The story of the plumber illustrates the problems of message coding, decoding, and transmission. We have suggested that in order for communication to be effective, we should adapt the process to the situation. We have suggested that when communicating with the outside community, a more structured process may be appropriate, while when communicating with the inside community a less-structured process might be more appropriate. This approach is in concert with one of the underlying themes of this text, that, whether we are speaking about organizational structure, leadership, motivation or communication, the situation determines the appropriate approach. In performance appraisal, the administrator and employee share information about the employee's performance to date and future development.

NOTES

1. K. J. Krone, F. M. Jablin, and L. L. Putnam, Communication Theory and Organizational Communication: Multiple Perspectives, in *Handbook of Organizational Communication: An Interdisciplinary Perspective*, ed.. F. Jablin, L. Putnam, K. Roberts, and L. Porter (Newbury Park, Calif.: Sage, 1987) 105–136s; P. G. Clampitt, *Communication for Managerial Effectiveness* (Newbury Park, Calif.: Sage, 1991).

2. G. L. Kreps, *Organizational Communication*, 2nd ed. (New York: Longman, 1990).

3. J. Sullivan, N. Kameda, and T. Nobu, Bypassing in Managerial Communication, *Business Horizons* 34, no. 1 (1991): 71–80.

4. R. C. Huseman and E. W. Miles, Organizational Communication in the Information Age, *Journal of Management* 14, no. 2 (1988): 181–204.

5. D. B. Rogers and R. E. Farson, Active Listening, in *Organizational Psychology: Readings on Human Behavior in Organizations*, ed. D. Kolb, I. Rubin, and J. McIntire (Englewood Cliffs, N.J.: Prentice-Hall, 1984).

6. E. W. Morrison and R. J. Bies, Impression Management in the Feedback-Seeking Process: A Literature Review and Research Agenda, *Academy of Management Review* 16, no. 3 (1991): 522–541.

7. P. V. Lewis, *Organizational Communication: The Essence of Effective Management*, 3rd ed. (New York: Wiley, 1987).

8. L. Copeland, Making Costs Count in International Travel, *Personnel Administrator* (July 1984): 47.

9. J. R. Gibb, Defensive Communication, *ETC: A Review of General Semantics* 22 (1965).

10. J. Hall, Communication Revised, *California Management Review* 15 (1973); J. Luft, *Group Processes: An Introduction to Group Dynamics* (Palo Alto, Calif.: Mayfield, 1970).

11. R. E. Zuker, *Mastering Assertiveness Skills* (New York: AMACOM, 1983), p. 79.

12. A. J. Lange and P. Jakubowski, *Responsible Assertive Behavior* (Champaign, Ill.: Research Press, 1976).

13. Wayne Hoy and Cecil Miskel, *Educational Administration*, 5th ed. (New York, McGraw-Hill, 1996), p.360.

14. See, for example, R. Jacobs and S. W. J. Kozlowski, A Closer Look at Halo Error in Performance Ratings, *Academy of Management Journal* 28 (1985): 201–212.

6

CONFLICT MANAGEMENT

The adventurer is within us, and he contests for our favour with the social man we are obliged to be. These two sorts of life are incompatible; one we hanker after, the other we are obliged to.

—William Bolitho

A few years ago, we invited Dr. Janet Baker, a well-known authority on conflict, to address a group of principals at a Principal's Academy that we were offering at St. Joseph's University in Philadelphia. We introduced Dr. Baker's topic as "conflict resolution." Upon taking the podium, Dr. Baker quickly corrected us and said that she was there to talk about "conflict management," not conflict resolution. "If your goal as a principal is to resolve conflict, you will be doomed to frustration and failure," she said. "The best that you can hope for is to manage conflict."

In this chapter, we begin our study of conflict management by considering the nature of conflict in organizations, especially schools. We look at its levels, stages, and consequences. We then introduce special issues associated with intergroup relations. We describe the typical ways groups interact, as well as the behavioral and attitudinal consequences of these interactions. We examine three influences on these interactions: perceptual differences, task issues, and power differences between groups. We conclude the chapter by examining prescriptions for dealing with conflict and improving the relations between groups.

THE NATURE OF CONFLICT

Conflict can be public or private, formal or informal, rational or nonrational. The likelihood of conflict increases when parties have the chance to interact, when the parties see their differences as incompatible, and when one or both parties see some utility in engaging in conflict to resolve incompatibility. Some individuals are more likely to engage in conflict than others. In one study, for example, individuals with a Type A behavior pattern (intense, assertive, and direct) had a higher frequency of conflict than those with a Type B pattern (more passive, low key, and diplomatic); women reported a lower frequency of conflict than men.[1]

Conflict most commonly results in four circumstances. First, when mutually exclusive goals or values actually exist or are perceived to exist by the groups involved, conflict can occur. In the collective bargaining process, for example, the teachers' union might perceive that the administration's goals conflict with those of the teachers, and vice versa. Second, behavior designed to defeat, reduce, or suppress the opponent can cause conflict. Again, union and management have historically experienced conflict for this reason. Third, groups that face each other with mutually opposing actions and counteractions cause conflict. For example, if the second-grade teacher does not follow the curriculum, the third-grade teacher will be affected because the students will not have been properly prepared. Finally, if each group attempts to create a relatively favored position, conflict might occur. If the English department attempts to show administration that it is superior to the other departments by demonstrating the others' ineptness, conflict occurs.

Conflict may be even more problematic in multinational or multicultural situations. Here basic differences in language, norms, personal styles, and other cultural characteristics hinder effective communication and set the stage for conflict. Cross-cultural sensitivity and understanding are the ingredients for minimizing dysfunctional conflict.[2]

THE RESULTS OF CONFLICT

Conflict can have functional or dysfunctional outcomes. Whether conflict takes a constructive or destructive course is influenced by the sociocultural context in which the conflict occurs, because differences tend to exaggerate barriers and reduce the likelihood of conflict resolution. The issues involved will also affect the likely outcomes. Whether the parties have cooperative, individualistic, or competitive orientations toward conflict will affect the outcomes as well. Obviously, those with cooperative attitudes are more likely to seek a functional outcome. Characteristics of the conflicting parties also affect conflict behavior. Finally, misjudgments and misperceptions contribute to dysfunctional conflict.

Effective managers learn how to create functional conflict and manage dysfunctional conflict. They develop and practice techniques for diagnosing the causes and nature of conflict and transforming it into productive force in the organization. Many colleges, for example, have a healthy competition between and among schools within the university for the recruitment of the most qualified students.

Some conflict is beneficial. It can encourage organizational innovation, creativity, and adaption. For example, a number of nonpublic school systems, and even some public school systems, allow schools within the system to compete for the same students. This "open enrollment" policy often spawns innovation in marketing techniques, and more importantly, in curriculum and programs. In these cases, conflict can result in more worker enthusiasm and better decisions. Can you think of a situation where such positive outcomes occurred? Perhaps during a disagreement with a colleague, you came to hold a different perspective on an issue or learned that your own perceptions or information had been inaccurate.

On the other hand, conflict can be viewed as dysfunctional for organizations. It can reduce productivity, decrease morale, cause overwhelming dissatisfaction, and increase tension and stress in the organization. It can arouse anxiety in individuals, increase the tension in an organizational system and its subsystems, and lower satisfaction. In addition, some people, often the losers in a competitive situation, feel defeated and demeaned. As the distance between people increases, a climate of mistrust and suspicion can arise. Individuals or groups might focus more narrowly on their own interests, preventing the development of team-work. Production and satisfaction might decline; turnover and absenteeism can increase. Diagnosing the location and type of conflict, as described next, is a first step in managing conflict so that it results in functional outcomes.

LEVELS OF CONFLICT

To manage conflict effectively, administrators must pinpoint precisely where it exists so they can choose appropriate management strategies. We can describe six levels on conflict: (1) intrapersonal, (2) interpersonal, (3) intragroup, (4) intergroup, (5) intraorganizational, and (6) interorganizational.[3]

An individual might experience internal conflict in choosing between incompatible goals. For example, a teacher who has recently assumed increased family responsibilities, might be torn between remaining in the profession that he or she prefers or moving to a less-preferred job that would pay more. In making such choices, the individual experiences intrapersonal conflict.

Intrapersonal conflict can be cognitive or affective. *Cognitive conflict* describes the intellectual discomfort created by incompatible goals. The teacher might be forced to sacrifice his or her job preference for one that pays better. Such conflict might have production consequences. For example, the teacher might be so obsessed with the decision he or she has to make that it negatively affects his or her classroom performance.

Affective conflict occurs when competing emotions accompany the incompatible goals and result in increased stress, decreased productivity, or decreased satisfaction for the individual. The teacher in our example might be so emotionally distraught that it affects him or her physically.

When two individuals disagree about issues, actions, or goals, and where joint outcomes become important, there is interpersonal conflict. A disagreement between a teacher and a department chair over grading standards might result in this level of conflict. Interpersonal conflict often arises from differences in individuals' perceptions, orientations, or status. It could motivate individuals to surface additional relevant issues or prevent any further communication.

A group might also experience either substantive or affective conflict. Substantive conflict is based on intellectual disagreement. For example, when university colleagues disagree on whether a new program is consistent with the mission of the university, they may experience substantive conflict. Such conflict often results in better information exchange and decision making. Affective conflict is based on the emotional responses to a situation. For example, the English department members might feel passionate about the need for writing across the curriculum, while the social studies department might feel that doing so would take valuable time away from the study of content in the various social studies classes. Both parties, therefore, have conflicting emotions about the same issue. Affective conflict can also result when interacting individuals have incompatible styles or personalities.

Intergroup conflict exists between or among groups, such as a the teachers and the custodians. The custodians, for example, might feel that the teachers should share in the responsibility to keep the school building clean. The teachers, on the other hand, might not consider this as part of their function. "We were trained and hired to be teachers, not janitors" is a common lament heard in faculty rooms. When conditions such as this exist, the instances of intergroup conflict are frequent.

Though, in one sense, it encompasses all of the previous levels, typically intraorganizational conflict is diagnosed when conflict characterizes overall organizational functioning. Vertical conflict is that between supervisors and subordinates. Administration and faculty may differ about the best ways to accomplish their tasks or institutional goals; union representatives and administration might disagree about the interpretation of the contract regarding working conditions in the school. Horizontal conflict exists between employees or departments at the same level, like that which could occur between a music and a physical education teacher. Diagonal conflict often occurs over the allocation of resources throughout an organization. For example, the percentage of the budget devoted to instruction versus the percentage devoted to operation and maintenance could be the source of diagonal conflict. Finally, role conflict can be pervasive in the organization. Department chairs in high schools often experience role conflict. They have both instructional and administrative responsibilities. However, they are not considered to be administrators by the school administration, and the teachers consider them to be more an administrator than a teacher. They do not fit into either category, therefore, and often experience role conflict. A moderate level of conflict throughout the organization can energize the employees and inspire innovation; but uncontrolled and unmanaged conflict can demoralize employees and cause performance to deteriorate.

Conflict can also exist between organizations. The amount of conflict can depend on the extent to which the organizations create uncertain conditions. An example of intraorganizational conflict would be a disagreement about funding in a large urban school system between the board of education and the city council. Recent attempts to manage such conflict and ensure that it has a positive impact on organizational performance have emphasized the formation of strategic alliances and partnerships. Identifying the level of conflict is a prerequisite to selecting appropriate strategies for managing it.[4] Accurate diagnosis also involves specifying the stage of conflict, as described next.

STAGES OF CONFLICT

Understanding the nature of conflict is aided by considering it as a sequence of stages. Regardless of the level of conflict, a historical, but still useful, view of the progression of conflict suggests that each episode proceeds through one or more of five possible stages: (1) latent, (2) perceived, (3) felt, (4) manifest conflict, and (5) conflict aftermath. By specifying the stage of conflict, a manager can determine its intensity and select the best strategies for managing it.[5]

Conflict begins when the conditions for conflict exist. Individuals or groups might have power differences, compete for scarce resources, strive for autonomy, have different goals, or experience diverse role pressures. These differences provide the foundation for disagreement and ultimately conflict. Departments, such as academic services and financial services, frequently experience latent conflict. Inherent differences in perceptions and attitudes contribute to their relationship.

In the next stage, individuals or group members know that conflict exists. They recognize differences of opinion, incompatible goals or values, efforts to demean the other party, or the implementation of opposing actions. If financial services feels a need to have students' financial responsibilities satisfied before they can attend class, and academic services believes that the students have a right to an education, regardless of the their financial status, a state of perceived conflict exists.

When one or more parties feel tense or anxious as a result of such disagreements or misunderstandings, conflict has moved beyond the perceived to the felt stage. Typically, there is a time lag between intellectually perceiving that conflict exists and then feeling it. Here, the conflict becomes personalized to the individuals or groups involved.

Observable behavior designed to frustrate another's attempts to pursue his or her goals is the most overt form of conflict. Both open aggression and withdrawal of support illustrate the manifest stage. At this stage, conflict must be used constructively or resolved for effective organizational performance to occur. If a teacher confronts an assistant principal about the severe lack of discipline in a school, manifest conflict could ensue. Demonstrated anger and refusal to listen to reason would further reflect this stage on conflict. However, so would a high level of creative tension. If properly managed, new and creative solutions can emerge.

The conflict episode ends with the aftermath stage. After the conflict has been managed, and the resulting energy has been heightened, resolved, or suppressed. The episode results in a new reality. Unresolved conflict, which exists everywhere, simply sows the seeds for manifest conflict later. The process continues and is a normal part of organizational life. The fact that organizations are composed of large numbers of interacting individuals and interacting groups increases the likelihood of conflict.

INTERACTING GROUPS

With the current stress on the open system model of organizational structure, it becomes important that managers understand the nature of interacting groups or subsystems. No two groups in an organization can exist truly independently. Rather, one group may depend on another for resources, information, or assistance in performing a task or providing a service. We can describe this interdependence in transactional terms, referring to the exchange of resources, such as budgeted funds, support services, and information.[6]

Managers should assess the nature and extent of interdependence in an organization so that they understand the potential for conflict and the impact on action one part of the organization will have on another part. Interdependence occurs in one of four ways: pooled, sequential, reciprocal, and team. Although any group may demonstrate any of these types of interdependence at specific times, one type will predominate in a group's relationship with other groups. Next, we examine each of these types.

Groups that rely on each other only because they belong to the same parent organization show pooled interdependence. Two schools in the same school district show pooled interdependence because their reputations can depend on the overall reputation of the school district. The maintenance workers and the cafeteria workers in an educational institution are two departments that, for the most part, demonstrate pooled interdependence. Groups with pooled interdependence may obtain their reputation, staff resources, financing, or other services from the central office. Basically, however, they operate as separate groups or organizations.

Because these groups have limited interactions, pooled interdependence has few potentially dysfunctional consequences for groups until their representatives need to work together. Such groups might be required to compete for resources, but such interactions are limited.

Sequential interdependence occurs when one group's operations precede and act as prerequisites for the second group's. In an elementary school, the first-grade teachers and the second-grade teachers are sequentially interdependent. The second group in the sequence might experience difficulty in accomplishing its tasks if its members do not interact effectively with its predecessor. As a result, the members in the second group might resent the first group and limit their interactions with it. This type of interdependence can easily be a source of conflict.

When two groups must repeatedly interact to perform their jobs effectively, they are said to have reciprocal interdependence. The registrar's and the treasurer's offices in an educational institution would be an example of two groups that would have reciprocal interdependence. Two groups whose operations precede and act as prerequisites to the other's have this type of interdependence. As the interdependence increases, the potential for conflict and dysfunctional behavior increases correspondingly. Reciprocal interdependence often results in dysfunctional behaviors and attitudes. Because each group relies on the other to perform its own job effectively, any problems between them could result in reduced productivity or decreased worker satisfaction.

Team interdependence occurs where multiple groups interact. The interdependence in the various academic departments in a high school or college are examples. Groups with team interdependence have the greatest potential for conflict and the highest requirements for effective communication and management.

TASK RELATIONS

The activities or processes that interdependent groups perform and the way these activities interrelate play a significant role in intergroup relations. Both the sequencing of task activities and the clarity and certainty of the tasks themselves have consequences for intergroup relation. Tasks performed by group members can be independent, dependent, or interdependent of tasks performed by members of the same or different groups. Often, there is a correlation between the nature of task interactions and the relationships between interdependent groups.

When one group's task can be done without any relationship to another group's, the task relations are independent. The English teacher and the school custodian can each perform his or her tasks without any assistance from the other. When one group's task follows another group's task that is a prerequisite to it, the second group has a task that is dependent on the first group's. The assistant superintendent for personnel who recruits new employees depends on the school principals to identify the types of personnel required. Where each group's task follows the other's and is prerequisite to it at some time, their tasks are interdependent. In the example given earlier, if the assistant superintendent followed through and sent the principal a cadre of five prospects to interview for a position and authorized the principal to make the selection, the two administrators' tasks would be interdependent.

The nature of task relations generally resembles the nature of interdependence among groups described earlier. Groups showing pooled interdependence most often have independent task relations, groups showing sequential interdependence most often have dependent task relations, and groups showing reciprocal or team interdependence most frequently have interdependent task relations.

Groups with independent tasks have much less potential for problematic relations with other groups than those with dependent or interdependent task relations because the independent task groups have less interaction. Interdependent tasks most frequently contribute to problematic relations between interacting groups.

The ambiguity or certainty of the task relationships describes whether the interacting groups have clear, predetermined processes of activity. Ambiguity in the task often contributes to difficulty in the group's interactions. Often, a particular group does not understand its responsibilities and the requirements of its task. This situation also results in more task uncertainty. The academic departments in a school might not understand their responsibilities vis-a-vis the interdisciplinary task force. If this is the case, conflict could arise and contribute to dysfunctional interactions between the two groups.

POWER DIFFERENCES

Interacting groups often experience performance difficulties when they differ in the power, or amount of influence and control over others, they have. Here we highlight three ways in which power differences affect intergroup relations, perceptions of substitutability, ability to cope with uncertainty, and control of and access to resources.[7]

If the activities of a group are viewed as replaceable, or if another group can perform the same work, the group is considered substitutable. If a nonpublic school system is considered able to provide programs parallel to those of a public school system, the public school establishment might consider the nonpublic schools to be substitutable, thereby diminishing the public schools' power. The more a group performs unsubstitutable tasks, the more power it possesses. When one group considers another group as substitutable, conflict can arise between the groups.

How well a group can deal with and compensate for a rapidly changing environment also influences its power. Typically, adult education programs are able to cope and adjust to changing needs quicker and better than traditionally aged educational programs because of their freedom from elaborate governance structures. Thus, in many cases, the adult education division might have an advantage on the traditionally aged division. Any difference such as this would contribute to power differentials between the two groups and potentially to dysfunctional intergroup relations.

The amount of material resources at a group's disposal also influences its power. The greater the amount of resources it controls, the more power the group has. In universities, business schools often have a larger share of the budget than arts and sciences schools. This disparity often leads to conflict between the two groups.

STRATEGIES FOR MANAGING CONFLICT

Administrators might encourage individuals or groups to use at least five behaviors or strategies for dealing with conflict: avoidance, accommodation, compromise, forcing, and collaborating. These differ in the extent to which they satisfy a party's own concerns and the other party's concerns. For example, a person or group that uses an avoiding mode is unassertive in satisfying its own concerns and uncooperative in satisfying others' concerns. In contrast, a person or group that uses a collaborating mode is assertive and cooperative.[8]

Each style is appropriate to different situations that individuals or groups face in organizations. Once again, the underlying theme of contingency theory applies. Table 6.1 summarizes the use of these five modes by a group of administrators. The behavior an individual or group chooses depends on that party's experiences in dealing with conflict, his or her own personal dispositions in interpersonal relations, and the specific elements of a particular conflict episode.

Avoidance

Individuals or groups may withdraw from the conflict situation. They act to satisfy neither their own or the other party's concerns. Avoidance works best when individuals or groups face trivial or tangential issues, when they have little chance of satisfying their personal concerns, when

Table 6.1 Uses of the five conflict modes

Conflict Handling Modes	Appropriate Situations
Competing	1. When quick, decisive action is vital—e.g., emergencies. 2. On important issues where unpopular actions need implementing—e.g., cost cutting, enforcing unpopular rules, discipline. 3. On issues vital to institutional welfare when you know you are right.
Collaborating	1. To find an integrative solution when both sets of concerns are too important to be compromised. 2. When your objective is to learn. 3. To merge insights from people with different perspectives. 4. To gain commitment by incorporating concerns into a consensus. 5. To work through feelings that have interfered with a relationship.
Compromising	1. When goals are important, but not worth the effort or potential disruption of more assertive modes. 2. When opponents with equal power are committed to mutually exclusive goals. 3. To achieve temporary settlements to complex issues. 4. To arrive at expedient solutions under time pressure.
Avoiding	1. When an issue is trivial or more important issues are pressing. 2. When you perceive no chance of satisfying your concerns. 3. When potential disruption outweighs the benefits of resolution. 4. To let people cool down and regain perspective. 5. When gathering information supersedes immediate decision.
Accommodating	1. When you find you are wrong—to allow a better position to be heard, to learn, and to show your reasonableness. 2. When issues are more important to others than yourself—to satisfy others and maintain cooperation. 3. To build social credits for later issues. 4. To minimize loss when you are outmatched and losing. 5. When harmony and stability are especially important.

conflict resolution will likely result in significant disruption, or when others can resolve the conflict more effectively. If two secretaries in the secretarial pool, for example, have an argument, the most appropriate strategy for managing the conflict might be avoidance. Let the secretaries resolve the conflict in their own ways. It is like the proverbial story of the next-door neighbors whose children got into an argument and the adults tried to intervene on behalf of their respective children. The adults ended up being lifelong enemies and the children were playing with each other again within the hour.

Accommodation

Individuals or groups who use accommodation demonstrate a willingness to cooperate in satisfying others' concerns, while at the same time acting unassertively in meeting their own. Accommodating individuals often smooth over conflict. This mode builds social credits for later issues, results in harmony and stability, and satisfies others. An assistant principal might capitulate on a disagreement with the principal over a minor matter in hopes that he or she can prevail on a larger issue in the future, thus building political capital to be used later.

Compromise

The compromise mode represents an intermediate behavior on both the assertiveness and cooperation dimensions. It can include sharing of positions, but not moving to the extremes of assertiveness or cooperation. Hence, it often does not maximize satisfaction of both parties. In one study, compromisers had a different communication style from avoiders; they were more likely to focus on communicating information about the job product or plan than messages about rules, regulations, or policies. This style works well when goals are important but not sufficiently important for the individual or group to be more assertive, when the two parties have equal power, or when significant time pressure exists. For example, if two grade partners disagree over what supplementary materials should be used for a certain lesson, they might compromise and use some of each teacher's suggestions.

Forcing

Using the forcing mode, a party tries to satisfy its own concerns while showing an unwillingness to satisfy the other's concerns to even a minimal degree. This strategy works well in emergencies, on issues calling for unpopular actions, and in cases where one party is correct in its position or where one party has much greater power. For example, if a child tries to commit suicide, the principal might wish to inform the parents immediately and the guidance counselor might wish it to remain confidential. If the principal arbitrarily informs the parents, he or she is using a forcing behavior.

Collaborating

The collaboration mode emphasizes problem solving with a goal of maximizing satisfaction for both parties. It means seeing conflict as natural, showing trust and honesty toward others, and encouraging the airing of every person's attitudes and feelings. Each party exerts both assertive and cooperative behavior. Parties can use it when their objectives are to learn, to use information from diverse sources, and to find an integrative solution. If the teacher's union and the school board establish a mutually satisfactory way of working together, they are taking a collaborative or problem-solving approach to resolve or avoid conflict.

CONFLICT INTERVENTION ACTIVITIES

Certain types of conflict, such as disagreements about goals or values, might call for the parties to control the differences by acknowledging their existence and then acting without attempting to resolve them. Such differences might be so ingrained in the conflicting parties that effectively managing those involved may preclude resolution of the differences within any reasonable period of time or without changing underlying value systems.[9]

Occasionally, in small-group situations, individuals escalate the conflict as a way of ultimately resolving it. An outsider purposely seeks to increase the frustration of the parties as a way of redirecting the conflict's course, increasing participants' understanding of the situation, or leading to a search for adequate behaviors. Three specific intervention techniques typify the strategies that focus on improving the process of interactions between two or more groups: confrontation meeting, organizational mirror, and other third-party interventions.

A confrontation meeting addresses problems experienced by interacting groups that result in dysfunctional organizational performance. It is a one-day meeting where two interacting groups air the problems they face and offer solutions for resolving them.

The one-day meeting occurs in the following way: First, a top manager introduces the issues and goals that are the focus of discussion during the day and on which the various groups or individuals experience problems; the manager may have identified these issues on the basis of prior discussions with group members. Then, in small subgroups from the various interacting groups, the participants gather more detailed information about the problems they face. Next, representatives from each subgroup report on their list of items to the entire group. In natural work groups, participants set priorities for the problems and determine early action steps; they set a concrete agenda about the steps they will take to resolve their problems. Implementation of the plan follows. A review committee continues to meet to plan and monitor follow-up action. Four to six weeks later, the group reconvenes to report its progress. The confrontation meeting is most effective in dealing with intergroup problems when the following conditions exist: There is a need for the total institution to examine its own workings, very limited time is available for the activity, top administration wishes to improve the conditions quickly, there is enough cohesion in the top team to ensure follow-up, there is real commitment to resolving the issues on the part of all parties, and the institution will experience or has recently experienced some significant change. An example of an issue that might be best resolved at a confrontation meeting would be the development of an accelerated degree program in a school. Such a program might be needed by the school to compete effectively with other schools offering these programs. However, a significant change such as this can be very controversial and cause considerable conflict among the various constituencies in the school community. The confrontation meeting could resolve these differences.

The organizational mirror is a set of activities that structures the provision of feedback from representatives of various organization groups to a host group about the way the host group is perceived. A consultant begins by conducting preliminary interviews with all members of the groups. Then, the consultant reports data from these interviews to the invited and host groups. The groups then discuss the data presented. Small, heterogeneous groups with representatives from the diverse groups meet, discuss the data further, and develop action plans for the problems identified. Implementation of the action plans should follow. Like the confrontation meeting, the organizational mirror requires institutional commitment and follow-up for effective action to result. If a school is suffering from morale problems because of a lack of communication between the administration and the faculty, the organizational mirror technique might be useful.

Third parties frequently intervene to resolve serious intergroup conflicts. Employing professionally trained management consultants can be effective in resolving conflicts, especially if they affect the entire institution and cannot be resolved internally.[10]

Third-Party Interventions

The third party can assume one of two roles: interpersonal facilitator or interface conflict solver. As an interpersonal facilitator, the third party assumes an active role of identifying areas of agreement and disagreement between the parties. Contact between parties occurs primarily through the facilitator, who acts as a go-between, a message carrier, a spokesperson for one or both groups, or a solution proposer. The facilitator deals with the leaders or key members of disputing parties who meet to exchange positions and formulate proposals or counterproposals. This model works best when two people are involved and personal chemistry prevents quality discussion.

As an interface conflict solver, the third party leads key members of opposing groups through a series of meetings and activities that identify and resolve differences. He or she sets expectations, establishes group rules, determines the sequence of speaking, ensures candor, curbs the expression of hostility, avoids evaluation, introduces procedures to reduce disagreements, ensures understanding of positions or statements, and checks implementation of agreed-upon changes. Each group first meets separately to prepare a description of the ideal relationship between the groups and then selects a spokesperson who presents the conclusions at a general meeting of the groups. After the large group meeting, each participant identifies similarities and differences in the two descriptions to develop an integrated model that can direct the functioning of both groups. Next, each group characterizes the actual conditions at that time. The groups then jointly formulate a statement of problems. Together, they propose steps for improving the situation. This approach works best when support of group members is key to change, when leaders do not know the entire problem, or when the problem is inherent to the culture of the groups involved. There are a number of equally effective third-party interventions to those mentioned. However, in order to be properly implemented, they require the services of a professional management consultant. If the conflict cannot be managed internally, and if it is one the permeates the entire institution, the services of a third party might be required.

CONFLICT RESOLUTION PROCESSES

Three types of formal processes can address conflicts in organizations and attempt to resolve them: grievance procedures, mediation and arbitration, and negotiation.[11]

Grievance procedures provide a formal process by which school personnel can complain to administration if they feel that they have not been treated properly or if their rights have been violated. A formal grievance procedure provides a mechanism for responding to employee complaints or clarifying an individual's or management's rights and obligations; formally brings the matter to the attention of the proper official, defines the nature of the conflict or complaint, and provides a structure for addressing the issue.

In unionized situations, the aggrieved employee presents the complaint orally to the union representative. Unresolved grievances then can proceed through the following steps until they are satisfactorily resolved. The union representative forwards the grievance in writing to the principal or other designated administrator. If not able to be resolved at that level the grievance is raised to the next appropriate level until it is resolved. If it cannot be resolved internally, an outside third party might be necessary.

In a nonunionized situation, the grievance procedure might be less formal, but a prudent administration will be certain that a grievance procedure is part of the policies and procedures of the institution. This system of due process is a very effective means of resolving conflict before it gets out of hand.

Mediation and arbitration are third-party interventions that use trained individuals to help resolve conflict in organizations. In mediation, a neutral party tries to help disputing parties reach a settlement of the issues that divide them. The mediator focuses on bringing the parties to agreement by making procedural suggestions, keeping channels of communication between the parties open, helping establish priorities, and offering creative solutions. A good mediator tries to determine the true intentions of each party and communicate them to the other. The mediator, however, does not make the decision. If mediation does not work, perhaps an outside arbitrator should be engaged.

An arbitrator, in contrast to a mediator, acts as a judge in a dispute. Arbitration is a quasi-legal proceeding that resembles a formal judicial procedure but does not take place in a court of law. In arbitration, each party presents its position on disputed matters to the arbitrator, who then judges the situation and decides on the disposition of the case. For example, if a teacher files a grievance against the principal for scheduling the teacher to too many class preparations, an arbitrator will listen to evidence about the matter from both sides and reach a judgment about the teacher's claim. Once again, mediation and arbitration can be valuable techniques in resolving conflict and should be part of an educational institution's employee relations policies whether or not the institution is unionized.[12]

The negotiations process can also be utilized as conflict resolution technique. Its use will be discussed in detail in Chapter 9.

STRUCTURAL MECHANISMS

Redesigning formal reporting relationships, adding special managerial roles, or using standard operating procedures more extensively and effectively can improve the management of conflict and intergroup relations. Altering the nature of task relations between two groups can also improve intergroup behavior or reduce conflict. Next, we examine some structural mechanisms that can improve employee relations.

Hierarchy

In this approach, a common superior is assigned to coordinate the work of two or more interacting groups or individuals. This position acts as a conduit for information, often setting priorities for interfacing groups or individuals and resolving disputes between them. Having a Guidance Counselors' Committee in a large school district would be an example of this strategy. If a central office administrator chaired such a committee, it would allow guidance counselors from various schools to air their common concerns before they reached the point where resolution becomes more difficult. This approach works best when interacting groups or individuals are reasonably close in function or work on similar projects.

Plans and Goals

Plans and goals direct the activities of interacting groups while minimizing their interaction. When plans are used, even the integration of groups geographically distant can be effective. The use of common goals can have an influence similar to plans because they create a common focus for the groups' activities. If the superintendent has a shared educational vision, for example, conflict can be reduced. If there is broad acceptance and understanding of the school or school system's educational vision, as expressed through its goals and objectives, conflict between individuals and groups that arise in attaining these goals will be minimized.

Linking Roles

Individuals are temporarily placed in positions to act as conduits between interfacing groups. They expedite communication by resolving issues through a person at the same level in the organization, rather than by using a common supervisor to solve them. A master teacher in a career ladder program can serve this function. He or she would be on the same level as a teacher, but would have added responsibilities to resolve conflict before it reaches extreme proportions.

Task Forces

Special groups with members representing each component of the school community can be convened to work on problems faced by interacting groups. Task forces integrate by presenting the ideas of their group to the others' representatives. Task forces typically include one representative from each group affected by or involved in a particular problem or task. A student retention task force, for example, could study a problem in student retention that affects many levels in an educational institution and thus prevent any one part of the institution from being "blamed" for the problem and experiencing conflict.

Integrating Roles and Units

Analogous to the typically more informal linking roles, a permanent coordinating individual or group of people can be appointed to act as an interface between interacting groups. A grade leader, for example, coordinates the decisions and materials used by such interdependent individuals as teachers who teach the same grade. Again, such an individual can be invaluable in preventing conflict from becoming problematic.

Project or Product Structure

Individuals who work on the same product or project can be grouped together. In the case of a student with a disability, the classroom teacher, the special education teacher, the parent, and the student might be part of the Individualized Education Program (IEP) team that determines the best program to meet the special student's needs. By using this approach, conflict can be precluded or at least reduced.

Matrix Organization

As mentioned in chapter 4, matrix organization is a highly sophisticated organizational design that integrates both functional departments and support groups through a multiple authority and reporting system. Its goal is to facilitate communication and thereby reduce conflict. But this structure itself can be inherently conflict ridden because of the multiplicity of command. However, it has been effective in help-ing organizations cope effectively with very complex, uncertain, and dynamic environments. Because educational institutions meet these criteria, it can be an effective mechanism to improve communication and reduce conflict. In a college setting, for example, a director of continuing education could report to the deans of the various colleges rather than to one dean or provost. This mechanism facilitates com-munication because it flattens the chain of command and allows indi-viduals to deal with whoever can best resolve a problem or provide needed information.

CULTURAL DIVERSITY

Managing culturally diverse groups poses special challenges depending on the extent of the differences. Cultural diversity exaggerates differ-ences between groups and may call for additional strategies and tech-niques. Managers must be trained to identify cultural differences and then use them for the organization's benefit. In addition, managers need to emphasize a vision, equalize power, develop mutual respect groups, and facilitate feedback on process and outcomes between groups. Ob-jectifying and sharing perceptions about the groups involved and reduc-ing task interdependence can also help alleviate potential dysfunctions between culturally diverse groups. In an educational setting, however, this last suggestion might be inappropriate.

SUMMARY

Conflict frequently characterizes individuals and groups in organiza-tions. It can exist at the intrapersonal, interpersonal, intragroup, inter-group, intraorganizational, and interorganizational levels. As a dynamic force, conflict progresses from latent to perceived, felt, and manifest stages, and finally to a conflict aftermath. Its consequences can be func-tional, such as increased creativity and exchange of ideas, or dysfunc-tional, such as increased stress, absenteeism, and turnover or decreased satisfaction and performance.

Interacting groups are especially prone to conflict. Effective intergroup relations require managers and other organizational members to diagnose the extent and causes of their interdependence. Groups can demonstrate pooled, sequential, reciprocal, or team interdependence. Groups experiencing reciprocal or team interdependence more often experience dysfunctional conflict and other problems than those showing pooled or sequential interdependence.

Task relations reflect the nature of group interdependence and can reinforce problematic interactions. Power differences, including the extent of a group's substitutability, its ability to cope with uncertainty, and its access to resources, influence the effectiveness of its interactions with other individuals or groups.

Conflict can be caused by scarce resources, jurisdictional ambiguities, communication breakdowns, personality clashes, power and status differences, and goal differences. However, we have a variety of strategies at our disposal for managing conflict. Conflict can be managed by applying the appropriate intervention style to the situation. Conflict intervention styles, such as avoidance, compromise, forcing, accommodation, and collaboration, can be applied depending on the vagaries of the situation. Other intervention techniques for more serious problems include the confrontation meeting, the organizational mirror, and third-party interventions.

Conflict resolution processes include grievance procedures, mediation, and arbitration. Such intervening structural mechanisms as hierarchical considerations, plans and goals, linking roles, task forces, integrating roles and units, project and product structures, and the matrix organization can be helpful. As with the areas of educational administration examined earlier, the ability to adopt the proper conflict intervention strategy in a given situation will determine effective administration and leadership.

CASE STUDY 6.1: THE FORT WASHINGTON SCHOOL

Fort Washington Elementary School attempts to provide opportunities for all students to experience success in a caring, secure environment where academic and cultural sensitivity exists and where educational, social, and emotional needs of students are addressed. These opportunities include a broad, flexible interdisciplinary curriculum, which is subject to review/revision on a regular basis, special education for exceptional learners, computers to enhance instruction, extracurricular activities, facilities designed for optimal student use, part-time support services for service and crisis intervention, and a dedicated and informed staff that is encouraged to participate in a wide variety of staff development activities that promote success for all students.

BACKGROUND INFORMATION (PERSONAL)

In 1995, I was hired as a fifth-grade long-term substitute. At the end of the year, I was offered a contract and gladly accepted. As a second-year teacher, I was asked by my principal to be her administrative assistant. Although apprehensive, due to my lack of experience, I accepted. The role of administrative assistant at Fort Washington has no definitive job description. Much of my time is spent carrying out monotonous tasks such as writing monthly board reports and sitting in meetings where I have no influence.

SCHOOL CULTURE

Fort Washington is a solidly upper-middle-class community. It has a strong tax base and a population that is very concerned with the public schools. Parental involvement on ancillary school functions frequently leads to parental influence on academic matters. Consequently, the school relinquishes its prerogative as purveyor of the curriculum.

School discipline is the area of professional responsibility where Fort Washington is most derelict. Codified school district procedures are ignored in favor of a laissez-faire approach, permitting a myriad of inappropriate behaviors. Attempts to gain control of the learning environment lead to parental complaints. Parental complaints are given forum by an extremely political administration that disenfranchises the teaching staff. The general population of children at Fort Washington attends school in a disciplinary environment with no consequences.

FW is also the home of St. Jude's Villa. St. Mary's is a live-in institution for abandoned children. These children are frequently the abused products of the inner city. They are asked to compete with children from stable families. In addition, the juxtaposition between their life of institutional regulations and the life of kids jetting off to Colorado for a week of skiing creates frustration and anger. In sharp contrast to the disciplinary approach of the general school population, sanctions leveled on St. Jude's students tend to be draconian.

PERSONAL EXPERIENCE

During the summer of 1996, an elevator was being installed in our school. The construction was not yet completed by September. Necessary equipment and materials were stored on the recess yard where children play. The area was sectioned off with yellow caution tape to ensure student safety during recess.

At FW, we have two periods for recess. One period is supervised by teachers, one by aides. There have been countless discussions concerning the effectiveness of the aides' supervision. Many factors contribute to these discussions. These aides are not schooled in effective management control and do not believe they have control, which the children can sense immediately. Even though the aides go through school district in-service, they hold no power for following through on disciplinary actions. The aides and students scream at each other. Students write notes expressing their frustrations, blaming the aides. Rather than believing the adult, who has no motive to fabricate stories of misbehavior, parents will support their children and blame the aides as well. Parents claim the aides capriciously yell at their children.

This past September, teachers at my grade level were informed about the inappropriate behavior at lunchtime in the cafeteria as well as on the recess yard. Our principal, Donna Cannon, chose to supervise the cafeteria because the aides "couldn't handle it." She also threatened to fire the entire team of aides. She came to fifth-grade lunch one day and asked my team members if we could brainstorm ideas on how to handle these children. Craig Parsons, a teacher for over twenty years, suggested non-negotiable after-school detention. Donna would not agree with that option, fearing even more complaints. No solution was found and the fifth-grade teachers were frustrated because our input was requested but not considered and ultimately our time was wasted. Two weeks had passed and a solution was still not resolved. Students continued to be disrespectful and the aides still lacked control.

I was returning to my classroom from lunch a bit early when I happened to glance outside into the recess yard. Twenty-five to thirty fifth-graders were on a tear. They were jumping on top of one another, causing classmates to fall to the ground. Their behavior was creating a safety hazard. They had broken through the caution tape from the construction site and wrapping the brightly colored plastic around their necks and waists. What was even more appalling was that the aides were standing right there not taking command. A school's first responsibility is to ensure the safety of its students.

I went to each fifth-grade teacher and announced that the entire fifth grade was going to receive assigned seats in the cafeteria. This procedural strategy, which had successfully been enacted in the past, would allow for a more orderly line when exiting the cafeteria. I acted as an administrative assistant, consulted my fellow team members, and they supported me on my judgment.

The following morning, I went to Donna, explained the situation, and told her what I had implemented as a procedural improvement. She, however, characterized my decision as a punishment. She began to explain how I was not allowed to impose the consequences that I choose because Dr. Ricci, our superintendent, does not support group punishment. My principal was not only unsupportive of my decision, but also took away my authority as a teacher. What Dr. Ricci and Ms. Cannon refer to as group punishment, I consider crisis management. Students were not given assigned seats, those who misbehaved had no repercussion and my professional credibility was undermined by the administration.

NOTES

1. B. Kabanoff, Potential Influence Structures as Sources of Interpersonal Conflict in Groups and Organizations, *Organizational Behavior and Human Decision Processes* 36 (1985): 115.

2. D. M. Kolb and L. L. Putnam, The Dialectics of Disputing, in *Hidden Conflict in Organizations*, ed. D. M. Kolb and J. M. Bartunek (Newbury Park, Calif.: Sage, 1992), 18.

3. C. H. Coombs, The Structure of Conflict, *American Psychologist* 42, no. 4 (1987): 355–363.

4. J. Pfeiffer, Beyond Management and the Workers: The Institutional Function of Management, *Academy of Management Review* 1 (1976): 26–46; H. Assael, Constructive Roles of Interorganizational Conflict, *Administrative Science Quarterly* 14 (1968): 573-581.

5. K. W. Thomas, Organizational Conflict, in *Organizational Behavior*, ed. S. Kerr (Columbus, Ohio: Grid, 1979).

6. J. E. McCann and D. L. Ferry, An Approach for Assessing and Managing Interunit Interdependence, *Academy of Management Review* 4 (1979): 113–119.

7. D. Hickson, C. Hinings, C. Lee, R. Schneck, and J. A. Pennings, A Strategic Contingencies Theory of Intraorganizational Power, *Administrative Science Quarterly* 23 (1978): 65–90.

8. D. Thomas, Conflict and Conflict Management, in *Handbook of Industrial and Organizational Psychology*, ed. M. D. Dunnette (Chicago: Rand McNally, 1976) 889–935.

9. E. Van de Vliert, Escalative Intervention in Small Group Conflicts, *Journal of Applied Behavioral Science* 21 (1985): 19–36.

10. R. Beckhard, The Confrontation Meeting, *Harvard Business Review* 45 (1967): 154, presents an early description of this intervention.

11. D. D. Morley and P. Shockley-Zalabak, Conflict Avoiders and Compromisers: Toward an Understanding of Their Organizational Communication Style, *Group and Organization Studies* 11 (December 1986): 387–402.

12. D. Q. Mills, *Labor-Management Relations* (New York: McGraw-Hill, 1978).

7

THE STRATEGIC PLANNING PROCESS

Planning is all, but plans are nothing.

—Dwight D. Eisenhower

Strategic planning is a process that was first developed and refined in business and industry, but has currently been adopted by a variety of educational institutions throughout the nation. In some states, the process is mandated for all public schools. In this chapter, we discuss the components of the planning process and some successful planning models.

AN ACADEMIC PLANNING PROCESS

Ten specifically identified activities would be included in a strategic plan for academic planning in educational institutions. They include the following:[1]

1. *Develop a Mission Statement.* The process of developing a mission statement involves establishing a strong group consensus about the unique purposes of the educational institution and its place in the community that it serves. The process of development of the mission

will set the tone for all further planning activity. Most often, educational institutions have an existing mission. However, the planning process should not begin until there is broad acceptance of the current mission. Many times, the mission needs to be revised to adapt to current circumstances before the process can continue.

The mission statement must, therefore, be developed through discussion among the various constituencies that make up the school community, be an outgrowth of a discussion of unique institutional purposes, and reflect the unique character of the institution.

The educational vision of the school is derived from the mission statement. It is often a concise summary of the mission or how you expect your mission to play out for the future.

2. *Develop a Set of Institutional Goals.* The institution should next develop a set of goals that it deems appropriate in the accomplishment of its mission. Goals are more specific and give direction to the action that needs to take place to achieve them. The goals should be expressed in terms that would promote easy assessment. It should be clear to an objective observer whether they have been achieved. An example of a goal that would be derived from the mission statement listed earlier would be, "to provide an education that addresses all dimensions of a student's character, mental, psychological, physical, and spiritual."

3. *Develop Learning Outcomes Statements.* The process of developing student learning outcomes statements, including transitional outcomes, should include the outcomes students must achieve in order to meet the institutional goals and progress from one level to the next. For example, from the primary to the intermediate level, intermediate level to middle level, and middle level to the high school program. An example of a typical outcome statement might be, "upon completing the American history course, the student will have the ability to research a topic in history, analyze its causes and effects and determine its implications for the future."

Ways of authentically assessing these educational outcomes also need to be developed. The current emphasis on outcomes-based education (OBE), authentic assessment and portfolio assessment focuses quite heavily on this step in the planning process.

4. *Describe Commencement Requirements.* The logical next step to developing outcome statements is to establish a set of criteria that will be used to determine achievement of student learning outcomes that will be required for graduation. In other words, the number and the degree to which the outcomes must be mastered in order to receive the culminating credential of the institution.

5. *Develop Planned Courses.* The essence of the conversion from a class time–based system to a student learning outcomes–based system is the revision of all academic courses to reflect student learning outcome statements. The courses should be developed to include a number of the learning outcomes determined earlier. Courses should be developed until all of the learning outcomes have been incorporated into at least one of the courses.

6. *Plan and Conduct a Comprehensive Needs Analysis.* The needs analysis is a crucial part of the strategic planning process. It must involve a comprehensive identification of both internal and external strengths and weaknesses and include an analysis of instructional practices. The process should rely on quantitative data whenever possible. It should involve all "stake holder" groups within the local community, giving each an opportunity to provide both hard data and informed opinion. The result of the needs analysis should be the main tool in developing priority goal areas for action planning.

7. *Develop a List of Priorities for Action Planning.* Priorities are identified by a process that applies the information accumulated during the needs analysis to the list of general institutional goals identified earlier. Those goals that show need for developmental action are prioritized on the basis of their relationship to the identified mission and on the severity of the need. One or more action plans or strategies are developed for each of the priorities.

8. *Develop Specific Action Plans.* One or more action plans or strategies are to be developed for each of the priority goal areas. The action plans are to identify specific actions to be taken to meet the identified priority needs. Action plans should include:
   a. Objectives
   b. Major strategies to be completed
   c. Projected time lines or completion dates

   d. The person or group responsible
   e. Estimated costs, if any
   f. Evaluation or assessment questions
 9. *Develop an Assessment Plan.* The assessment plan ascertains the
    degree to which the student learning outcomes are achieved. The
    assessment plan should include the following:
    a. The general purpose of the assessments
    b. A description of the process to be used to develop and analyze
        portfolios of student work, including a variety of strategies
    c. A description of assessment procedures to be used
    d. A description of how the assessment results will be used
    e. A description of how the school will assist students who have
        not demonstrated mastery of the outcomes
    f. A description of the process for notifying the public of assess-
        ment results
10. *Prepare a Professional Development Plan.* The final step in the
    academic planning process is to prepare a professional develop-
    ment plan to train and prepare the staff to implement the plans.
    This step is especially important if new and innovative ap-
    proaches are required to implement the strategic plan.

STRATEGIC PLANNING

The planning mentioned earlier focuses exclusively on the academic program in an educational institution. A more comprehensive strategic planning process would involve similar steps and utilize a similar rationale.

There are a variety of positions taken by educators concerning the
meaning and the use of the term *strategic planning*. In 1980, William
Cook defined strategic planning as a voluntary commitment to generate
rational decisions about the deployment of resources toward fixed goals
and functions. He states further that strategic planning is a prescription
that is formulated by the combined expertise within the organization
and represents a consensus plan derived through the application of basic principles of participative management. In a more recent publication, Cook defined strategic planning as a means by which an organization constantly re-creates itself to achieve extraordinary purpose.

Implied in this meaning is the concentration of all efforts, resources, and energies toward a single goal.[2]

A strategic planning approach for education is provided by Kaufman and Herman who define strategic planning as long-range planning with a vision. They present a strategic planning process that covers nursery school through higher education.

In general, then, strategic planning is a process by which an organization identifies objectives and unfolds strategies for achieving them. Although it can be built into existing structures, it is common practice to create a task force composed of representatives from all levels of the organization that is responsible for planning and making decisions. The process must look forward to the future. It must start with a statement of mission, which should be brief but adequate enough to clearly express the organization's commitment to selective academic, social, and career outlines for students, faculty, staff, and other stake holders. The mission statement should be the basis for planning and decision making in an institution.[3]

COMPREHENSIVE STRATEGIC PLANNING

An example of a more comprehensive strategic planning process is one developed by a number of local school districts. The plan begins under the direction of a strategic planning facilitator and twenty or so team members. This step is followed by 8 action teams with a total composition of approximately 175 members spread over the 8 teams. The statements of the school's and the community's beliefs are next, followed by the mission statement, objectives, parameters, and strategies. A series of action plans is determined and specific administrative responsibility is established for monitoring the achievement of each plan and for meeting realistic time lines.[4]

STRATEGIC PLANNING AND HUMAN AND MATERIAL RESOURCES

It is essential that the relationship between strategic organizational planning and human and material resources planning be understood. Human resource directors must be concerned with meshing human resources planning with strategic educational planning. The financial directors of the institution must do likewise. Strategic planning is setting management organizational objectives and developing comprehensive plans to support those objectives. It involves deciding on the priority of the organization, its process, and the interrelationship with human and material resources.

Human and material resources planning and strategic planning become effective when there is reciprocal and interdependent relationship between the two functions. Strategic planners should recognize that their decisions affect and are affected by human and material resources.

In any planning where human and material resources are concerned, there comes a time when one must define the difference between what is and what is not desired. Planning should be based upon what is feasible within the human resource and financial capabilities of an institution. To do otherwise is an exercise in futility and frustration.

SYSTEMS PLANNING

Roger Kaufman has devised a planning process that is particularly effective within the context of the open system approach to organizational development mentioned in chapter 1. He calls his process "systems planning," and although it has many similarities to the processes already discussed, its approach is somewhat unique.

A system approach, as described here, is a six-step process for realizing valid planned change. The six steps are quite general, and a self-correcting process is built into the approach. Thus, the administrator has a "road map" for achieving the desired change. The tools of system analysis can be used at each step of the process and, in fact, are used to plan each step of a new educational program. The six steps are as follows:[5]

1. Identify problem (based upon documented needs).
2. Determine solution requirements and solution alternatives.
3. Select solution strategies (from among alternatives).
4. Implement selected strategies.
5. Determine performance effectiveness.
6. Revise, as required, at any step in the process.

The foregoing is a continuous process and actually consists of the subelements of (1) problem identification and (2) problem resolution. Problem identification is the primary concern of steps 1 and 2 and problem resolution is the concern of steps 3, 4, and 5 of educational management. The sixth step is used in both problem identification and problem resolution. This process for educational management is also called a system approach.

Step 1, identify problems from documented needs: Earlier, educational needs were defined as measurable discrepancies between a current situation and a required or desired situation. An example of such a need might be: Learners in the Radner School District have a mean reading score of 32nd percentile and a standard deviation of 7 on the Iowa Test of Reading Achievement. The district school board has required that the learners perform at the 50th percentile or better with a standard deviation not to exceed 5 on this test before June 13.

This example shows a measurable discrepancy between "what is" and "what should be," namely, of a mean score difference of 18 and a standard deviation of 2. This stating of needs in measurable performance terms is a crucially important feature of a system approach because it provides a tangible, quantified stating referent for the design of a responsive educational system. A statement of need describes outcome gaps and, therefore, must be free of any solution or "how-to-do-its."

Educational management using a system approach starts with an assessment of educational needs. The importance of starting system design from documentable needs cannot be overemphasized. It prevents selection of solutions before the identification and specification of problems. Thus, the first step of an educational management process called a system approach is to identify problems based on documented needs. These problems should be stated in measurable, performance terms.

Step 2, determine solution requirements and solution alternatives: The needs assessment process has identified discrepancies for resolution on the basis of priority and has provided overall requirements for an educational system. These overall requirements serve as the "mission objective and performance requirements" for system design. By comparing the statement of the problem with the situations and outcomes currently experienced, the system planner can find out where he or she is going and how to tell when he or she has arrived.

Having used the statement of needs to describe both the current situation and the success they seek, the educational manager and the educational system planner must decide on the requirements to solve the problems they face. Using educational "system analysis," one can determine system requirements and possible solution strategies and choose in layers or levels of details from the most general to the most specific.

The tools of educational system analysis include:

1. Mission analysis
2. Function analysis
3. Task analysis
4. Methods–means analysis

Let us take a closer look at these tools for system analysis, for each contribute a little more to the determination of what is required to meet the identified need, what alternatives are available to achieve each requirement, and what the advantages and disadvantages are of each alternative solution possibility.

The mission analysis tells us about requirements for the total problem, function analysis tells about more detailed aspects of each part of the total problem, and finally, task analysis breaks the problem down into the smallest units we will require for planning. After we have identified all the parts of this system, we can identify possible methods and means for each of the requirements we have unearthed during mission, function, and task analysis. We match requirements against possible solutions and note the relative advantages and disadvantages of each so that we can later pick the best ones for solving our problem.

MISSION ANALYSIS

Proceeding from the needs assessment and problems delineation, the mission analysis states the overall goals and measurable performance requirements for the achievement of system outcomes. These required outcome specifications are closely related to the previously identified needs. The mission objective and its associated performance requirements state the appropriate specifications for the system being planned and designed.

Because, as we know, an educational system design procedure must take the planner from where he or she is to where he or she needs to be, the next part of mission analysis is the statement of a management plan showing the major milestones or the central pathway for solving a given problem.

It is possible that the overall process model for a system approach may also be shown as a mission profile. Such a profile, containing a management plan for identifying and solving problems in a logical, orderly manner, can be developed. Flow charts provide a tool for displaying a system and its components and subsystem relationships in a simple format. A flow chart, which identifies functions and their interrelations, can be read by following the solid lines and connecting arrows and by noting the order of the numbers.

FUNCTION ANALYSIS

The mission profile has provided the basic functions, or milestones, that delineate the major duties that must be performed. The next part of an educational system analysis is to identify and define what is to be done to get each one of the milestones in the mission profile accomplished.

Function analysis is the process for determining requirements and subfunctions for accomplishing each element in the mission profile. As such, it can be considered a vertical expansion of the mission profile.

Again, as was true for the mission objectives, each function in the mission profile will have performance requirements, and a miniature mission profile can be constructed to describe the functions that will get one from where he or she is to the accomplishment of each mission profile function.

TASK ANALYSIS

Task analysis is the arbitrary end-point of the analysis of what is to be done in a system analysis. It differs from mission and function analysis only in degree.

The vertical expansion, or analysis, is continued through the function level until "units of performance" are identified. The identification of tasks and their ordering is the last "breaking down" step of an educational system analysis.

METHOD–MEANS ANALYSIS

Recalling that an educational system analysis is a tool for determining feasible "whats" for problem solution and that the second step in system approach to education is to "determine solution requirements and solution alternatives," let us look at the remaining step of a system analysis, the identification of possible methods and means (strategies) for achieving each of the performance requirements or group of performance requirements.

The methods–means analysis can be conducted after mission, function, and task analyses have been completed, or it can be conducted in parallel with each of them as the analysis of additional requirements progresses from level to level. A methods–means analysis identifies possible strategies and tools available for achieving each performance requirement and additionally lists the relative advantages and disadvantages of each for later selections in the next system approach step.

Methods–means analysis, like the other educational system analysis steps, determines what is to be done and not how it is to be done.

SYSTEM ANALYSIS SUMMARY

The steps and tools of an educational system analysis determine the feasible "whats" of problem solution. The tools of analysis and synthesis are used in determining requirements for system design. Again referring to the generic process model for educational management utilizing a system approach, needs assessment and system analysis deal with "what," and the balance of the model is concerned with "how." There is a relationship between educational system planning (needs assessment and system analysis—the what) and system synthesis (the how) for the overall design-process model, along with the interrelations among the various steps and tools of system analysis. Let us now continue with the "how" of system analysis.

PROBLEM RESOLUTION SUMMARY

Step 3—select solution strategies from alternatives: This third problem-solving step begins the "how-to-get-it-done" portion of the system approach process. Here, the appropriate tools and strategies for achieving the various requirements are selected. Frequently, a choice criterion of "cost-benefit" is used, that is, the selection from among alternatives that which will at least achieve the minimal requirements at the lowest cost. All too frequently, educators begin the system design procedure at this point, without the specific delineation of problems and requirements, and select the alternative methods and means on the basis of professional judgment or on a mere assumption of the problems and the requirements.

Selecting methods and means from alternatives requires that the various identified functions and tasks be allocated to (1) people, (2) equipment, and/or (3) people and equipment in combination.

Selection must be made on the basis of the system as a whole, noting the interactional characteristics of the various requirements of the system. Frequently, tools of modeling and simulation are utilized to determine the most effective and efficient means for meeting the requirements. By simulation, different tools and strategies can be tried in a fashion that will not compromise the current, ongoing educational activity.

Step 4—implement solution strategy(ies): It is at the fourth system approach step that the products of planning and selection are actually accomplished. The methods and means are obtained, designed, adapted, or adopted. A management and control subsystem is developed to ensure that everything will be available and utilized as required and that proper data will be collected to determine the extent to which the system is functioning as required. The system is put into operation, including all the complexities of utilization and acquisition of people, equipment, learners, facilities, budgets, and the many other factors necessary for a properly functioning educational system. Frequently, network-based management techniques, such as PERT (Program Evaluation Review Technique) and CPM (Critical Path Method), are quite useful in the management control of system implementation.

Step 5—determine performance effectiveness: Data are collected concerning both the process and the products of the system during and after the system's performance. Against the requirements established in the needs assessment and the detailed determination of requirements obtained from the system analysis, performance of the system is compared with the requirements. Discrepancies are noted between actual system performance and the performance requirements. This provides data on what is to be revised and thus gives diagnostic information that will permit valid system revision.

Step 6—revise system as required: Based on the performance of the system, as indicated by the performance data, any or all previous system steps can be modified and a system redesign job accomplished if necessary. This self-correctional feature of a system approach ensures constant relevance and practicality. An educational system is never considered to be complete, for it must be constantly evaluated in terms of:

1. its ability to meet the needs and requirements it set out to meet,
2. the continued appropriateness of its original needs and requirements. Thus, we must have not only internal consistency and performance, but also constant checking of needs and requirements to ensure external validity, as well.[6]

CASE STUDY 7.1:
REENGINEERING AT MACMILLAN STATE COLLEGE

It was 6:10 on an unseasonably warm Thursday evening in late April 1996. Scott Ferguson, the vice president for business affairs at Macmillan State College, was heading across the parking lot to his car when he crossed paths with faculty member Arnold Thompson. "I thought this morning's meeting was terrific," Thomas said. "I know reengineering is taking a tremendous amount of time and risk, but the things people have been complaining about on this campus for years are finally going to get fixed. You're doing a great job, Scott. Keep it up." "Thanks," Ferguson answered. He smiled and waved good-night as Thompson headed for his car.

A few seconds later, Ferguson heard his name being called by Beth Wilson, the director of undergraduate admissions. He turned as she approached. "Scott," she said, "I was going to call you about where we're going with this reengineering. You've got two of my staff spending time on these new working groups, and it's starting to eat into our ability to get our regular admissions work done. My office is understanding as it is. Don't get me wrong. I like what you're doing, but I just don't know how we can continue to participate in the process. Do you want me to give you a call in the morning to talk about this?" "No, I understand what you're saying," Ferguson answered. "Let me give it some thought. I know there are a lot of people with lots of different reactions to reengineering."

BACKGROUND

From the vantage point of the mid-1990s, life at Macmillan State College ten years earlier would have seemed relatively trouble free. In the mid-1980s, enrollments grew slowly but steadily, and the college was enjoying regular increases in legislative appropriations. But the economic downturn in the late 1980s altered many assumptions. State appropriations to the college were reduced, sometimes more than once a year. Macmillan State reduced its operating budget and searched for economies. Expenditures were carefully controlled. All vacant positions were reviewed by the business office before being refilled. By 1992, these actions, together with a state-sponsored early retirement program, had led to the elimination of 35 positions, mostly support staff, out of a workforce of 410.

In 1993, Scott Ferguson was hired as the new vice president for business affairs. Forty years old, Ferguson has started his career in academia as an assistant professor of finance. He had left teaching to accept a staff position in the office of the Undersecretary for Higher Education at the federal Department of Education, and he had been there for three years when he was tapped for the position at Macmillan State. Once he arrived on campus, his genial personality and his easy accessibility quickly differentiated him from his predecessor. He practiced "management by walking around" and soon was on a friendly first-name basis with many of the faculty.

Ferguson came onto a campus where money was tighter than it had been in the past, staff was smaller, and student enrollments continued to climb. And yet, he observed, administrative processes and work habits seemed not to have changed. Fewer staff were trying to deliver the same services using the same methods they had used for many years.

Turning to technology for improvements in productivity did not seem to be an option. The existing homegrown administrative information system

was, according to one veteran administrator, "hard to use. It doesn't encourage managers to become more computer literate." Data could not be
shared easily across departments. For example, human resources had to
create a special report whenever a department wanted an updated employee list. Most forms were still "paper-and-pencil" and required data to
be entered manually into the system.

In 1994, Macmillan State College decided to reform its computing and
information services, with special emphasis on new software to serve ac-
counting, admissions, development, and other administrative departments. The college made a commitment to spend $2 million on new soft-
ware and related hardware over the next two to three years. Ferguson
fought hard to allocate funds for the new administrative system.

Mark Harris, a consultant recommended by the software vendor, was
hired to help with the installation. He also happened to be a reengineering expert. In conversations with Harris, Ferguson became convinced that
there was no point in changing software at Macmillan if the system and
processes that used computers and software were not also changed.
"Mark kept calling it 'reengineering.' I was clueless about reengineering at
the time," Ferguson remembered, "although I had heard about the idea
from my corporate contacts. Educating me and the campus was the first
priority."

In the spring of 1995, Ferguson asked Mark Harris to conduct a seminar on campus on the topic of reengineering. Ferguson invited everyone
who had been involved in the software search or who had major administrative responsibility. He also made sure that faculty attended. The seminar was a great success; Harris's enthusiasm and his reengineering "war
stories" energized the participants. He explained the links among reengineering, the software, and the need for a reduced staff, in order to (in his
words) "work smarter and not just harder." As Ferguson walked out of
the seminar, he overheard many people saying approvingly, "It's about
time."

STEERING COMMITTEE

That fall, Ferguson convened a new steering committee to coordinate
reengineering activities. The steering committee would be responsible for

planning and communications and would manage the budget. (Ferguson reallocated $325,000 to reengineering from the original $2 million hardware/software budget.) Ferguson remembered that his becoming committee chair "was not a formal decision or a specific event. I suddenly realized one day I was viewed as the 'chief-reengineer.'" A faculty member claimed that Ferguson's selection was inevitable: "Scott was the one who started us thinking about reengineering. As vice president for business affairs, he had the power and access that the project would need to be successful."

Ferguson selected the other members of the steering committee. To ensure broad representation, he included the librarian, the registrar, the director of institutional research, a faculty member from the computing science department, and the computing services director. He also picked members of the support staff—one from the biology department and one from the development office—and one student who had been student body president the previous academic year.

"Instead of being a board of directors, the committee became a group of 'worker bees' with tasks carried out by individual members," Ferguson commented. The committee did not hire any staff; members thought they could do the work on their own, and some thought it would be embarrassing to add a position after the college had just finished downsizing. The computing director agreed to be the contact with Mark Harris for training the steering committee. The support staff members volunteered to become a communications subcommittee to develop a reengineering newsletter and other media. The librarian agreed to recruit and arrange training for team facilitators. Responsibility for taking minutes of the meeting rotated among all the members. Ferguson's office provided clerical support.

MISSIONS AND BELIEF STATEMENTS

One of Harris's first messages to the steering committee was that reengineering needed a statement of mission and underlying beliefs. These would clarify what reengineering was about at Macmillan State College, emphasize its priority, and serve as a communications tool. A three-person subcommittee, including Ferguson, wrote a first draft that was substantially edited by the full steering committee. The final version read as follows:

> *Macmillan State College believes that:*
>
> services and management processes can be restructured to be more responsive to constituents' needs, efficient and cost-effective, and contribute to the academic mission of Macmillan State College;
>
> all members of the community are at different times, both service providers and recipients;
>
> teamwork and collegiality are essential to the successful operation of the College;
>
> all information should be easily available, in keeping with College policies and procedures; and
>
> information technology should facilitate the process of change, leading to improved College services and job satisfaction supported by new training and employment opportunities.
>
> These beliefs lead to a mission statement that aims to create an environment in which:
>
> (1) services and management processes are continuously examined and improved in response to changing constituents' needs; (2) information systems enhance the capability to retrieve, exchange, and analyze institutional data; and (3) evaluation of success is based on responsiveness to constituents' needs, efficiency and cost effectiveness, and contributions to the academic mission of Macmillan State College.

"One significant change in the original draft of the mission statement was substituting the word 'constituent' for 'customer,'" recalled Barbara Miller, the computing services director. A faculty member concurred. "There was real apprehensive about the word 'customer.' The academic culture is very suspicious of any corporate approach toward education."

CAMPUS MEETING

A campuswide meeting was held in December 1995, a little more than three months after the steering committee was formed. The flyer that invited faculty, staff, and students to the meeting promised answers to such questions as "What is reengineering?" "Is it true that student registration will be reengineered first?" and "What's in it for me?" The state college systems office also sent a representative from the budget office who had been on staff at Macmillan State until two years ago.

"The meeting was a success," according to Arnold Thompson, the faculty member on the steering committee, "simply because more than 75 people showed up and were interested in the process. Many of my colleagues came to hear how reengineering might affect them after I had previewed the agenda at the monthly faculty meeting." The student member of the steering committee noted that "there were few students at the meeting because it was close to final exams. However, they could still read about it in the *Macmillan State Journal*, the student newspaper."

According to Professor Thompson, initial campus response to reengineering was positive. "I think there were three reasons for this. First, a clear mission was presented at the faculty meetings and the open meeting in December. Second, the president spoke on both occasions about the importance of reegineering to Macmillan State. Third, abstract corporate language was clarified and made less threatening by defining certain basic terms."

REEGINEERING OR RETRENCHMENT?

Despite the generally positive response to the meeting the prevailing assumption on campus was that reengineering would lead to the elimination of more positions. "Reengineering sounds better than retrenchment," remarked a library assistant, "but everyone knows what's going to happen in the end."

"That was not at all the spirit in which we started reengineering," said Ferguson afterward. "We had already eliminated thirty-five positions. But it is true that additional personnel reductions and productivity improvements were the main interests of any foundation or state budget officials that we approached for financial support. Potential funders always asked, 'How many positions will you cut by reengineering?'" One state legislator had commented: "If IBM can cut 40,000 positions to reduce its cost structure, why can't Macmillan State do likewise by cutting 40 more?" To lessen anxiety on campus, members of the steering committee agreed to communicate to the rest of the campus that while some positions might be defined or reorganized, reengineering would not lead to another round of layoffs campuswide.

PILOT TEST: REGISTRATION FOR CLASSES

Consultant Harris advised the steering committee to conduct a pilot test before deciding whether to start a comprehensive reengineering effort. Participants in the pilot test, and the steering committee, would learn what was involved in producing a successful redesign. "Only after you've finished the pilot," he argued, "will everyone have a thorough understanding of what reengineering is all about."

The steering committee was receptive to the consultant's idea. For the pilot test, they selected student registration for classes. Scott Ferguson noted that "this made sense to all of us, because registration, as a process, was broken. It concerned Macmillan State's most important customers—faculty and students. And there was a high probability that it could be improved through reengineering."

In late 1995, immediately after the all-campus meeting, the steering committee selected the twelve members of the registration pilot team. Ferguson met one-on-one with each prospective member. Subsequently, all pilot team members received a written explanation of reengineering and its importance to the college, as well as a description of their own role and how much time it would take. Following Mark Harris's suggestion, Ferguson promised that redesign would be complete within a six- to eight-week period (or "timebox"). Harris had consistently maintained that a process redesign would take 75 percent of a team member's time during that period. Ferguson worried that this would discourage people from joining the pilot team. Still, almost all those who were asked accepted Ferguson's invitation to participate. The team leader later claimed that "the process actually occupied 30 to 40 percent of our time, but 70 to 80 percent of our energy."

Ferguson also made a point of contacting the supervisor of each team member to ensure their cooperation, and supervisors received a copy of the introductory materials. Many supervisors were concerned about how reengineering would hamper their operations. "Almost all of the reengineering literature is based on large universities like Oregon State or M.I.T.," one commented, "where offices have more people to move around to cover for staff who are off reengineering. A small college like Macmillan has fewer people and less flexibility." Ferguson decided to make funds available for supervisors to hire temporary replacements. However, he heard back from several supervisors that much of the college's work could not be done by replacements, and most team members would be reengineering and doing their own jobs.

The team selected a college-owned house on the edge of campus as the headquarters where the team would do its work. This space was significant, according to the team leader, because "it was far enough away from the daily activity of Macmillan State. We were able to focus, without distractions, on the task of redesign."

Following the suggestions of Mark Harris, the team structured itself around four core positions:

1. The *team leader* had the role of motivating people and ensuring that the charge for the group was completed on time. An athletic coach was picked as the "perfect person for the job."
2. The *facilitator*, an accountant from the dining service, had the task of moderating discussion and ensuring that everyone participated.
3. The *technologist*, from computing services, aided the team by making sure that technology was used appropriately in redesigning the process.
4. The *process owner* represented the department that was principally responsible for the process being redesigned. This person, an assistant registrar, was the most knowledgeable about the process from the operational and management viewpoints.

Other team members had been chosen because they could provide different perspectives on registration. Two senior students and two faculty members represented the "customer" of the process. The bursar joined the team because of the link between the students paying their semester bills and being allowed to register for classes. An institutional researcher worried about the data and coding issues, and the interface of the student records systems with other information systems in both the admissions office and alumni relations office. Finally, the registrar was the liaison from the steering committee to the redesign team; she helped with training, logistics, and any issues that needed the attention of the steering committee.

TRAINING ISSUES

The pilot team's first two days together were spent on training, which was provided by consultant Mark Harris. The team rated Harris highly as a trainer. As one member observed, "He was clear, enthusiastic, and motivated the team with just enough structure." The team facilitator agreed, "We were all well trained and came away with a clear understanding of the process and the task. I was the only member trained separately as a facilitator by Macmillan Bank and Trust (a local bank that offered professional facilitator training to its own staff and guests). I understood what reengineering was about at the College."

Around this same time, Scott Ferguson and a member of the original steering committee began to feel some disenchantment with Harris. Ferguson commented that the steering committee received weak advice from Harris about their role in the redesign process and what their purpose would be in the long term. When asked questions, he had a different answer each time. The steering committee was first explained as a permanent fixture and then as a transitional body that would end after six months. Harris relied too much on anecdotes that never addressed what the steering committee was supposed to be doing, with whom, and when. Too often, it felt like the committee were muddling through and creating their own job descriptions. Ferguson chose not to complain to Harris. "The focus right now is on the redesign work being done by the pilot team. As long as they're happy with what they're getting from Mark and they're making progress, I'm not going to interfere."

REENGINEERING PROCESS

The registration pilot team started its work in January 1996 by "mapping" the current process. Among the elements of the system that the team noted were the following:

- Students preregistered in one semester for class the following semester and then had to register again after classes started.
- For preregistration, the student manually recorded his or her course selections on a card.

- The registrar's office hired temporary extra staff to enter the information from the preregistration cards into the computer, which was slow and prone to error.
- Students were allowed to propose only four courses on the preregistration card. Because of enrollment limits, prerequisites, and other factors, many students did not obtain a full four-course load and had to "shop around" for courses during the first week of the semester.
- Instructors did not have to specify their admission criteria in advance. They could edit their class lists almost until the day the semester started. This meant that many students could be dropped from courses that the registrar's office had confirmed in writing were on their schedules.
- Many students decided not to preregister at all and took their chances negotiating with individual instructors. (The two senior students on the pilot team wanted to retain the ability to negotiate; as one remarked, "after four years, we've figured out how to beat the system.")

Mapping was followed by "brainstorming," during which the pilot team members discussed various ideas for radically redesigning registration. These ideas include: a new registration schedule, much greater use of computers for advising and course selection, improved orientation materials for student and faculty advisors, and more consistent rules for adding and dropping courses. During this stage, members of the team also telephoned other schools to find out how they registered students for classes.

Meanwhile, the steering committee was wondering what role it should be playing during the pilot team's deliberations. According to Ferguson, first, the steering committee had never understood the importance of explicitly defined starting and ending points of the registration process that the team was supposed to redesign. For example, some of the brainstorming ideas that came out involved putting better information in the college catalog, or creating new class schedules that would spread the courses out more evenly during the week. Eventually, the committee recommended to the pilot team that they should limit their redesign work to the period starting with the publication of the class schedule and ending at the conclusion of the first week of the semester, when students could still add courses. The problems that the pilot team had identified with the class schedule and catalog were referred to the faculty and relevant administrative departments.

Second, the committee and the team were confused about which ideas involved changes in administrative processes that the team could tackle and which were higher-level policy issues that were the prerogative of the steering committee, president and senior staff, or the faculty. For example, the committee kept getting bogged down in arguments over whether the team had the power to redesign the class schedule. Third, the steering committee never defined the desired end-result of the redesign process. What would be an "acceptable" new registration process? We determined to keep it simple: the new process would result in every student who registered having a full four-course load without needing to shop around. In addition, the reengineering versus retrenchment issue emerged again. The steering committee failed to tell the team if they should strive to operate registration with fewer positions or, at the other extreme, if they could add positions to improve the process.

PILOT TEAM'S REPORT AND DEBRIEFING

The pilot team concluded its work in March 1996 with its recommendations to the steering committee. The written report included a brief list of problems with the old process, an explanation and defense of the newly redesigned registration process, and a description of the team's methodology. Two debriefing sessions were held between the steering committee and the pilot team. Despite their hard work, team members were unanimously enthusiastic about reengineering, the new registration system, and their own group process. One faculty member from the English department on the team had been critical of reengineering and business techniques in general. After participating in the pilot test, he spoke out in favor of reengineering at several faculty meetings and even volunteered to be a team leader in future redesigns.

IMPLEMENTATION

When it came time to make the transformation from the planning stage to the implementation stage, members of the steering committee discovered that they had a significant disagreement among themselves. Several members, including Ferguson, believed that the redesign process should be carried out exactly as proposed by the redesign team. "In fact, the redesign team and steering committee should have a 'contract' that if the team follows the charge of the committee in terms of the desired end-result and other guidelines, then no changes will be made at all," maintained computing director Miller. "Reengineering has to respect the hard work and careful research of the redesign team." Ferguson agreed: "Reengineering means delegating responsibility to where the work gets done. It's difficult but essential for senior administrators to let go and trust the process. Otherwise, the teams and other employees will feel that reengineering is just a game."

Other members argued that no administration could delegate so much responsibility to an ad hoc team. The administration, they said, must reserve the right to tailor any recommendations to fit budgetary and other realities. Dr. Susan Rivers, the director of student records, would be responsible for carrying out a new registration system. She argued that the pilot team's proposals could not be accepted "as is." "It's impossible for people from all over campus to create a new system and expect it to be implemented exactly as they want because, inevitably, they are going to overlook a lot of important details. Instead, we should consider that the most important outcomes of the redesign process are the new ideas they generate. For example, the idea of giving students more choices makes good sense. And we are certainly going to eliminate preregistration. But specific decisions about implementation can't be left in the hands of the pilot team." The president and academic dean let it be known that they concurred with Rivers' assessment.

Rivers explained later, "The most significant aspect of the proposed registration system that would not work was a complicated new system for selecting classes. Students would have to make choices for classes on a sheet that would then be inputted into a computer and processed. It was not practical from a student's point of view because it was not user-friendly." Further, she argued, such a method of registration "did not meet the needs of the academic culture here. For example, it did not give preference to seniors in classes."

A pilot team member protested, "We were shut out of the implementation. Susan never contacted us for advice or to clarify what we had recommended." Ferguson took a position in the middle, when he suggested that a detailed plan should be the responsibility of a separate implementation team, "although," he admitted, "the steering committee should have decided explicitly one way or the other at the start."

Implementation was hurried to give reengineering credit for a speedy impact on a key campus process and to build support for the process among faculty and students. That left only six weeks between the presentation of the pilot team's report and registration for the fall semester. Changes had to be made. The pilot team had wanted to have the entire registration process online. Because of time constraints in programming and the availability of computers, what was implemented was "batch" registration. Adding and dropping courses was online, but only for registration staff and not for students. There was no time to orient the registration staff, conduct test runs, or perfect the new system before going "live" with the students. An article in the April 7 issue of the student newspaper announced the new process to the campus community. Rivers and computing services spent much of their time reacting to questions and complaints. In retrospect, Ferguson admitted that "the implementation was too hasty and might have been postponed for a semester, despite the political consequences."

FUNCTIONAL WORKING GROUPS

While the pilot team was meeting to rethink the registration process, Mark Harris recommended that the steering committee identify additional business processes that needed to be redesigned and reengineered. However, this was unacceptable to the steering committee because, as Ferguson said, "we wanted the whole community to take an interest and become involved. Otherwise, given our participatory culture, reengineering might be dismissed as more top-down manipulation by the administration."

In February 1996, the steering committee identified six functional working areas within the college: academic information, alumni and community, admissions and student records, facilities, finance, and human resources and payroll. Separate groups were formed and charged with figuring out which processes in each area were "broken." Each had a leader, called a "convener," who was selected by the steering committee and then trained in reengineering and the task at hand. The conveners, in turn picked the members of their groups. In total, about eighty faculty, staff, and students were chosen to participate.

Each functional working group was charged with identifying between twenty-five and forty business processes in its area and then recommending up to six processes for redesign. The criteria for recommending processes for redesign included: "opportunity for improvement, visible impact, potential use of technology, measurability of success, probability of success, impact on culture, need for cross-departmental interaction and ability to redesign within a reasonable time."

Ferguson noted that "at the start, it was difficult for most people in the groups to understand what a business process was, even after it had been explained. It was also tough to take a process and think about whether it could be redesigned in a six- to eight-week timebox. Nevertheless, the groups did identify more than 250 business processes and recommended 38 for redesign. All the information from the six groups was given to the steering committee as well as to the president and senior staff.

Two meetings were held at which the steering committee and conveners discussed the recommendations of the working groups. The criteria that the steering committee used to rank the business processes for redesign were the same ones that the working group used. In April 1996, the thirty-eight business processes were narrowed to twenty. Besides registration, these included: processing of admissions applications, authorization to hire nonfaculty staff, budget formulation, cash handling, catalog information, course textbooks and material ordering, faculty research grant support, first-year student orientation, gift processing, hiring casuals and temps, miscellaneous billings, purchasing, employment of returning students, and room and events scheduling.

INVOLVEMENT OF SENIOR STAFF

The president and senior staff at Macmillan State College were periodically updated about reengineering by Scott Ferguson in his role as steering committee chair. About once a month, he discussed reengineering at a senior staff meeting, and he copied his colleagues on many communications to the steering committee and other reengineering participants. The senior staff also formally approved the core members of each team and the list of twenty processes to be redesigned.

The president was concerned that some processes selected for redesign were too narrow and trivial, given the amount of money being invested in reengineering. Also among the thirty-eight processes recommended for resign by the functional working groups, three troubled the academic dean, and, to a lesser extent, the president. These were off-campus study, student advising, and faculty hiring—even though the faculty and others on the working groups thought that these processes needed significant reform. The dean felt that reengineering was really an administrative matter and not appropriate for aspects of the academic program. He added that there was already a faculty committee looking into the off-campus study program.

Ferguson was disappointed, but he conceded, "There is enough to do on the administrative side." He also pointed out that "many faculty members who have been involved in reengineering consider the process interesting and worthwhile. It's only a matter of time before reengineering comes to the classroom and other parts of the academic program."

According to Ferguson, "One of our problems at Macmillan State is that we have a separate steering committee. At most colleges, I believe, the senior staff constitutes the steering committee. And that make it easier to get funds, recruit process teams, and ensure that implantation takes place properly. The senior staff here is already overcommitted on other projects, so I don't see them being very involved with reengineering." A steering committee member declared that "one of the reasons for the muddled relationship between the senior staff and the steering committee rests in the fact that the entire effort is seen to be to let Scott handle it."

Ferguson observed, "My involvement is seen as a power grab by some. This is not what was intended. Reengineering is not part of my job description." "That's exactly the problem," complained one observer; "he has too much to do in his regular administrative position to be able to spend the time on reengineering that it needs."

REFLECTIONS

In April 1996, Scott Ferguson reflected on the progress of Macmillan State's reengineering efforts.

One of the things that keeps nagging me is the question of communications. We do not have articles about reengineering in the administrative newsletter and in the student newspaper. But reengineering lacks a consistent message in terms of purpose, and many people still view it as another excuse for downsizing the staff.

I don't think we've done a good enough job documenting our experiences with the pilot team. We don't have job descriptions for the team leader and other core process participants. The details of the reengineering steps in the pilot test—mapping, brainstorming, and building the prototype—were never documented. The steering committee liaisons had no checklist of what the process teams would need in order to get started, such as a meeting location. This means that future teams and participants will have to rely on oral tradition and also trial and error (or, as one person put it, "trial and success").

When I look at this campus, I see people who are really turned on by reengineering, and people who aren't even aware that anything is happening. We've got supporters, who see the real potential, and we've got some serious cynics. And now we're planning to launch two new process redesigns this summer. It's really important that they go well.

SUMMARY

The strategic planning process should be understood as a dynamic ebb and flow of events in the life of an educational institution. The so-called chaos theory tells us that life is a process, constantly changing and evolving. Therefore, it should not be surprising for some of the best-laid plans become obsolete before they see the light of day. Mirror Lake, for example, is slowly drying up and evolving into a meadow. If you were planning strategically for the future, you would do well to buy your grandchild a kite rather than a boat, if he or she lived near Mirror Lake.

The moral of the story, therefore, is to plan for the unexpected as well as the expected. Even though your school system might currently be prosperous and healthy, the only way to sustain this success is to plan for the possibility of difficult times. How do we know that the unexpected will eventually occur? One need only look at history.

What prevents us from planning accurately is our paradigm for how things are. We want to find order when the reality is chaos. We like to think that events occur in a linear way. The reality is that events occur in a sporadic an unpredictable way. Our mission, then, is find order in this apparent chaos. Thus, we must see our plans as constantly evolving and changing. The process is continuing. The plans themselves change so frequently that they are of limited value. We prefaced this chapter with Dwight Eisenhower's apt words, "Planning is all, but plans are nothing." The primacy of the planning process over the plan itself is a notion that the astute administrator will constantly keep in mind.

NOTES

1. Professional Development Plan Guidelines, 1992 ed., Strategic Planning in Pennsylvania. Harrisburg: Pennsylvania State Department of Education.

2. Roger Kaufman and Jerry Herman, *Strategic Planning in Education: Rethinking, Revitalizing* (Lancaster, PA: Technomic Publishing 1991), 41.

3. James J. Jones and Donald L. Walters, *Human Resource Management in Education* (Lancaster, PA: Technomic Publishing, 1994).

4. K. J. Hatten and M. L. Hatten, *Effective Strategic Management: Analysis and Action* (Englewood Cliffs, N.J., Prentice-Hall, 1988), 27.

5. Roger A. Kaufman, *Educational System Planning* (Englewood Cliffs, N.J.: Prentice-Hall, 1972).

6. Roger A. Kaufman, The System Approach, Programmed Instruction and the Future, paper presented to the New York University Thirty-Fifth Annual Junior High School Conference, May 1962.

8

EFFECTIVE DECISION MAKING

The fine art of executive decision consists in not deciding questions that are not now pertinent, in not deciding prematurely, in not making decisions that cannot be made effective, and in not making decisions that others should make.

—Chester I. Barnard

Suppose Will Smith was appointed to the position of superintendent of schools for the Rose Tree School District with the expressed purpose to rightsize the school district in light of its declining student population. Having been successful in a similar situation in another school district, how should Will Smith proceed?

In this chapter, we begin by examining the nature of decision makers. Next, we look at the types of decisions managers and other organizational members make and the information they use to make decisions. Then, we specify the characteristics of effective decisions, including issues of quality, acceptance, and ethical decision making. We also compare and contrast individual and group decision making. Finally, we propose ways of improving decision making.

DECISION MAKERS

Individuals or groups of individuals with a set of skills, knowledge, experiences, and values make decisions in organizations. Obviously, the skills, knowledge, and experiences correlate with the type and amount of expertise an individual or group brings to decision making. The personal value systems of individuals influence the decision-making process and outcomes by affecting perceptions of situations, problems, individual and organizational success, the choice process, interpersonal relations involved in decision making, limits of ethical behavior, and acceptance of organizational goals.[1]

Personal style also plays a major role in decision making. Figure 8.1 shows one model of style. It considers the dimensions of cognitive complexity, or an individual's ability to tolerate ambiguity, and values orientation, or the propensity for logical as opposed to relational thought. High cognitive complexity also describes a leader who is proactive and has a high tolerance for ambiguity; low cognitive complexity depicts an administrator who is action oriented and reactive and has a high need for the structure. The resulting four styles suggest the way a decision maker would approach the decision-making process. Groups of decision makers might use a common or hybrid style; analyzing its appropriateness is one element in diagnosing decision-making effectiveness. An individual's personality might further affect the attitude toward uncertainty and risk, as well as his or her perception of the decision and the decision-making process.[2]

EFFECTIVE DECISIONS

A good-quality decision brings about the desired result while meeting relevant criteria and constraints. What would constitute a good-quality decision in the situation in Rose Tree School District? Certainly a decision that reduces costs while maintaining educational quality would be considered a good-quality one. Also, a decision that met the needs of those affected by the decision, including students, faculty, staff, administrators, and the taxpayers, would qualify. So, too, would a decision that meets the financial, human, time, and other constraints existing in the situation.

The quality of the decision depends in part on the level of the decision maker's technical or task skills, interpersonal or leadership skills, and decision-making skills. *Technical* or *task skills* refer to the individual's knowledge of the particular area in which the decision is being made. In the decision that Will Smith must make about right-sizing, *task skills* refer to a knowledge of labor costs, projected revenues, educational product information, and school system overhead costs. Interpersonal or leadership skills relate to the way individuals lead, communicate with, motivate, and influence others. Will Smith, for example, must be able to get the other stakeholders in the school system to accept the decision for which he is responsible. Effective communication should facilitate understanding and acceptance of the decision in the implementation. Decision-making skills are the basic abilities to perform the components of the decision-making process, including situational analysis, objective setting, and generation, evaluation, and selection of alternatives, as discussed later in this chapter.

Will Smith and any advisors he involves in the decision making must produce a decision that they and the rest of the school system community can accept, one that they are willing to "live with." For example, closing two schools might be a high-quality decision, but the teachers' union might oppose it so much that the union members would cripple the work at other schools. Alternatively, reducing the teaching staff may be a high-quality decision, but the students and parents might resist the change because they feel that they are not receiving a quality education. Thus, "acceptance" of the decision is a characteristic that needs to be considered along with the "quality" of the decision.

VROOM–YETTON DECISION-MAKING MODEL

The administrative and organizational theory literature are in agreement about the two most important factors to be considered in determining the decision style that will produce the most effective decisions. While Vroom and Yetton's model includes the additional dimensions of shared goals and conflict possibility, the two key elements are the quality and the acceptance of the decision, as described earlier. Figure 8.1

The administrative and organizational theory literature (Maier, 1962; Bridges, 1967; Vroom and Yetton, 1973) are in total agreement about the two most important factors to be considered in determining the decision style which will produce the most effective decisions. While Vroom and Yetton's model adds the additional dimension of shared goals and conflict possibility, the two key elements are also stressed: QUALITY and ACCEPTANCE. The diagram below summarizes Maier's work in identifying the decision style which is most appropriate for particular problem types. The two key elements are defined as:

(1) Quality (Q) - The importance of quality, i.e., one solution is likely to be more rational than another.

                 The extent to which the leader possesses sufficient information/ expertise to make high-quality decisions by him or herself.

(2) Acceptance (A) - The extent to which acceptance or commitment on the part of subordinates is crucial to the effective implementation of the decision.

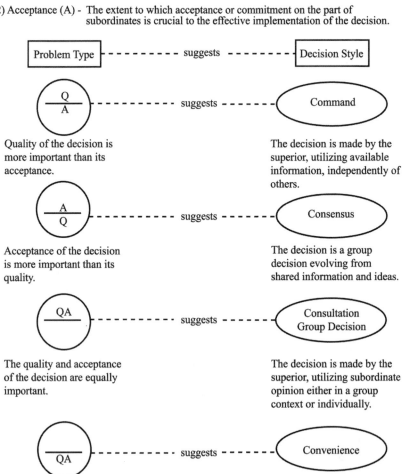

Figure 8.1.　The Dimensions of Effective Decisions

summarizes the identification of the decision style that is most appropriate for particular problem types.[3]

The two key elements are "quality," or the likelihood of one decision to be more rational than another, and "acceptance," or the extent to which acceptance or commitment on the part of subordinates is crucial to the effective implementation of the decision.

For example, if a new law is passed regarding education and the administrator has to include it in the revised edition of the student handbook, the quality of the decision would be more important than its acceptance. Therefore, the appropriate decision style is command. On the other hand, if acceptance is more important than quality, as in the development of a new teacher evaluation instrument, the proper decision style would be consensus.

If both the quality and acceptance are of equal importance, like whether to adopt a whole language approach to reading, consultation or group decision making would be the appropriate style. Finally, if neither the quality nor the acceptance is important, like deciding what color to paint the school lockers, convenience would be the applicable style.

THE DECISION TREE

An effective tool in determining the appropriateness of group versus individual decision making is the "decision tree." An extensive discussion of this decision-making model took place in chapter 3. This model can be used in conjunction with any of the decision-making processes that we consider.

ETHICAL DECISION MAKING

In addition to evaluating a decision in terms of its quality and acceptance, we can also assess how well it meets the criterion of ethical fairness and justice. Consider for example, a disastrous decrease in standardized test scores in a certain high school. Top administrators are faced with the decision of whether to risk public outrage and the possible transfer of significant numbers of students or ignore the situation.[4]

Administrators and staff can assess whether the decisions they make
are ethical by applying personal moral codes or society's codes of values;
they can apply philosophical views of ethical behavior; or they can assess
the potential harmful consequences of behaviors to certain constituencies. One way of thinking about ethical decision making suggests that a
person who makes a moral decision must first recognize the moral issue
where a person's actions can hurt or help others, second make a moral
judgment, third decide to attach greater priority to more concerns than
financial or other concerns, or establish their moral intent, and finally
act on the moral concerns of the situation by engaging in moral behavior.[5]

THE RATIONAL DECISION-MAKING PROCESS

In many situations, using a rational, step-by-step decision-making
process increases the likelihood that a high-quality, accepted, and ethical decision will result. Consider Will Smith's charge to rightsize the
school district. He can proceed to a solution by performing the five steps
of situational analysis: objective setting, generation of alternatives, evaluation of alternatives, making the decision, and evaluation of the decision. Let us look at each of these steps in turn.

Decision making first requires the recognition that there is a problem
to be solved or a decision to be made, followed by the exploration and
classification of the decision situation.[6] Decision making then requires
asking such questions as: What are the key elements of the situation?
What constraints affect the decision? What resources are available?
How would Will Smith answer these questions? The key elements include the past performance of various schools and faculties, the academic reputation of the schools and the school district, the projected
demographic information, the profit margin in each school, the overhead costs for each school, and contractual issues, among others. Will
must consider his previous experience in effecting restructuring and
how the various components of the school community reacted to his efforts. He must assess whether approaches successful in the past can be
effective in the Rose Tree School District.

Constraints on the decision will include the state laws regarding faculty downsizing, as well as the local labor agreement constraints. Although limitations on resources and constraints, such as those mentioned, can be debilitating, they can also generate creative alternatives. For example, if simply laying people off is restricted, one can offer early retirement and voluntary severance packages to achieve the rightsizing objectives. From this situational analysis, the decision maker begins to formulate the issues to be addressed.

The way the decision makers frame the problem has a significant impact on its ultimate resolution. Subsequent steps may differ, for example, if Will Smith frames the problems as cost reduction, downsizing, or an opportunity to serve our constituencies in a more effective and efficient way that will ensure the long-range future of the school district. Errors in problem definition may be hard to identify and even harder to correct. The decision maker should carefully identify the goals and objectives that the decision must accomplish and specify the criteria that will be used to assess its quality, acceptance, and ethical appropriateness. The accomplishment of these goals and objectives serves as one measure of the effectiveness of the decision and the decision-making process.[7]

Often, decision makers err at this step by confusing action plans with objectives. Decision makers must first set their goals and then determine ways of accomplishing them. For example, offering all eligible teachers early retirement is one way of accomplishing the goal of rightsizing. In this case, the early retirement program is not the goal, but a means to a goal.

When possible, decision makers should establish objectives that specify observable and measurable results. Certainly, reducing absenteeism and costs or increasing standardized test scores by a specified percentage or amount are objectives that are observable and measurable. Objectives related to employee attitudes, such as satisfaction, commitment, or involvement, might be more difficult to measure and observe. Still, skillful crafting of the objectives by the decision maker can accomplish the need for quantifiable and observable results—even in these difficult-to-measure instances.

The decision maker specifies a set of realistic and potentially acceptable solutions to the problem or numerous ways of meeting the objectives specified earlier as part of the searching for alternatives phase. What alternatives are available to Will Smith? He can close no schools but offer early retirement incentives to decrease costs; he can close one or two schools and lay off a number or teachers; he can reduce the administrative layer; he could increase the class sizes and lay off a number of teachers; or he could effect efficiencies throughout the school system in both academic and non-academic areas.[8] Techniques for generating alternatives are described later in the chapter.

The decision maker next appraises each alternative. Criteria for evaluation include the alternative's feasibility, cost, and reliability. In addition, the decision maker must assess the risks involved and the likelihood of certain outcomes for each alternative. What other criteria might be used in evaluating the alternatives Will Smith faces? For example, what will the taxpayers think of the alternatives? What about the school board? Will local or national politicians prefer one alternative above another? Are there advocacy groups to be considered? All of these factors, and more, need to be considered before making a decision.

Quantifying the alternatives can systematize their evaluation, dramatize differences among them, and even improve the quality of decision making. For example, we might score each of the alternatives on its feasibility, cost, potentially adverse consequences, and probability of success. Summing the scores of each alternative would allow us to rank-order them and ultimately select the highest one. The process assumes that the criteria are equally weighted, that the numerical values are exact, and that ranks alone are sufficient to provide the best choice. More sophisticated statistical techniques can also be used for such an evaluation. Obviously, this approach to quantifying the evaluation of alternatives is highly subjective because the decision maker's rating of each criterion is incorporated into the overall evaluation. Recent research suggests that decision makers evaluate alternatives using a compatibility test.[9] In decision making, which can be either intuitive or deliberative, the decision maker compares each alternative with a set of standards, such as values, morals, beliefs, goals, and plans, called *images*. The decision maker rejects incompatible alternatives and adds compatible ones to the set of feasible alternatives.

The next step in the process is making the decision. Ideally, a decision maker should select the optimal, or best, alternative. Notice, however, that the decision maker's knowledge, abilities, and motivation will affect the choice. In addition, each alternative had disadvantages as well as advantages. If the cost criterion outweighs all others, then closing schools and laying off teachers and staff would be the best solution. If a moderate cost reduction is acceptable and low likelihood of adverse consequences is desired, then offering early retirement or some other less-drastic alternative might be acceptable.

Next comes evaluating the decision. Review of the decision is an essential step in effective decision making. Too often, selecting an alternative and reaching a decision comprise the final step. Individuals must pause and recheck their decisions and the process that led to them as one way of increasing their effectiveness. Once Will Smith determines how to handle the situation he faces, he must review the steps that led to that decision. Where possible, he might check his thinking with another person. Together, they can evaluate the planned implementation of the decision by assessing its likely or actual outcomes and comparing them to the objectives set earlier. Evaluation performed prior to implementation is part of decision making. Evaluation performed after implementation is part of management control and can call for corrective action and follow-up.

ALTERNATIVE DECISION-MAKING MODELS

Some researchers have argued that the decision-making processes just described do not adequately consider the complexity and ambiguity of organizational life. Next, we present three alternative models, Simon's bounded rationality, decision making by objection, and the "garbage can" approach.

Simon's Bounded Rationality

Herbert Simon, a Nobel Prize winner, was an early critic of the rational model. In his three-step decision process, the decision maker first scans the environment for conditions that call for a decision. He called this the "intelligence" stage, when the administrator listens to reports from various other representatives of the organization and generally monitors the workplace. In the second step, the decision maker "designs" possible solutions to the problem; he or she develops and analyzes possible courses of action. Finally, the decision maker must make a "choice" among the available alternatives. Here, in the interests of efficiency and because of an individual's limited information-processing capability, the decision maker will "satisfice," or sacrifice the optimal for a solution that is satisfactory or "good enough."

Simon's bounded rationality approach places greater emphasis on the creative generation of reasonable alternatives to identify an optimal one than the basic decision-making model. Finding the best alternative, as required by the rational model, might be unrealistic because of conflicting aspects of the situation, such as constituencies with opposing objectives, lack of information, time and cost constraints, communication failures, precedent, or perceptual limitations, making satisficing an appropriate and effective strategy.[10]

Decision Making by Objection

In the model known as decision making by objection, the decision makers do not seek an optimal solution to a problem, but a course of action that does not have a high probability of making matters worse.[11] The decision makers first produce a rough description of an acceptable resolution of the situation. Then, they propose a course of action, accompanied by a description of the positive outcomes of the action. Objections to the action are raised, further delimiting the problem and defining an acceptable resolution. The decision makers repeat this process, creating a series of courses of action, each one having fewer objections than the previous one. Will Smith might start by proposing the closing of three schools and the laying off of twenty teachers, but actually implement a decision requiring much less drastic consequences?

The Garbage Can Model

In contrast to the decision-making processes proposed earlier, the garbage can model emphasizes the unsystematic quality of much decision making in organizations.[12] In an organization with unclear goals, uncertain means of achieving the goals, and changing participants in decision making, a diverse set of problems and solutions are presented simultaneously. The decision maker should recognize that nonrational decisions may occur. Sometimes decisions fit solutions to problems in a way that resolves the problem, removing both the problem and solution from further consideration. The researchers note that this matching often occurs somewhat at random, and use the image of participants dumping problems and solutions into a garbage can to reflect how problems and solutions can be mixed together. If solutions and problems meet at the right time to make a choice, a rational outcome or choice is made. Otherwise, no decision results. Because solutions go in search of problems, the stream of problems must coincide with the stream of solutions for the optimal decisions to be made. More recent expansions of this model try to make the decision maker a more explicit part of the action by citing him or her as able to take advantage of opportunities when problems and solutions match. For example, an unexpected new industry might move into the Rose Tree School District and the influx of new students might solve Will Smith's rightsizing problem.[13]

INDIVIDUAL VERSUS GROUP DECISION MAKING

The decision-making processes described thus far can apply to decisions made by individuals or groups. Yet, group decision making brings different resources to the task situation than does individual decision making. When a group makes a decision, a synergy occurs that causes the group decision to be better than the sum of the individual decisions. The involvement of more than one individual brings additional knowledge and skills to the decision, and it tends to result in higher-quality decisions. However, the same caveat holds for decision making as we have reiterated throughout this book. That is, decision making is situational, and the idiosyncrasies of the moment dictate the decision-making approach to be taken. For example, if your school building is on fire, a participative decision making approach is not appropriate.[14]

CULTURAL DIVERSITY

As the group becomes more diverse, attitudinally, behaviorally, and culturally, the advantages of cultural diversity increase. Cultural diversity provides the greatest asset for teams with difficult, discretionary tasks requiring innovation. Diversity becomes least helpful when working on simple tasks involving repetitive and routine procedures.[15]

TIME REQUIRED

Group decision making generally takes more time than decision making by individuals. The exchange of information among many individuals, as well as effort spent on obtaining consensus, is time consuming. Sometimes, to reach a decision more quickly or to reach a decision all group members will accept, groups satisfice rather than optimize.

RISKINESS OF DECISIONS

Early research suggested that groups tend to make riskier decisions.[16] More recent research suggests that this "risky-shift" phenomenon is actually a "polarization" phenomenon. Groups become more extreme in the direction of the initial predominant view. Because no single person shoulders the consequences of the decision made by a group, individuals might feel less accountable and will accept more risky or extreme solutions. When a problem occurs in a school, the parents do not complain to the committee, they complain to the principal. Thus, a committee feels free to make a decision that is more risky.

RECOGNIZING EXPERTISE

Groups might ignore individual expertise, opting instead for group consensus. Particularly as a member of a group of peers, an individual might be reluctant to discriminate among individuals on the basis of their expertise. Groups then may develop "groupthink," a mode of thinking with a norm of concurrence-seeking behavior, as described later. When group members choose a colleague's solution that they consider to be good, the resulting decision equals the quality of a decision obtained by group decision making and is no riskier than a group decision. But the effectiveness of such a "best member strategy" depends on the probability of the group's selecting the real best member and on the potential for subjectivity in the solution. Even then, research suggests that many groups can perform better than the most knowledgeable member.[17]

GROUPTHINK

Irving Janis first identified groupthink as a factor that influenced the misguided 1961 Bay of Pigs invasion. The symptoms of groupthink arise when members of decision-making groups try to avoid being too critical in their judgment of other group members' ideas and focus too heavily on developing concurrence. It occurs most frequently in highly cohesive groups, particularly in stressful situations. For example, group members experiencing groupthink might feel invulnerable to criticism and hence believe that any action they take or decision they make will be positively received. They might also ignore external criticism, choosing instead to rationalize their actions or decisions as optimum. Some group members might also pressure other group members to agree with the group's decision; deviant opinions are either ignored or not tolerated; members can neither question views offered nor offer nonconforming information. All of these aspects were present in the Bay of Pigs decision.[18]

CHOOSING GROUP DECISION MAKING

We have suggested that the Vroom–Yetton decision tree is an appropriate tool to determine the extent of group participation appropriate in decision making. In general, however, group or individual decision-making choices can be made by considering the type of problem encountered, the importance of its acceptance, the desired solution quality, the individuals involved, the organizational culture, and the time available, as shown in Figure 8.2.

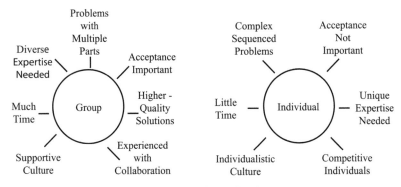

Figure 8.2.   Individual Versus Group Problem Solving

Group decision making is superior when a task or problem requires a variety of expertise, when problems have multiple parts that can be addressed by a division of labor, and when problems require estimates. Individual decision making results in more efficiency if policy dictates the correct solution. Individual decision making also tends to lead to more effective decisions for problems that require completion of a series of complex stages, so long as the individual receives input from many sources, because it allows better coordination of the phases in solving the problem.[19] In Rose Tree School District, for example, the main decision that Will Smith and his colleagues must make is how to reduce costs without reducing quality. This type of problem requires diverse knowledge and skills, creativity, and completion of a series of complex stages, calling most likely for a combination of individual and group decision making.

Group decision making more often leads to acceptance than does decision making by individuals. In addition, because individuals involved in making a decision generally become committed to the decision, use of group consensus expedites acceptance of the decision by the group, thereby increasing individual and group commitment to the decision. Acceptance of the decision about rightsizing at Rose Tree can affect its implementation in the short run, and because school employees cannot easily be replaced, can also affect it in the long run. Therefore, the acceptance is as important as the quality of the decision.

Group decision making generally leads to higher-quality solutions unless an individual's expertise in the decision areas is identified in the beginning. At Rose Tree, Will Smith has had successful experience in rightsizing, therefore, he has less need for group input to make a high-quality decision. However, he needs the input because the acceptance of the decision is so important.

The personalities and capabilities of the people involved in the decision will help or hinder group decision making. Some individuals have difficulty collaborating in a group setting, whereas others are used to dealing with diverse viewpoints and attitudes. Also, groups can ignore individual expertise, creating tension, distrust, and resentment, which can hinder the identification of effective solutions.

The organizational culture provides a context in which the rational or alternative decision-making processes occur. Supportive climates encourage group problem solving; competitive climates stimulate individual responses.

The amount of time available will determine whether group problem solving is feasible because group decision making takes much more time than individual decision making. Rose Tree School District must resolve its problem in a timely manner or risk a taxpayer revolt; therefore, the amount of group participation might be somewhat limited.

WAYS TO IMPROVE DECISION MAKING

How can decision makers overcome barriers, reduce biases, and make more effective decisions? At least five techniques can improve decision making: brainstorming, the nominal group technique, the Delphi technique, consensus mapping, and creative thinking.

Brainstorming

Groups or individuals use brainstorming when creativity is needed to generate many alternatives for consideration in decision making. In brainstorming, they list as many alternatives as possible without simultaneously evaluating the feasibility of any alternative. For example, Will Smith might charge a task force with listing all the ways of reducing costs in the Rose Tree School District. The absence of evaluation encourages group members to generate rather than defend ideas. Then, after ideas have been generated, they are evaluated, and decisions are made. Although brainstorming can result in many shallow and useless ideas, it can also motivate members to offer new ideas. It works best when individuals have a common view of what constitutes a good idea, but it is harder to use when specialized knowledge or complex implementation is required.[20]

Nominal Group Technique

The nominal group technique is a structured group meeting that helps resolve differences in group opinion by having individuals generate and then rank-order a series of ideas in the problem-exploration, alternative-generation, or choice-making stage of group decision making.[21] A group of individuals is presented with a stated problem. Each person individually offers alternative solutions in writing. The group then shares the solutions and lists them on a blackboard or large piece of paper, as in brainstorming. The group discusses and clarifies the ideas. They then rank and vote their preference for the various ideas. If the group has not reached an agreement, they repeat the ranking and voting procedure until the group reaches some agreement. Figure 8.3 illustrates the steps.

A more recent version of the nominal group technique emphasizes anonymity of input, pursuing a single purpose in any one group meeting, collecting and distributing inputs before a meeting, and delaying evaluation until all inputs are displayed. It also ensures opportunities for discussing displayed items before voting and limiting discussion to their pros and cons, allowing any individual to reword items, always using anonymous voting, and providing a second vote option.

The size of the group and diverse expertise of its members increase the usefulness of the nominal group technique. It encourages each group member to individually think about and offer ideas about the content of a proposal and then directs group discussion. It moves the group toward problem resolution by focusing on top-ranked ideas and eliminating less valued ones systematically. The nominal group technique also encourages continued exploration of the issues, provides a forum for the expression of minority view points, gives individuals

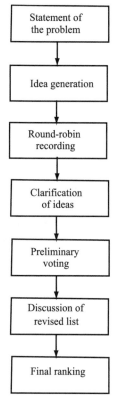

Figure 8.3.   Steps in Nominal Grouping

some time to think about the issues before offering solutions, and provides a mechanism for reaching a decision expediently through the ranking-voting procedure. It fosters creativity by allowing extensive individual input into the process. Strong personality types will dominate the group less often because of the opportunity for systematic input by all group members. It encourages innovation, limits conflict, emphasizes equal participation by all members, helps generate consensus, and incorporates the preferences of individuals in decision-making choices. However, unless the administrator is trained in the use of this technique and the ones that follow, it would be more prudent to employ an organizational consultant trained in these techniques to act as a facilitator in the process.

Delphi Technique

Basically, the Delphi technique structures group communication in dealing with a complex problem in four phases: exploration of the subject by individuals, reaching understanding of the group's view of the issues, sharing and evaluation of any reasons for differences, and final evaluation of all information. In the conventional Delphi, as shown in figure 8.4, a small group designs a questionnaire, which is completed by a larger respondent group; the results are then tabulated and used in developing a revised questionnaire, which is again completed by the larger group. Thus, the results of the original polling are fed back to the respondent group to use in subsequent responses. This procedure is repeated until the issues are narrowed, responses are focused, or consensus is reached. In another format, a computer summarizes the results and thus replaces the small group. Such group decision support systems have increased the focus on the task or problem, the depth of analysis, communication about the task and clarifying information and conclusions, effort expended by the group, widespread participation of group members, and consensus reaching.[22]

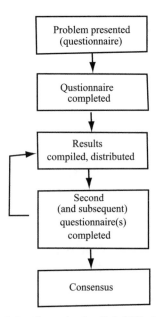

Figure 8.4. Steps in the Delphi Technique

Delphi is very helpful in a variety of circumstances. First, if the decision makers cannot apply precise analytical techniques to solving the problem but prefer to use subjective judgments on a collective basis, Delphi can provide input from a large number of respondents. Second, if the individuals involved have historically failed to communicate effectively in the past, the Delphi procedures offer a systematic method for ensuring that their opinions are presented. Third, the Delphi does not require face-to-face interaction and thus succeeds when the group is too large for such a direct exchange. Fourth, when time and cost prevent frequent group meetings or when additional pre-meeting communication between group members increases the efficiency of the meeting held, the Delphi technique offers significant value for decision making. Fifth, the Delphi can overcome situations where individuals greatly disagree or where the anonymity of views must be maintained to protect group members. Finally, the Delphi technique reduces the likelihood of groupthink; it prevents one or more members from dominating by their numbers or the strength of their personality.

Consensus Mapping

Consensus mapping, which works best with multidimensional, complex problems that have interconnected elements and many sequential steps, begins after a task group has developed, clarified, and evaluated a list of ideas. First, a person acting as a facilitator encourages participants to search for clusters and categories of listed ideas. This search for structure includes the listing and discussion of alternative clusters and categories by the entire group or subgroups and then production of a single classification scheme by group members working as a group or in pairs or trios.[23] Then, the facilitator consolidates the different schemes developed by subgroups into a representative scheme that acts as a "straw-man map" for the entire group. Group members next work to revise the straw man into a mutually acceptable solution. When there is more than one task group, a representative from each task group presents its revised map to members of other task groups. Finally, representatives from each task group produce a single, consolidated map or solution.

Creative Thinking

Creativity in decision making is concerned with changing traditional patterns of thinking. Individuals try to restructure a pattern to reassemble it and view the problem differently. Like brainstorming, which is a type of creative or lateral thinking, such thinking should focus on the generation of ideas, not on the evaluation of alternatives. Suspending judgment about the correctness of an alternative facilitates creative thinking. Individuals can delay judgment about the relevance of information to the decision being considered, the validity of an idea for themselves or others, or the validity of an idea offered by another person. Delaying judgment encourages ideas to survive longer and spawns other ideas. It also motivates other people to offer ideas they normally would reject and stimulates new ideas, and it can result in the development of a new, more useful frame of reference for assessing them.[24]

Individuals can use a variety of techniques to encourage their creative thinking. First, they can use alternative thinking languages, such as expressing a problem in mathematical rather than verbal language or using visual models rather than verbal expressions of a problem. For example, we might suggest that Will Smith express his alternatives graphically, in the form of a decision tree. Decision makers can also develop a questioning attitude as a way of gaining additional information. They might also make lists as a way of increasing their ability to process the information gained. Creative decision makers repeatedly challenge their assumptions; for example, Will Smith may repeatedly ask the question "why" about information gathered. Or other individuals or group members might take a devil's advocate approach to evaluating alternatives and choosing final solutions to a problem. Educators have a head start in assuming this role, since we have been trained to be inquisitive. Creating analogies, reversing situations, and breaking alternatives into their component parts also foster more creative decision making.

CASE STUDY 8.1: THE HILLSIDE MIDDLE SCHOOL

Hillside Middle School is an inner-city public school with 403 students on roll. Ninety-three percent of the students are African American, 5 percent are of Spanish descent, and 2 percent are Asian. Ninety-eight percent of the students come from homes that are below the poverty level, therefore every child in the school receives the free breakfast and lunch program. Students are from the local area; many students are from the Richard Allen projects, some from public housing as well as private homes/apartments, and a few from shelters.

Hillside Middle School is in the Mountain School District, the largest district in Pennsylvania. The Superintendent of the District, Herbert White, has been with the district for two years. Mr. White's plan is for Children to Achieve, he believes all children can learn and should have every opportunity to do so. Mr. White wants students to become active participants in the learning process; therefore our mode of teaching should be child centered. Mr. White has implemented "standards" into the curriculum, a series of outcomes students must meet before graduating or before being promoted to the next grade level. The facilitation of the teacher is crucial in order for the child to meet the requirements necessary in relation to the standard. Mr. White also believes that the teacher should be held accountable for having the students achieve.

Accountability has set the tone for many schools in the district. Many schools are reevaluating the way in which they implement and teach their curriculum. Hillside is one of those schools. Before Mr. White revealed his student-centered agenda, Hillside was very laid back with its curriculum. Each teacher had his or her own style, plan, and set of goals they hoped to achieve. Teaching strategies varied from classroom to classroom. The principal's theory was simple: If your class is quiet and students are working on something, "Hillside is doing its job as a school!"

All of this changed when the plan was revealed by Dr. White, and a new principal was appointed to Hillside, Mr. James Host. Mr. Host immediately went to work. He revamped the entire school. He changed everything from the subjects teachers taught to the way the teachers taught them. A major change to the curriculum was a teaching strategy Mr. Host would pilot in the school, Problem Based Learning (PBL). PBL would add a new dimension to student learning and teacher facilitation in the classroom. Dr. Alice Gray, a Medical College professor from a local hospital, would train selected staff members in how to implement PBL into the curriculum, since she was the founder of this successful teaching/learning strategy. Mr. Host's plan was to start small in the school. He decided to offer this invaluable learning opportunity to only a small group of children, one full class of thirty-three students and eight staff members. The pilot group was selected from three sixth-grade classes. Student acceptance was based on interest, motivation, and parental support. The coordinator was chosen by the principal, as were the other staff members. The secretary, school coordinator, school nurse, four teachers, and Mr. White, himself, made up the PBL team.

PBL divided students into four groups of eight children with one facilitator and a back up. Students were given a case study, developed by Dr. Gary, and were required to generate data, questions, hypothesis, and learning issues. Cases were based on a medical issue. Students were required to use critical thinking and cooperative learning strategies to diagnose and come up with a solution to the problem.

A typical PBL session lasts one week. The first day of PBL, the students are required to read part one of the case study, generate data, ask questions, relate to the information given, come up with hypotheses based on the facts, and list learning issues they feel should be researched in the case. Day two and three are planned research days. The children go to the school library and investigate their learning issues. They may use all resources available. The facilitators, school nurse, and Dr. Gray gather and display various sources for the children. The students may work alone or with a partner, depending on what learning issues they chose. Students are encouraged to help one another out during this time.

Once they finish their research, it is time to come back and meet as a small learning group again. Day four enables the students to summarize what they have found thus far by using a concept map. The map integrates data from the case as well as research findings; students are now able to holistically make connections. The students next finish reading the case. This enables them to rule out any hypotheses they may have come up with that do not agree with the new data. On the last day of PBL, students usually follow up with a field trip that extends the health issue discussed in their PBL session.

The program had proven to be very successful. Students are more motivated to learn, attendance has increased, many students have selected health-related High School Career Programs, their research skills have dramatically improved, cooperative learning strategies have been enhanced as well as higher order thinking strategies, students have become

critical thinkers, and the list goes on. (Many forms of evaluation and assessment are unable to measure the benefits of PBL.)

Because the benefits of PBL are many, Mr. Host has decided to implement PBL across the curriculum, involving all grade levels. Staff development has been offered several times to accommodate all teachers, and
other PBL grade groups have been identified. The principal, staff, students,
and parents are very excited about the integration of PBL into the curriculum because this change has proven to be beneficial to the entire
school community.

SUMMARY

Decision making is a basic and important process in educational institutions. The success experienced by educational administrators depends
largely on their mastery and effective implementation the decision-making process. In this chapter, we described the nature of the decision being made in rightsizing the Rose Tree School District. We noted that to
make such decisions effectively individuals must have technical, interpersonal, and decision-making skills. We outlined basic decision-making
processes that help improve the quality of a decision and encourage its
acceptance by others. We noted that quality and acceptance are the two
most important factors to be considered in making a decision. Decision
makers must systematically analyze the situation; set objectives; generate, evaluate, and select alternatives; make the decision; and evaluate
the decision made. We also identified some alternative decision-making
processes such as Simon's concept of bounded rationality, decision making by objection, and the garbage can model of decision making. In all
of this, we stressed the situational nature of effective decision making.
No one singular decision-making style is effective at all times and in all
situations.

Next, we compared decision making by individuals and groups. The
advantages and disadvantages of group versus individual decision making
were presented, as were the factors that determine the extent of group
participation. We concluded by suggesting some techniques to improve
decision making, including the nominal group technique, brainstorming,
the Delphi technique, consensus mapping, and creative thinking.

NOTES

1. E. F. Harrison, *The Managerial Decision Making Process*, 3rd ed. (Boston: Houghton Mifflin, 1987).

2. A. J. Rose, R. O. Mason, and K. E. Dicken, *Strategic Management: A Methodological Approach* (Reading, Mass.: Addison-Wesley, 1987).

3. V. H. Vroom and P. W. Yetton, *Leadership and Decision Making* (Pittsburgh: University of Pittsburgh Press, 1973) is the original version; V. H. Vroom and A. G. Jago, *The New Leadership: Managing Participation in Organizations* (Englewood Cliffs, N.J.: Prentice-Hall, 1988).

4. L. K. Trevino, Ethical Decision Making in Organizations: A Person-Situation Interactionist Model, *Academy of Management Review* 11 (1986): 601–617.

5. J. R. Rest, *Moral Development: Advances in Research and Theory* (New York: Praeger, 1986); T. M. Jones, Ethical Decision Making by Individuals in Organizations: An Issue-Contingent Model, *Academy of Management Review* 16, no. 2 (1991): 366–395.

6. J. S. Carroll and E. J. Johnson, *Decision Research: A Field Guide* (Newbury Park, Calif.: Sage, 1990).

7. P. C. Nutt, Types of Organizational Decision Process, *Administrative Science Quarterly* 29 (1984): 414–450.

8. D. Braybrooke and C. Lindblom, *A Strategy of Decision* (Glencoe, Ill.: The Free Press, 1963).

9. T. R. Mitchell and L. R. Beach, ". . . Do I love thee? Let me count . . ." Toward an Understanding of Intuitive and Automatic Decision Making, *Organizational Behavior and Human Decision Processes* 47 (1990): 1–20.

10. H. A. Simon, *The New Science of Management Decision* (New York: Harper, 1960).

11. P. A. Anderson, Decision Making by Objection and the Cuban Missile Crisis, *Administrative Science Quarterly* 28 (1983): 201–222.

12. For a discussion of this model, see most recently J. G. March and J. P. Olsen, Garbage Can models of Decision Making in Organizations, in *Ambiguity and Command*, ed. J. G. March and R. Weissinger-Baylon (Marshfield, Mass.: Pitman, 1986), 11–53; and earlier works including M. D. Cohen, J. G. March, and J. P. Olsen, A Garbage Can Model of Organizational Choice, *Administrative Science Quarterly* 17 (1972): 1–25; J. G. March and J. Olsen, *Ambiguity and Choice in Organizations* (Bergen, Norway: Universitetsforlaget, 1976).

13. M. Masuch and P. LaPotin, Beyond Garbage Cans: An AI Model of Organizational Choice, *Administrative Science Quarterly* 34 (1989): 38–67.

14. Recent research continues to confirm this observation. See, for example, J. P. Wanous and M. A. Youtz, Solution Diversity and the Quality of Group Decisions, *Academy of Management Journal* 29 (1986): 149–159; and P. C. Bottinger and P. W. Yetton, An Integration of Process and Decision Scheme Explanations of Group Problem Solving Performance, *Organizational Behavior and Human Decision Processes* 42 (1988): 234–249.

15. N. J. Adler, *International Dimensions of Organizational Behavior*, 1st ed. (Boston: Kent, 1986), 113.

16. K. Dion, R. Baron, and N. Miller, Why Do Groups Make Riskier Decisions Than Individuals?, in L. Berkowitz, *Advances in Experimental Social Psychology*, vol. 5 (New York: Academic Press, 1970), 96–125 presents some of the earliest work in this area.

17. L. K. Michaelsen, W. E. Watson, and R. H. Black, A Realistic Test of Individual vs. Group Consensus Decision Making, *Journal of Applied Psychology* 74, no. 5 (1989): 834–839.

18. G. Whyte, Groupthink Reconsidered, *Academy of Management Review* 14 (1989): 40–56.

19. L. N. Jewell and H. J. Reitz, *Group Effectiveness in Organizations* (Glenview, Ill.: Scott, Foresman, 1981).

20. J. L. Adams, *The Care and Feeding of Ideas: A Guide to Encouraging Creativity* (Reading, Mass.: Addison-Wesley, 1986).

21. G. P. Huber, *Managerial Decision Making* (Glenview, Ill.: Scott, Foresman, 1980); and A. Delbecq, A. Van de Ven, and D. Gustafson, *Group Techniques for Program Planning* (Glenview, Ill.: Scott, Foresman, 1975), provide an early discussion. See J. B. Thomas, R. R. McDaniel, Jr., and M. J. Dooris, Strategic Issue Analysis: NGT + Decision Analysis for Resolving Strategic Issues, *Journal of Applied Behavioral Sciences* 25, no. 2 (1989): 189–200, for more recent examples.

22. K. L. Kraemer and A. Pinsonneault, Technology and Groups: Assessment of the Empirical Research, in *Intellectual Teamwork*, ed. J. Galegher, R. E. Kraut, and C. Egido (Hillsdale, N.J.: Erlbaum, 1990): 375–405.

23. S. Hart, M. Boroush, G. Enk, and W. Hornick, Managing Complexity through Consensus Mapping: Technology for the Structuring of Group Decisions, *Academy of Management Review* 10 (1985): 587–600.

24. E. DeBono, *Lateral Thinking: Creativity Step by Step* (New York: Perennial Library, 1990); E. DeBono, *Lateral Thinking for Management: A Handbook of Creativity* (New York: American Management Association, 1971).

9

POWER AND THE
NEGOTIATIONS PROCESS

The power of a man is his present means to obtain some future apparent good.

—Thomas Hobbes

Charlotte Burton is the new principal of Springfield High School. She met Marie Wilson, the teacher union representative, on her first day at the school. The two women were both strong-willed individuals who had reached their respective positions by aggressively pursuing their professional goals. They were both intent on showing the other who was "boss."

The scenario here is not unlike many that occur at educational institutions of all levels. This situation reflects the exercise of power in an organization. Power is the potential or actual ability to influence others in a desired direction. An individual, group, or other social unit has power if it controls information, knowledge, or resources desired by another individual, group, or social unit. Who has the power in the situation described at Springfield High School? Recognizing, using, and dealing with power differences is implicit in negotiation, which is a process for reconciling different, often incompatible interests, of interdependent parties. At Springfield High School, both Charlotte Burton and Marie

Wilson have power. How well each one uses her power and negotiation skills will determine her effectiveness.

In this chapter, we examine power and the negotiation's process. We begin by considering the reasons individuals or groups exert power. We then examine the sources from which they derive power. Next, we examine the use of negotiations. We describe two bargaining paradigms, the negotiation process, and strategies and tactics of negotiations.

POWER IN THE ORGANIZATION

Organizational researchers have increasingly cited the value of identifying and using power behavior to improve individual and organizational performance, even calling its development and use "the central executive function."[1] Theorists and practitioners have transformed an early view of power, which considered it evil and as mainly stemming from coercion, into a model of viable political action in organizations. Yet, although functional and advantageous in many situations, power behavior can also create conflict, which frequently is dysfunctional for the organization.[2]

Different individuals and groups within and outside the organization can exert power. Individual employees, including top and middle management, technical specialists, support staff, and other nonmanagerial employees, can influence the actions an organization takes to reach its goals.[3]

Individuals can exert influence in a variety of ways. They can exert regular ongoing influence, such as when the college president exerts authority over the faculty. Or, they can make attempts to exert influence periodically, when unique circumstances occur, such as the expiration of a labor contract or a change in the economic or technological environment. Some individuals use their personal charisma or network of contacts to create personal influence, while others remain more detached. They might try to influence rules, regulations, policies, and procedures rather than individuals. Attempts to exert influence can be constructive or destructive. How would you characterize the situation that is about to unfold at Springfield High School?

ETHICAL ISSUES

How legitimate is the use of power in organizations? Certainly, if the use of power is manipulative and autocratic, it raises questions about the ethics of power. The abuse of power is evident not only in politics, but also in schools and school districts across the nation.

But the use of power, so long as it does not abuse the rights of others, has been encouraged in organizations. It helps administrators attain institutional goals, facilitate their own and others' achievements, and expedite effective functioning in the workplace. Power viewed in this way is an essential part of effective administration and leadership.

Administrators must establish guidelines for the ethical use of power in their organizations. They and other organizational members must emphasize its contribution to organizational effectiveness and control its abuses. Ensuring that the rights of all organizational members are guaranteed is one criterion for its ethical use. This is especially appropriate in institutions that are not unionized, where the employee handbook should outline employee rights in a way similar to that of a labor agreement.

POWER AND DEPENDENCE

We can initially diagnose power by measuring the extent or force of the dependence that flows in the opposite direction from power in a relationship.[4] In other words, the power that Charlotte Burton has over Marie Wilson is determined by the degree of dependence that Marie Wilson has on Charlotte Burton. Individuals can initiate an act of power to counteract their job-related dependence.

Dependence arises in part because a person, group, or organization relies on another person, group, or organization to accomplish his, her, or its tasks. It might also arise for other reasons, such as a previous history of assistance by one person or a psychological reliance by one person on another. A subordinate depends on his or her ordinates for assistance in accomplishing a task and identifying obstacles to achieving a work goal. The person being relied or depended upon automatically has some power to influence the other. Individuals who are dependent attempt to secure power to neutralize their dependence on others.

Individuals engage in power-oriented behavior to reduce their dependence on others; they also try to increase the dependence of others on them, thus increasing their own relative power. Marie Wilson, for example, might attempt to have the nontenured teachers believe that their continued employment depends largely on her support as a way to increase their dependence on her. On the other hand, Charlotte Burton might circumvent Marie Wilson as much as possible to display her independence from union influence and demonstrate to the teachers that their future employment depends more on Charlotte Burton than on Marie Wilson.

POWER AS EXCHANGE

Recent definitions of power have described power as a property of a social relationship. This definition derives from an historical view of power as an exchange process where a person who commands services needed by others exchanges them for compliance with his or her requests. For example, Charlotte Burton accedes to Marie Wilson to avoid a potential bargaining impasse. In the exchange relationship, each party exercises a kind of power in providing something of value to the other.[5]

A social exchange network exists when an individual or group negotiates with another over the allocation of valued resources.[6] Charlotte Burton, the principal, has significant power since in the exchange of resource transaction, she controls the financial resources of the school.

PERSONALITY AND POWER

A third way of viewing power, in addition to a response to dependence or a part of an exchange relation, looks at individual needs for power.[7] You may recall from our discussion of motivation that individuals with a high need for power try to influence and control others, seek leadership positions in groups, enjoy persuading others, and are perceived by others as outspoken, forceful, and demanding. Often, politicians, school administrators, or informal leaders are perceived as having a high need for power.

An individual's personality can also affect his or her exertion of power and influence. One recent study showed, for example, that personality

explains the type of influence tactics used. People high on Machiavellianism more often used nonrational and indirect tactics (e.g., deceit,
thought manipulation), and people low in Machiavellianism more often
used rational and direct tactics (e.g., reason, persistence, assertion).
Those high on need for approval used rational and indirect tactics (e.g.,
hinting, compromise, bargaining), and those low on need for approval
used nonrational and direct tactics (e.g., threat, evasion, reward).[8]

POWER RELATIONS

Most influence attempts we have described are directed downward in
the organization. Principals, for example, can give direct instructions to
faculty, establish guidelines for their decision making, approve or reject
their decisions, or allocate resources to them. Individuals can also exert
upward influence. To promote or protect their self-interests, they can
control the type of information passed to superiors or withhold information they feel is detrimental to themselves. For example, a principal
might withhold negative information from getting to the superintendent
of schools for fear that the principal will "look bad" as a result.[9]

Lateral influence can also occur. Peers can offer advice or provide
service; or they can use power to control others. Marie Wilson might use
her influence as union representative to control her peers, for example.
Influence attempts between entities at the same level often results in
competition.[10] The parties involved often resort to power struggles that
result from the tendency to try to strengthen one's own position vis-à-vis
the other individual. For example, one college professor might try to
strengthen his or her position at the expense of the other when two professors seek tenure from the same department. As the parties' interdependence increases, however, they can less afford conflict. Thus, they
might rely more on negotiation and cooperation, rather than on a power
struggle to resolve their differences.

EMPOWERING OTHERS

Recent research suggests that individuals often can increase their own
power by sharing power with others. Administrators can facilitate the

sharing by helping colleagues to understand and tap into the sources of power described in this chapter. They can also give them empowering information, such as providing emotional support and affirmation, serving as a role model, and facilitating successful accomplishment of a task. Other strategies for a leader include providing a positive emotional atmosphere, rewarding staff achievements in visible and personal ways, expressing confidence in subordinates' abilities, fostering initiative and responsibility, and building on success.

In a site-based or school-based management situation, for example, superintendents and principals are relinquishing some of their power. Task forces, whose membership reflects the make-up of the school community, are given either advisory or governance power in making decisions. This process empowers faculty and staff and, ultimately, enhances the power of the administration because the school is more likely to achieve its goals.

SOURCES OF POWER

There are at least three sources of power in an organization: position power, personal power, and information or resource power.

Possessing position power, administrators can exert influence over others simply because of the authority associated with their jobs. It results in subordinates obeying the instructions given by a principal, for example, simply by virtue of the position that he or she holds. In education, the union contract and tenure mitigate the principal's position power to a significant degree. Thus, it is inappropriate to rely on position as the only source of power. One study showed, for example, that as a supervisor's position power increased, a subordinates's compliance increased, but his or her satisfaction with supervision decreased.[11] So, in the long run, the abuse of position power can have diminishing returns.

Power accrues to other positions because of their centrality. The more the activities of a position are linked and important to those of other individuals or subunits, the greater their centrality. A superintendent of schools, for example, has greater centrality than the school board because the activities of more jobs are linked to him or her than to the elected school board. Thus, even though the school board has technically more position power, in reality, the superintendent has more power because of the centrality of his or her position.

Personal Power

Personal power is based on the knowledge or personality of an individual that allows him or her to influence the behavior of others. An individual who has unique or special knowledge, skills, and experience can use this expertise as a source of influence and as a way of building personal power. When the use of computers first made its impact on schools, for example, the "computer guru" on the faculty oftentimes wielded personal power based on special knowledge and skills. As schools and other organizations have become increasingly technology-oriented, technical support staff have acquired increased power.

Some individuals influence others because they have charisma or because others identify with them. An individual with charisma often exerts power because he or she attracts others to follow. Oftentimes, when lateral dependence occurs among peers, it is the result of personal power based on the individual's charisma.

Another type of personal power is coercion. If a superintendent can exert power over his or her principals because they fear the superintendent, he or she is using coercive power. If the teachers are on strike, the superintendent might threaten to replace them with nonunion teachers. This would be another example of coercive power.

The use of coercive power often has dysfunctional consequences. It can create ongoing stress and anxiety for employees. In extreme cases, it can result in increased absenteeism, increased turnover, and even sabotage in the workplace.

Access to resources or information provides a third major source of influence. This differs from expert power in its greater transience. Expertise is more permanent than information-based power. For example, the first individuals to learn to use a new computer system might initially derive their power from having information that others do not, but if their power persists even after the average teacher becomes computer literate, he or she has developed personal power based on expertise.

Power can come from the control of scarce resources, such as money, materials, staff, or information. In a school setting, the business manager oftentimes has this type of power. Even the audiovisual director can have this type of power if there is a greater demand than there is a supply of these types of resources in a school.

THE NEGOTIATION PROCESS

Negotiation is a process by which two or more parties attempt to reach an agreement that is acceptable to both parties about issues on which they disagree. Negotiations typically have four key elements.[12] First, the two parties demonstrate some degree of interdependence. Charlotte Burton and Marie Wilson demonstrate such an interdependence. Second, some perceived conflict exists between the parties involved in the negotiations. Ordinarily, the teachers' union and the school administration differ in their views on how the school should operate. Third, the two parties have the potential to participate in opportunistic interaction. Therefore, each party tries to influence the other through various negotiating actions. Each party cares about and pursues its own interests, by trying to influence decisions to its advantage. Finally, the possibility of agreement exists.

BARGAINING PARADIGMS

Basically, two bargaining paradigms are in current use, distributive bargaining, which takes an adversarial or win-lose approach, and integrative bargaining, which takes a problem-solving or win-win approach.[13]

The classical view considers bargaining as a win-lose situation, where one party's gain is the other party's loss. Known also as a *zero-sum type of negotiation*, because the gain of one party equals the loss of the other and hence the net adds to zero, this approach characterizes the great majority of the negotiations taking place in educational settings today.

Recent research encourages negotiators to transform the bargaining into a win-win situation. Here, both parties gain as a result of the negotiations. Known also as a *positive-sum type of negotiation*, because the gains of each party yield a positive sum, this approach has recently characterized the negotiations in a few school districts, especially those that have had a history of strikes and are looking for an alternative to the classical model of collective bargaining.

COLLABORATIVE BARGAINING

Even when an agreement is reached, distributive bargaining tends to lead to a win-lose conclusion between the parties. Both parties tend to depict the other as the loser to their respective constituencies. When the negotiations break down into a serious impasse, the probability of a lose-lose outcome increases. In this circumstance, not only are the parties frustrated from achieving a satisfactory agreement, but those whom they serve are affected adversely. The teaching-learning environment can be disrupted by the hostility between the parties. Parents, students, and the community in general can become angry when the school is unable to function properly because of unsettled disputes between the school's management and its employees.[14]

An alternative form of bargaining has emerged as a way to avoid or minimize the negative aspects of adversarial bargaining. Collaborative bargaining represents a cooperative process that focuses on problem solving and other activities that identify, enlarge, and act upon the common interests of the parties. Its objective is to increase the joint gain of the parties, the win-win outcome.

The pressure for educational reform in the last two decades of the twentieth century has stimulated teachers and school boards to negotiate collaboratively over policy issues dealing with class size, staff development, and teacher appraisal methods. Collaborative bargaining is a timely method for joining the general trend of school reforms that seek to institutionalize collaborative decision making into the daily operations of schools. Collaborative bargaining rests on the assumptions that both parties want to achieve a mutually satisfactory agreement and that the agreement will lead to an improved school environment for students.

An example of an integrative or collaborative bargaining approach is the win-win process developed by Irving Goldaber. In this process, the parties are given a fixed period of time in which to negotiate a contract. In so doing, the parties are to arrive at shared solutions without either being forced to give up its desired goals.

Goldaber's win-win approach is organized into ten phases depicted in Table 9.1. The preliminary phases entail each party receiving the protocols for structuring the process and preparing lists of questions, concerns, and expectations. These lists are copied onto large sheets of paper for posting around the room during the first formal meeting of the process.[15]

The third and fourth phases occur during the first two weekends that bound the fixed time period (usually thirty days) for reaching an agree-

Table 9.1 Goldaber's win/win contract development program

Phase	Activity
1	Both sides receive protocols governing the process.
2	Each side lists questions and concerns for Phase 3
3	Weekend 1: The Communications Laboratory
4	All participants and the facilitator meet.
	Issues are identified for inclusion in the contract and contract matter committees are appointed.
5	Committees discuss issues, finalize agreements, and list unresolved issues (approximately thirty days allowed).
6	Weekend 2
	All participants and the facilitator meet to reach agreement on the contract.
7	The writing committee writes the proposed contract.
8	All participants review the proposed contract and recommend its approval to their constituencies.
9	Each side votes on the proposed contract.
10	All participants meet to witness the signing of the contract.

ment. This weekend is conducted as a communications laboratory to deal with areas of distrust and to reach the realization that each side needs the other to resolve their conflicts. The questions prepared in phase two provide a way for the parties to communicate and share their concerns with each other.

The laboratory usually begins on a Friday evening and extends through all day Saturday. The participants are representatives of the two parties (an equal number from both sides, plus resource persons they invite) and an external facilitator who conducts the laboratory. The end goal of the laboratory, the fourth phase, is to identify issues for collective bargaining and to appoint contract matter committees.

During the next thirty days, the fifth phase, the contract matter committees meet, discuss, and attempt to reach agreement on issues to be included in a collective bargaining agreement. One committee might address salary and benefits; a second, working conditions; and a third, rights and responsibilities. A fourth committee might be established to deal with any items not assigned to the other committees. Their job is to finalize agreement on as many items as possible. Unresolved issues are to be listed and brought to the second weekend meeting of the entire group.

Collective bargaining itself takes place during the committee meetings. But rather than following the traditional distributive approach, the parties are urged to seek new and creative solutions to problems. They are also encouraged to concede voluntarily on positions whenever it is possible to do so. Mutual respect and empathy for the greater good of the school should guide the deliberations.

At the end of the fixed period for bargaining, All participants reconvene for a second weekend (phase six). Agreed upon items are confirmed, and unresolved items are addressed. When success is achieved in reaching agreement on all items, a contract writing committee is appointed to put the agreement in final form. The remaining phases, seven through ten, deal with reviewing and recommending the proposed agreement, formal ratification, and the signing of the contract.

The use of the Goldaber model has been more successful in affecting attitudes than the content of the agreements. The model has had an astounding success rate, with management and employees citing a freer, more open exchange and the problem-solving approach promoted greater awareness of the other side's point of view on issues. One of the drawbacks to the process, however, is that both managements' and employees' constituencies are locked into the distributive paradigm of negotiations. There is a tendency to think that the best possible agreement has not been achieved because negotiations do not necessarily continue until Labor Day. In order for the process to be effective, then, a great deal of staff development needs to take place before negotiations even begin so that both parties' constituencies have realistic expectations of what the results of the process will be.

EFFECTIVE NEGOTIATION

We can identify at least four basic steps in effective negotiation for either distributive or integrative bargaining. First, the parties prepare for the negotiations. Second, they determine the model they will use and develop their bargaining strategies. Third, they negotiate a settlement, and fourth, they administer the agreed-upon contract.[16]

PRE-NEGOTIATION PREPARATION

The preparation phase of the negotiation process is as important as the negotiations themselves. It is with proper preparation that many problems during the actual negotiations can be precluded. The preparation phase begins the day after the last contract is signed. It continues until the next contract is negotiated, but picks up in intensity about six months before the negotiation sessions begin. One of the first steps in the preparation process is to anticipate the issues that will be negotiated. An effective way of doing this is to review the grievances that have occurred during the administration of the current contract. This review will identify the problematic areas of the present contract and be an accurate indicator of what will most likely be the substance of the upcoming negotiations.

Another step in the preparation process is the gathering of information regarding comparable settlements in other school districts and institutions similar to your own. Data regarding the Consumer Price Index is also important to have. Demographic data regarding the school district, like the average age of the faculty, student enrollment projections, property tax expectations, and budget projections, should be gathered. Finally, the negotiation team should be assembled during this phase.

The make-up of the negotiation team should reflect appropriate levels of the school community. From management's point of view, the team should include representatives from the central office, local school administrators, and a member of the school board. Many times, legal counsel is part of the team and frequently serves as the chief negotiator. It is not advisable for the superintendent or the highest-ranking administrative officer to be on the team because that person needs to remain as the respected leader of the school district after the contract is negotiated and should not be associated too closely with what is too often an adversarial process.

The choice of chief negotiator is the next step in constituting the negotiating team. This person must be knowledgeable of the prevailing collective bargaining laws and the bargaining process itself. The abilities to plan, analyze, and coordinate the activities of the team are essential. Being able to articulate the various positions is also extremely important.

The personal qualities of tolerance and persistence are needed to ensure that the process is conducted in a rational, calm manner and is kept on course toward achieving an agreement.

From a practical perspective, team members should be identified according to the expertise needed in the process. One person, generally the chief negotiator, should be a skilled spokesperson. Another member should be a specialist in the wording of proposals; another in cost analysis; another in keeping written records of key discussions; and at least one who knows the current contract provisions thoroughly.

DEVELOPING A BARGAINING STRATEGY

The second phase of the negotiation process is developing the bargaining strategy. This phase includes the mutual decision of whether a distributive or an integrated model is to be used. Once a model is selected, the identification of key issues takes place. Management must determine what goals it plans to achieve as a result of the process. For example, management might wish to hold the line on school governance issues, or hold the line on salary and fringe benefit costs to 1 percent above the cost-of-living increase. Management might wish to rectify a salary inequity between junior and senior faculty or address a class-size issue. Once the broad based goals are developed, a rationale for each proposal needs to be prepared.[17]

THE BARGAINING PROCESS

Maintaining an atmosphere of reasonableness and civility during the bargaining process is important if a settlement is to be reached. Certain protocols should be maintained so that common courtesy prevails. Once the proper atmosphere is established, the negotiators can go about their business of presenting, evaluating, and responding to each others' proposals. Once proposals are presented, those that have cost implications need to be identified and "costed out." It is an effective tactic to consider the cost items as a "package," rather than individually.

It is essential that the negotiation team presents a united front. Never disagree on an issue at the bargaining table. If there is disagreement or misunderstanding among members of the team, a private caucus should be called to resolve the differences before returning to the table. In addition, a careful rationale for each proposal should be developed and a reasoned response to the other parties' proposals should be articulated. It is also effective to accept certain of the other parties' proposals as a "trade-off" for the acceptance of one of your own proposals. Finally, when reaching agreement on an issue, be certain that the proper wording is incorporated into the contract because the parties will have to live with it for the duration of the agreement.

When the parties fail to reach a settlement, an impasse may be declared. In the case of many educational institutions, state law determines how an impasse is handled. In general, however, the process may proceed from mediation to fact finding and then to arbitration.

The mediation process is one through which a third party seeks to facilitate the process and resolve the impasse. The objective is to assist the parties to arrive at an agreement of their own creation. The mediator typically meets with each party's negotiating team separately to explain the process and to ascertain each party's view of the disputed issues. Then, in a joint meeting, the mediator summarizes the issues with the effort to ensure that each party's position is understood clearly by the other. After further meetings with each team, the mediator develops a proposed settlement for presentation to both parties that will end the impasse.

The fact-finding process leads to a set of independently developed recommendations for a settlement of the impasse. Prior to fact finding, the parties prepare their cases with supporting documentation and arguments. The fact-finder considers the cases and develops a report. The fact-finder's report may be accepted or rejected by one or both parties. If the report is made public, it may be persuasive in the parties' eventual acceptance.

If neither mediation nor fact finding is effective in resolving an impasse, binding arbitration is often the result. The arbitration can be voluntary or mandatory, advisory or binding. However, if mediation and/or fact finding has not been successful, binding arbitration is the only viable solution short of a strike.

In an arbitration, the parties usually have the right to select or reject names from a list of potential arbitrators. The selected arbitrator conducts a hearing at which each party presents its written exhibits and oral testimony. Within a reasonable period after the hearing, the arbitrator's decision is issued. If binding arbitration is used, the decision resolves the impasse and the arbitrator's report becomes the "settlement."

CONTRACT ADMINISTRATION

A successful collective bargaining process leads to an agreement or contract that determines the conditions of employment for its duration. If an educational administrator is to be an effective and respected leader in the school community, it is essential that he or she "know the contract." Failing to do so will lead to embarrassing contract breeches that will undermine the administrator's competence and any culture of trust that has been established. Thus, principals and other administrators should participate in training sessions about the newly adopted contract. Preparation of an administrator's manual, which includes interpretation of contract clauses, procedures for processing grievances, and contractual deadlines should take place.

CASE STUDY 9.1: ACADEMIC UNIVERSITY

THE PRESIDENT—DR. JOHN SMITH

In front of Dr. John Smith sat a pile of manila folders. He had been putting off going through them since about this time last Monday but now commencement had come and gone and he had run out of excuses.

As the new college president at Academic College, Dr. Smith was both well liked and well respected. He brought to Academic a long list of accomplishments at past colleges and was quickly gaining a reputation of a doer—someone whom most all liked because of a natural affinity for his calm but persuasive drive and vision. Dr. Smith's main vision for Academic College was to transform Academic into a more competitive, nationally recognized institution—a college able to compete with other schools he believed Academic could compete with for high-end academic high school students. Academic College was already known locally as a quality small liberal arts school but not quite considered in the elite category . . . and so lost some academic recruiting wars.

In keeping with its institutional mission, Dr. Smith had slashed many continuing education programs. This had upset some around campus who feared both for their job safety and a shift in the basic institutional mission of the school. Dr. Smith had also cut down significantly the amount of transfers admitted to Academic.

The first folder was perhaps the most interesting of all the student folders in front of Dr. Smith. It was a folder that contained the high school transcripts and academic profile of a local student named Kevin Small. Dr. Smith had been approached several times by both his director of admissions, Dr. Jim Admit, and the men's basketball coach Sid Hoops, about making an exception to their already-full 1997 class of freshman. Kevin Small's grades certainly were not outstanding. Nor were Kevin's SAT scores even close to what the revamped Academic College standards for admissions in 1996–1997 were.

However, in this particular case, there seemed to be some extenuating circumstances: for starters, beyond the fact that Kevin was a standout basketball player and someone for whom the coaches were actively petitioning, Kevin was just the type of kid who seemed to slip through the cracks of any large high school—he was capable of better academic performance but because he went to a large school and had very little direction from both school and home he was left to his own decisions— namely sports not studies. Moreover, Kevin was a minority and one of Dr. Smith's new institutional goals was to help produce a less-homogenous campus student body; a fact not lost on Dr. Smith as he looked at Kevin's folder—for the college had had another surprisingly poor recruiting year in terms of minority enrollment.

As Dr. Smith rose to grab a cup of coffee his phone rang—it was Dr. Admit coincidentally calling about Kevin Small. Jim had an intriguing message from an alumnus about Kevin's admission to Academic.

THE ADMISSIONS DIRECTOR—DR. JAMES ADMIT

The admissions director—Dr. James Admit, an unassuming middle-aged father of two known just as Jim throughout the college community—was in his fifth year at Academic. He was extremely well liked by all—faculty as well as staff and coaches, a rare combination at any school of Academic's size, where often the faculty and athletic departments seem pitted against each other. Dr. Admit had gone to Swarthmore College and had even worked there for some time, so he was well versed in the rigors of admissions to an academically challenging institution like Academic College. Last week, Jim had received a phone call from a prominent alumnus who was calling on behalf of Kevin Small and Kevin's mother, Marge. It seemed that Kevin's high school coach was an employee of the alum and really wanted Kevin to go to a quality program and school. He had asked for the alum's help. The alum had since called both Jim and Coach Sid Hoops to strongly argue for Academic to allow Kevin admission—knowing full well what Kevin's academic portfolio looked like. In fact, the alum had gone so far as to intimate some rather large potential donation if the school would see fit to admit Kevin and help Kevin along in his development as a student.

THE COACH—SID HOOPS

Sid Hoops was in his third year at Academic. He had been hired to return Academic's once nationally prominent men's basketball program to its previous glory. The program had badly atrophied over the past decade or so because of poor recruiting by its coaches—they never seemed to land the top-level players or bring in a class of athletes that would have immediate success. So it was with some surprise that Coach Sid first heard about the possibility that Kevin Small would be coming to Academic.

There was some ambivalence about Kevin for the coach. On the one hand, a player of Kevin's caliber rarely lands in a coach's lap like this. Kevin could certainly help the team. In point of fact, he would probably "start" right away as a freshman. On the flip side, Kevin was going to require a great deal of help. Coach Sid worried that it was a disservice to bring Kevin to a school in which he might not survive academically. The alum's possible donation only exaggerated the problem for Coach Sid because then there would be that much more pressure on Kevin to do well at Academic.

THE RECRUIT—KEVIN SMALL

Kevin Small sat in his room spinning a ball on one finger and occasionally lying back and mimicking the slow process of shooting. He had drawn a circle on his ceiling as a target for his shooting exercise. His mother would often shout from the kitchen below to stop that dribbling—little did she know about the ceiling. Kevin was waiting for a phone call; a call so important he had been too nervous to go to his summer league game for fear of missing it.

Kevin's mother knocked on the door and softly opened it. She saw a scared and small child—hardly the massive forward and local hoops star all the others saw. She saw a child who didn't deserve to be going through this. Hadn't he stayed in on weekends to study? She knew he sometimes cheated out after she had gone to bed—but just to go to the park next door where she could hear his dribbling and shooting deep into the night. She only wanted her baby to go to college—that's all she had ever wanted for her only child . . . and now the phone, so loud and active in December and January, had slowly gone quiet. No more coaches calling. No more coaches offering this deal or that. Where had they all gone?

SUMMARY

Power might be one of the least understood, but most important, areas of educational administration. Individuals exert power to overcome job-related dependencies; social exchanges can create power; or individuals might have a need for power. This chapter described the sources and uses of power in institutions. We identified position power, personal power, and resource- and information-based power.

We continued by looking at negotiation as the ritualized use of power in organizations. Two bargaining paradigms, distributive and integrative, were described and compared. Then, the process of negotiation was outlined; the steps include preparation, model selection and strategy development, negotiating an agreement, and contract administration.

It is likely that most educational administrators will not be integrally involved in the bargaining process because that duty is usually assigned to a collective bargaining specialist. However, all educational administrators will be responsible for the administration of the contract. It is important, therefore, to know the process whereby the contract was established and to know the nuances of its implementation. Many an administrator has been rendered ineffective, and even incompetent, because of an insufficient knowledge of the implications of the labor agreement. Thus, a thorough understanding of the document and a humane implementation of it, are essential elements to an educational administrator's eventual success.

NOTES

1. J. P. Kotter, Why Power and Influence Issues Are at the Very Core of Executive Work, in *Executive Power,* ed. S. Srivastva and Associates (San Francisco: Jossey-Bass, 1986).

2. A. Kaplan, Power in Perspective, in *Power and Conflict in Organizations*, ed. R. L. Kahn and E. Boulding (London: Tavistock, 1964); M. Weber, *The Theory of Social and Economic Organization* (Glencoe, Ill.: Free Press, 1947).

3. H. Mintzberg, *Power in and around Organizations* (Englewood Cliffs, N.J.: Prentice-Hall, 1983).

4. This discussion of dependence is based in large part on J. P. Kotter, Power, Dependence, and Effective Management, *Harvard Business Review* 55 (1977): 125–136; and J. P. Kotter, Power, Success, and Organizational Effectiveness, *Organizational Dynamics* 6 (1978): 27–40.

5. R. M. Emerson, Power-Dependence Relations, *American Sociological Review* 27 (1962): 31–41.

6. B. Markovsky, D. Weller, and T. Patton, Power Relations in Exchange Networks, *American Sociological Review* 53 (1988): 220–236.

7. D. McClelland and D. H. Burnham, Power Driven Managers: Good Guys Make Bum Bosses, *Psychology Today* (December 1975): 69–71; D. McClelland, *Power: The Inner Experience* (New York: Irvington, 1975).

8. W. C. Grams and R. W. Rogers, Power and Personality: Effects of Machiavellianism, Need for Approval, and Motivation on use of Tactics, *Journal of General Psychology* 117 (1990): 71–82.

9. J. Gabarro and J. Kotter, Managing Your Boss, *Harvard Business Review* 58 (1980): 92–100.

10. W. F. G. Mastenbroek, *Conflict Management and Organization Development* (Chichester, England: Wiley, 1987).

11. M. A. Rahim, Relationships of Leader Power to Compliance and Satisfaction with Supervision: Evidence from a National Sample of Managers, *Journal of Management* 15, no. 4 (1989): 545–556.

12. D. A. Lax and J. K. Sebenius, *The Manager as Negotiator* (New York: Free Press, 1986).

13. Lax and Sebenius, *Manager as Negotiator*.

14. R. Fisher and W, Ury, *Getting to Yes: Negotiating without Giving In* (Boston: Houghton Mifflin, 1981) was an early call for this approach.

15. Larry James and Ned Lovell, *A Systematic Labor-Relations Model: Returning the Principal to the Driver's Seat*, NASSP Bulletin, 66: 77 (1982).

16. See the following publications of Irving Goldaber, *The Communication Laboratory: A Collaboration between Adversaries to Generate Social Change* (Pittsburgh: Pittsburgh Tri-State Area School Study Council, University of Pittsburgh, 1984). *The Goldaber Win/Win Contract Development: A Thirty Day Process* (Miami, FL: Center for the Practice of Conflict Management, 1987).

17. R. Fisher and S. Brown, *Getting Together* (Boston: Houghton-Mifflin, 1988).

10

THE CHANGE PROCESS

To live is to change, and to be perfect is to have changed often.

—John Henry Newman

Changing an educational institution or system has been described as being like making a U-turn with the Queen Elizabeth II. In some cases, resistance to change is so extreme that this can be considered an understatement.

Despite its difficulty, the process of change is absolutely necessary if an organization is to continually improve. Thus, to be an effective leader, especially in the transformational style, an administrator must become a change agent and master the process that can bring it about effectively. In this chapter, we discuss a variety of processes and techniques that will enhance the administrator's chances of effecting change successfully.

MODELS OF CHANGE

Suppose the Washington School received a mandate to introduce school-based management, the objective of which was to empower a team of faculty and staff to assist the administration in the operation of the school. And suppose the principal, Rita Curran, had successfully run the school in a relatively autocratic manner for the last ten years. The faculty leader of the school-based management team was Jodi Jones, who felt that giving the staff a voice in decision making was long overdue.

How will the Washington School move to school-based management? What changes will be required? Who will implement them? What resistances will they face? These are just a few of the questions that need to be posed and answered if the Washington School is to move successfully toward school-based management. In order to effectively bring about this change, a model of planned change needs to be developed.

The model of planned change suggested here includes seven steps that reflect a systematic approach to introducing change. These steps include assessment, entry, diagnosis, planning, action, evaluation, and termination. Although this model was developed more than two decades ago, it remains a robust and useful approach to introducing change and implementing action in organizations. It can be applied in a setting with a multicultural work force, as well as a traditional work force.[1]

The first step in the process is assessment. Change begins by obtaining preliminary information about those involved in the change situation. In particular, the person(s) responsible for making the changes or for ensuring that they occur must assess the organization's readiness for change, including a consideration of the environment in which it functions and the nature of its work force. In the case of the Washington School, Rita Curran, Jodi Jones, and the others involved in the school-based management must assess the organization before implementing the new form of administration. They might consider, for example, how the various members of the faculty and staff will react when given the news that such a change will be taking place. They might also wish to collect data on the work force's openness to change and engage in a full-needs assessment process.

The change agent(s) next attempts are to negotiate a formal or informal agreement with the organization. In the entry phase, the change agent identifies a reasonable point or person of contact in the organization and then must develop an effective working relationship with him or her, or with the group or committee responsible for the change. In the situation at Washington, for example, proponents of school-based management must talk to faculty, staff, administrators, and parents about its implications for the school and ideally secure their approval of and commitment to the change. Organizational members who will serve as the primary implementers of change, such as those on the school-based management committee, must be identified.

The diagnosis step involves problem definition, further goal specification, and an evaluation of the resources available to deal with the problem. It is during this phase that a Force Field Analysis can be helpful. We discuss this technique later in the chapter.

During the planning phase, the change agent and client generate alternative strategies for meeting the objectives of the change. They outline the prescription for change, determine the steps in its implementation, and detail the nature, cost, timing, and personnel required for any new system. This step also requires anticipating and planning for all possible consequences of the change effort. Jodi Jones or other faculty members might take major responsibility for planning action, repeatedly testing support for the proposed action with the rest of the school's faculty, staff, and parents.

In the action phase, the change agent(s), Jodi Jones, Rita Curran, other faculty and administration, parents, or top administrators in the school system, implements the best strategies that arise out of the planning phase.

The change agent(s) collects data about the nature and effectiveness of the change as it occurs. The results of the evaluation indicate whether the change process is complete or whether a return to an earlier stage should occur. The criteria for success should be specified in advance of a change effort; these criteria may be culturally linked and varied. If ineffective outcomes result from the introduction of school-based management, the process should return to an earlier stage, for example, assessment (to determine if the client is really committed to the change), diagnosis (to determine the real nature of the problems), or planning (to determine the best strategy for meeting the change objectives).

During the termination phase, plans for continuing the change into the future or for knowing when it will end should be specified. Ensuring the institutionalization of effective changes should also occur as part of this step. Successful changes should become institutionalized; that is, the changed processes should be established as permanent ways of operating, otherwise, when the present change agent(s) leave, the change might not be perpetuated. Ideally, the change should become part of the organizational culture. Failures may terminate the change process or may signal a need for other changes, such as different staffing activities, a new reward system or new technology.

THE CLINICAL STRATEGY

Another change strategy, called the *clinical strategy*, involves the manipulation of intergroup and interpersonal interactions and proceeds through the following steps:[2]

1. *Gaining knowledge of the organization:* The approach begins with a thorough knowledge of the dynamics of the organization. Such knowledge, of course, comes through careful observation, analysis, and study. The perceptive principal, for example, might have acquired much of this knowledge through experience, but typically, a more systematic analysis is enlightening and valuable. As a prelude to such a study, he or she must understand the salient aspects or organizational life, including the basic norms and values of the faculty. The conceptual perspectives provided by such measures as the Organizational Climate Description Questionnaire, the Organizational Health Inventory, and the Pupil-Control Ideology Form can substantially aid this learning about the school organization.

2. *Diagnosis:* The second step in the process is diagnostic. Here again, conceptual capital, from a variety of perspectives, can provide labels for diagnosing potential trouble areas. Poor esprit, high disengagement, custodialism, distorted communication, unilateral decision making, weak motivation, and low academic expectations are examples of such conceptual labels. The extent to which these concepts are clearly defined in the mind of the administrator and fit together in a broader perspective probably mediates the effectiveness of the diagnosis.

3. *Prognosis:* In the third step, the change agent(s) judges the seriousness of the situation and develops a set of operational priorities to improve the situation.

4. *Prescription:* The appropriate course of action is often hidden. Suppose we decided that the school's atmosphere is too custodial

in pupil-control orientation. How can the situation be remedied? We might replace the number of "custodial" teachers with younger "humanistic" teachers. Research suggests, however, that the pupil-control ideology of beginning teachers becomes significantly more custodial as they become socialized by the teacher subculture, which, in this case, tends to equate tight control with good teaching. Merely replacing a number of custodial teachers without altering basic teacher norms about pupil control will probably have little or no impact. Altering basic teacher norms calls for a more sophisticated strategy. A first step in such a strategy is to eliminate teacher and administrator ignorance about the pupil-control ideology. Teachers generally think that principals are much more custodial in pupil-control ideology than they themselves are, and conversely, principals typically believe that teachers are more custodial in pupil-control orientation than they report themselves to be. These common misperceptions need to be swept away if a more humanistic perspective is to be achieved. In other words, developing prescriptions at first seems easy enough, but experience shows that solutions to various school problems are usually oversimplified and often irrelevant. If administrators are going to be successful in changing the school climate and culture, for example, they must change the norms and values of the teacher subculture, as well as the basic, shared assumptions of the faculty and staff. These types of strategies are developed during the prescription step. The best strategy is then implemented.

5. *Evaluation:* The last step in the clinical strategy is to evaluate the extent to which prescriptions have been implemented and are successful. Because planned change in social systems is often slow, continuous monitoring and evaluation are required.

THE GROWTH-CENTERED STRATEGY

A growth-centered strategy simply involves the acceptance of a set of assumptions about the development of personnel and the use of these assumptions as the basis for management decision making. The assumptions are the following:[3]

1. *Change is a property of healthy organizations.* The administrator should see organizations, and hence organizational climate, in a constant state of flux.
2. *Change has direction.* Change can be positive or negative, progressive, or regressive.
3. *Change should imply progress.* Change should provide movement of the organization toward its goals. Of course, not all change represents progress; yet the administrator's stance is progress oriented.
4. *Employees have high potential for the development and implementation of change.* Administrators are always ready to provide employees with more freedom and responsibility in the operation of the organization.

These basic assumptions, if acted upon, would allow for a growth policy, which in turn leads to increased opportunities for professional development. From this perspective, administrators would remove obstacles from the path of professional growth and not manipulate people. Finally, the approach should help facilitate a climate of mutual trust and respect among employees and management.

The clinical and growth-centered approaches do not conflict in their assumptions, although they have different focuses, organizational versus individual. The astute administrator draws on both strategies to bring about change in an institution.

FORCES INFLUENCING CHANGE

Whatever model is chosen, the change process calls for understanding and changing the forces that affect the change. We can use an analytical technique called *force field analysis*, which views a problem as a product of forces working in different, often opposite directions.[4] An organization, or any of its subsystems, will maintain the status quo when the sum of opposing forces is zero. When forces in one direction exceed forces in the opposite one, the organization or subsystem will move in the direction of the greater forces. For example, if the forces for change exceed the forces against change, then change likely will occur.

To move an organization toward a different desired state requires either increasing the forces for change in that direction, decreasing the forces against change in that direction, or both. Generally, reducing resistance forces creates less tension in the system and fewer unanticipated consequences than increasing forces for change. At the Washington School, for example, reducing the resistances to the changes created by the introduction of school-based management increases the likelihood of the changeover. Figure 10.1 shows what happens when a resistance force is eliminated. When the administrators and staff no longer resist change, the present state, as shown by the solid vertical line, moves closer to the desired state, as indicated by the broken vertical line. A complete analysis looks at ways to alter all forces, for and against change.

Let us consider again the situation at the Washington School. School-based management focused on changing school governance to greater participation by more diverse constituencies; it meant removing some control from the school principal and other top administrators. What forces for change, also known as driving forces, exist? Increased demands for parental involvement, an increasingly complex educational situation, and changes in state legislation are among the forces that might have spurred the change.

Changes in the organization's environment, such as new laws or regulations, rapidly increasing competition, or an unpredictable rate of in-

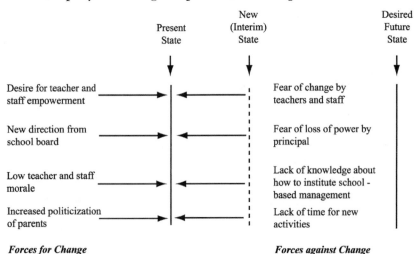

Figure 10.1.   Identifying target forces

flation might cause the organization to implement new structures or reward systems. New programs resulting from the availability of improved technology, changes in competition in the field, or unusual requirements of the new generation of students, like inclusion or mainstreaming, could also affect the institution. Finally, reduced productivity and effectiveness, product quality, satisfaction, commitment, or increased turnover or absenteeism might call for changes in intra- or interdepartmental relations. Frequently, one or two specific events external to the organization precipitate the change. For example, as mentioned previously, the publication of *A Nation at Risk* in the 1980s caused a flurry of educational changes and reforms that continue until today.

Forces known as *resistance forces* counteract the forces for change. Administrators might resist changes in their routines and supervisory activities; they might also be unwilling to relinquish their decision-making authority. Superintendents might be unwilling to allocate the resources required to change the culture. Identifying and then reducing resistance forces may be essential to making an individual or group receptive to change.

Forces against change often reside within the organization and stem from rigid organizational structures and rigid individual thinking. Specific forces against change include employee's distrust of the change agent, fear of change, desires for maintaining power, and complacency; lack of resources to support the change; conflicts between individual and organizational goals; and organizational inertia against changing the status quo. These forces frequently combine into significant resistance to change.

Resistance results from a variety of factors. First, it occurs when a change ignores the needs, attitudes, and beliefs of organizational members. If teachers, for example, have high security needs, they might perceive as threatening the increased attention in distance learning. Second, individuals resist change when they lack specific information about the change; they might not know when, how, or why it is occurring. Third, individuals might not perceive a need for change; they might feel that their organization is currently operating effectively and efficiently. In these cases, change often is neither voluntary nor requested by organizational members. Fourth, organizational members frequently have a "we-they" attitude that causes them to view the change agent as their enemy, particularly when change is imposed by representatives outside of the immediate worksite. Fifth, members may view change as a threat to the prestige and security of the institution. They might perceive the change in procedures or policies as a commentary that their performance is inadequate. Sixth, employees might perceive the change as threats to their expertise, status, or security. The introduction of a new computer-aided instructional system, for example, might cause teachers to feel that they lack sufficient knowledge to perform their jobs; the revision of an organization's structure might challenge their relative status in the organization, as our example of site-based management might do; the introduction of a new reward system might threaten their feelings of job security. For effective change to occur, the change agent must confront each of these factors and overcome the resulting resistance to change. It helps a great deal if the change agent has engendered a sense of trust in his or her colleagues.

BUILDING AN ACTION PLAN

Following the identification of the forces for and against change, the person responsible for implementing the change must identify alternative actions for changing each force and then organize them into an action plan. The analytical approach we are describing here must be supplemented with a consideration of individuals' psychological reactions to change and development of appropriate strategies for dealing with them. It can also use action research methodology as a basis of studying and intervening in organizational situations. In action research, the change agent collaborates extensively with the client in gathering and feeding back data. Together, they collect and discuss the data, and then use the data for planning.[5]

Consider the possible reluctance of the principal to reduce her involvement in decision making, a force against change in the school. The following actions could reduce this reluctance: implementing the change slowly, educating the principal about the value of the change, or testing an experimental version of new procedures to increase teacher and staff participation. Another intervention would be to identify a school where site-based management has been successful and have the principal visit that school (best practices approach). Table 10.1 lists these alternatives, as well as alternative actions for changing a second target force. It also cites the feasibility and action priority of each alternative.

Table 10.1. Analysis of Target Forces at the Washington School

Target Forces	Alternate Actions	Feasibility	Action Priority
Fear of change by the principal, teachers, and staff	Implement change slowly	Moderate; change can occur over a 12-month period	High
	Educate employees about the change	High; easy and relatively low cost	High
	Illustrate the benefits of site-based management	High; easy and relatively low cost	High
	Pilot-test the system for small group	Moderate; time-consuming; pilot may be difficult to design	High
	Involve employees in planning the change	High; time-consuming but important to acceptance	Medium-High
Lack of knowledge about how to institute site-based management	Revise and provide new policies and procedures	High: important to eventual implementation	Medium
	Offer professional development in the change	High; important to system implementation	Medium

Overcoming resistance to change is a key action issue for administrators or external change agents. Employees can sabotage change efforts and, ultimately, decrease their effectiveness. Resistance to change can result in behavior ranging from lowered productivity, increased absenteeism, and decreased motivation. In the extreme, it can lead to work stoppages. The change agent must plan ways to overcome resistance to change.

The person responsible for change should maintain open and frequent communication with the individuals, groups, or organizations involved; for example, he or she might schedule regular informational meetings for all employees affected by the change. The change agent should also consider the needs of individual employees because responding to needs when possible helps develop in the individuals a vested interest in and ultimately support for the change. Finally, where possible, the change agent should encourage voluntary change. Establishing a climate of innovation and experimentation can reduce the organization's tendency to maintain a status quo.

Development of an action plan concludes with a specification of each action in the order it will be performed. You can continue the analysis for the Washington School or try a similar analysis with an organizational change situation you have faced. Be sure to perform all the steps described earlier.

SELECTING A CHANGE AGENT

Who could make the changes inherent in school-based management at the Washington School described earlier? Should top administrators of the school system direct the proposed changes? Should the Washington School principal or other members of the school community be responsible? Or, should they use an outside consultant to facilitate the changes? Clearly, the use of internal as opposed to external change agents presents some trade-offs that need to be considered in the decision.

The school principal, faculty, and even some parents have firsthand knowledge of the institution, are known and immediately available to organizational members, and require almost no additional expenditures in fees or additional salary. However, because of their investment in the organization, insiders can be too close to the problem and not objective in looking at it, or they can be viewed as part of the problem.

Most frequently, the principal becomes the implementer of the changes. This selection occurs primarily because he or she is closest to the situation, has greatest knowledge of it, and has control over it. Further, the principal is already on board, which can reduce the time required to begin the change. In addition, other organizational members already know the principal and have clear expectations about actions he or she might take. However, if an atmosphere of mutual trust and respect has not been adequately established, either another person in the school community or an outside consultant might be more appropriate as a change agent.

Other organizational members can be used as internal consultants, likely reducing resistance to change from coworkers. If well-respected in the institution, these internal consultants can be effective in breaching divisions between faculty and administration and actually training both sides in appropriate problem solving activities that may close the communication gap that oftentimes exists between faculty and administration.

External consultants offer the opposite advantages and disadvantages. They tend to have more technical knowledge, especially regarding the communication techniques required to bring about effective change. They tend to have diverse competencies and objectivity. They might lack information about the particular situation, take longer to start implementing the change, and are costly. A general rule regarding the use of outside consultants is that they should only be considered if an appropriate and effective internal change agent cannot be identified. If a culture of trust and respect has been established in a school, for example, almost any change can be implemented internally.

IMPLEMENTING ORGANIZATIONAL CHANGES

Action follows the identification of target forces for change and the selection of the change agent and intervention strategy. Implementation must ensure that the strategies succeed. Although careful preparation for change, including description, diagnosis, and prescription, increases the chances of success, it does not guarantee effective action. Implementation requires an ongoing assessment of the reactions of organizational members to the change. Briefing sessions, special seminars, or other means of information dissemination must permeate the change effort. Implementation must include procedures for keeping all participants informed about change activities and effects.

The use of a broad-based steering committee to oversee the change may increase its likelihood of success. Such a group, composed or representatives of all areas of the organization can advise on issues related to program budget, as well as on organizational policies and priorities.

Further, the dynamic nature of organizational systems calls for flexibility in action. All efforts must include contingency plans for unanticipated costs, consequences, or resistance. A strong commitment to the change on the part of top management can buffer change efforts from such difficulties and can ensure the transfer of needed resources to the action program.

Managing large-scale organizational change might require a more elaborate approach. The process includes at least four components: (1) pattern breaking, (2) experimenting, (3) visioning, and (4) bonding and attunement. Pattern breaking involves freeing the system from structures, processes, and functions that are no longer useful. An organization can be open to new options if it can relinquish approaches that no longer work, if its managers are rewarded for weeding out unproductive programs and processes, and if it is willing to challenge long-held traditions. At the Washington School, replacing some of the structures and processes associated with the former, nonschool-based management workplace would be a first step in instituting change. Experimenting by generating new patterns encourages flexibility and yields new options. Training small groups of administrators to institute teamwork illustrates this element. To experiment, organizations must have a philosophy and mechanisms in place that encourage innovation and creativity. Visioning, the third element, calls for the selection of a new perspective as the basis of the change. Visioning activities, such as building shared meaning throughout the organization and using the current mission statement, generates support for and commitment to the planned changes. Schoolwide meetings at Washington to share ideal views about school-based management would help accomplish this step. In the last component, bonding and attunement, management attempts to integrate all facets of the organizational change to move members toward the new way of action by focusing them on important tasks and generating constructive interpersonal relationships.[6]

ETHICAL CONSIDERATIONS

Change agents often confront issues of integrity in their interactions with organizations. Five types of ethical dilemmas include misrepresentation and collusion, misuse of data in change efforts, manipulation and coercion, value and goal conflict and technical ineptness. Some managers implement their personal change agenda at the expense of solid diagnosis of the organization's needs. For example, a college dean might propose a doctoral program even though he or she knows that it might tax the institutions resources and negatively affect other programs. Still other managers promise more than they can deliver. For example, that standardized tests scores will improve if a new program is implemented. Some consultants fail to build ways of institutionalizing the change into their process so the organization must continue to rely on them. Organizational leaders, as well as internal and external consultants, should ensure that the selection and implementation of change strategies respond to well-documented organizational and individual needs. They must also ensure that the change process respects the rights of individuals in the workplace.

ORGANIZATIONAL TRANSFORMATION

Environmental pressures, government intervention, and societal reforms spur organizational transformations. Organizational growth or decline, pressure by specific constituencies, a real or perceived crisis, or atypical performance demands can also pressure the organization to change. Declining national achievement scores, as compared with those of other nations in the 1980s lead to educational reform in the United States. A number of the educational reforms of the 1990s have been transformational in nature.[8]

Even if managers and other organizational members diagnose a situation correctly and select appropriate prescriptions of improving it, the complementary action sometimes does not result in the intended outcomes. Sometimes more basic changes, including transformations of the organization itself, are required. *Transformation* means fundamentally changing organizations to function better in today's competitive world. Currently, there is some sentiment for using government vouchers to allow parents to make educational choices concerning which school, public or nonpublic, to send their children, as a way of allowing market forces to affect schooling. If adopted, this policy would be an example of structural or transformational change.

Four types of changes are transformational: (1) changes in what drives the organization, such as marketing or production; (2) changes in the relationship between parts of the organization, such as between administration and instruction; (3) changes in the way work is done; and (4) basic cultural changes, as described earlier in this chapter.

Transformational change, or paradigm-breaking change, differs from the more frequently observed, converging change, which involves fine-tuning in an institution or making incremental modifications to minor shifts in the work environment. Paradigm-breaking change involves redefining the organization's mission, changing the distribution of resources within the organization, restructuring, altering patterns of interaction, and hiring transformational leaders.[9]

An Alternative Model for Change

In an earlier work, *The Ten-Minute Guide to Educational Leadership*, we suggest that if the educational leaders systematically focus on ten aspects of their institution each day, that they will most likely be effective. These ten components include the school's organizational structure, its organizational climate, its leadership, motivation, communication, planning, decision-making and conflict-management processes, its power distribution, and its attitude toward change. Of these essential elements, I believe that an institution's tolerance of and ability to change is the most important element for success. I also believe that mastering the ability to effect change successfully to transform an institution is the *culminating* activity of the effective educational leader.

Successfully effecting change requires the educational leader to have mastered all of the other elements necessary for promoting organizational effectiveness. To effect successful change, the educational administrator must have outstanding leadership skills, ensure that the organizational structure is appropriate, engender a climate of trust and respect, motivate his or her colleagues to achieve a vision, communicate effectively, plan strategically, incorporate appropriate decision-making techniques, effectively manage conflict, and empower faculty and staff. This is a daunting task—so daunting that the average educational administrator is not able to cope with it. As a result, successful implementation of change in the form of educational reform remain the exception rather than the rule; and effective educational institutions remain the exception rather than the rule. The question now is: How do we incorporate the "philosophy of administration," espoused here, into the effective implementation of the change process?

Making Change Happen

Education, particularly urban public education, seems to be in a continual state of crisis. None of its constituencies seems to be satisfied with its outcomes. There is no dearth of remedies, however. Educational research has produced a variety of reforms that the scholars claim will resolve many of the problems encountered in American education. Until now, however, the major problem has been how to implement these reforms effectively. There have been sporadic successes, but generalizing from these effective models has been problematic.

Reforms, such as site-based management, charter schools, clustering, whole language instruction, cooperative learning, outcomes-based education, distance education, and the constructivist classroom, all have their advocates. Pilot programs using these approaches and others have been successful. The frustration lies in how to implement these reforms universally so that the schools where they are effective become the rule rather than the exception. In a nutshell, the issue becomes: How do we successfully effect change? Basically, looking at an institution in the terms described above is in the functionalism/structuralism tradition. The remaining question is: How do we imbue this approach with the principles of critical theory and the Ignatian vision? Emotionally, we seem to prefer the status quo. Intellectually, however, we all seem to realize that to progress, we need to experience change. Collectively, we have bought into Edwards Deming's notion that for any institution to thrive, "continuous improvement" is an absolute necessity. Earlier in this text, we have seen that the *magis* principle also implies change. But none of this rationalizing makes it any easier to accept change as a way of life. When dealing with the process of change, we seem to operate on a visceral level. Our security needs seem to clash with our achievement needs, and our security needs frequently prevail. Nevertheless, if our educational institutions are to progress, we need to overcome our instincts and implement the reforms that will make them effective in educating our children and adults.

An Integrated Approach to Change

The literature is replete with various suggested change processes, more or less based on functionalist/structuralist theory. Many of them contain elements that are helpful in leading to successful transformation, but few contain all of the necessary elements. As a result, through the process of trial and error, I have developed my own process for change. I call it an *integrated change* process because although there are distinct steps in the process, the key to their successful implementation is that many of them are implemented simultaneously rather than sequentially.

In an earlier work, entitled *Ten Steps to Educational Reform: Making Change Happen,* we suggest the following steps in the process:

- Establishing a climate for change
- Assessing the need for change
- Creating a sense of urgency
- Assessing favorable and opposing forces
- Selecting among alternatives
- Promoting ownership
- Providing professional development
- Operationalizing the change
- Evaluating the change
- Institutionalizing the change

Most attempts at effecting change in the form of educational reform fail because leaders have no plan at all or do not engage in all the steps in the process. Other failures occur when administrators try to implement the reform by following the change process steps sequentially rather than simultaneously and get bogged down in one or another of the steps, unable to bring the process to closure.

Whether it be an apparently insignificant change, such as deciding between the homogenous or the heterogeneous grouping of students (tracking), or what form of assessment should be used in college admission, or a more significant reform, such as whether tuition vouchers should be used to restructure and reform, public education, we are suggesting that the implementation of these steps be viewed through the lens of functionalism, critical theory, and the Ignatian vision, all of which are explained more fully in the next chapter. For now, functionalism is the belief that leading effectively requires a technical knowledge of the processes necessary for improving an organization. Critical theory and the Ignatian vision suggest that in addition to the technical aspects of leadership behavior, there is a moral or ethical component that requires leaders to keep in mind the underserved or marginalized elements in society. Let us now see how functionalism, critical theory, and the Ignatian vision impacts each of the steps in the integrated change process.

Establishing a Climate for Change

E. Mark Hanson, in his text entitled *Educational Administration and Organizational Behavior,* describes an incident regarding the process of change. Always interested in the processes of school improvement, he once asked the superintendent of a large, urban school district, "How does change come about around here?" She thought for a moment. "Well," she replied, "there is the normal way and the miraculous way. The normal way," she continued, "is where the heavens part and the angels come down and do the change for us. The miraculous way is when we do it ourselves."

If you have established a climate of change at your institution, change will come to be expected. It will be perceived as something positive and routine. The need for change in the context of continuous improvement should be articulated constantly by institutional leaders. College presidents, superintendents, and principals should set the tone for change by taking every opportunity to articulate its necessity and model it in their own leadership. For example, the faculty convocations can be occasions for articulating the notion that if the institution is to progress, academically and operationally, it must be open to change. At the initial meeting, the possible changes that are anticipated during the upcoming academic year can be shared. At subsequent faculty meeting, the need for change can be reinforced. Using the establishment of a climate for change as the first step in a systematic method of effecting change is a structural functionalism principle. Articulating the need for change, modeling change, and establishing trust and respect are behaviors that are the product of utilizing critical theory and the Ignatian vision, specifically the *magis (the more)* principle and secular humanism.

In addition to articulating the need for change, to promote a positive school climate the leader must model a tolerance for change. Even if it is something simple, such as changing the color of the school lockers every two or three years or changing the format of faculty meetings to incorporate innovative concepts like cooperative learning and shared decision making, the leader needs to lead by example. The leader must be perceived as being open to new ideas and providing a climate in which creativity is fostered. In other words, "be the change that you expect in others."

While fostering a climate for change, the leader must be careful not be perceived as being in favor of change for its own sake, or for his or her own sake. If this occurs, it can have a counterproductive or dysfunctional effect. One way of precluding such a perception is to mutually establish the basics or essentials of your institution—the things that are relatively constant and not subject to change—and those that must change for your institution to remain healthy. Such fundamentals as academic excellence, individual attention, community involvement, and an emphasis on educational outcomes might be identified as remaining constant, while instructional methods, curricular approaches, and organizational structure are subject to change. In other words, the *goals* can remain constant for awhile, while the *methods* of achieving them may be frequently changing. In establishing both the goals and the methods, however, remember to examine them under the lens of critical theory, by being aware of the equitable distribution of power, and so on, and the Ignatian vision, by being aware of the social justice implications, and so on.

Another way to avoid being perceived as in favor of change for change's sake is to be certain that when a change is implemented, all of the steps in the process are followed. If this is done, it is more likely that the change will be implemented successfully in the first place, and, second, if the change is not effective, the evaluation stage of the process provides an opportunity to move away from it gracefully. In addition, success breeds success. If the leader has a record of implementing change successfully, it paves the way for future change. If leaders also have a reputation for objectively evaluating the effectiveness of change and abandoning it if it is unsuccessful, they will foster a climate with a high tolerance for change.

If a positive climate for change is to be established, another requisite is an environment of trust and respect. Institutions do not amount to anything without the people who make them what they are. The individuals most influential in making institutions what they are, are essentially *volunteers*. Our very best teachers and administrators can work anywhere they please. So, in a sense, they volunteer to work where they do. As educational leaders, we would do far better if we looked on and treated our employees as volunteers. To engender trust and respect in the Ignatian tradition, we should treat our employees as if we had a *covenantal* rather than contractual relationship with them. We will speak more on covenantal relationships in the next chapter.

If an educational institution is to be a place where change is not only tolerated, but embraced, it must be successful in creating a culture of trust and respect so that everyone in it feels as if he or she "owns the place." We often hear educators refer to where they work as "school," such as "I will be staying at *school* late tonight, dear." On the other hand, beware of the teacher who says simply, "I will be staying at *work* late tonight." That teacher has likely not taken "ownership" in the place.

Taking ownership is a sign of one's love for an institution. In his book *Servant Leadership,* Robert Greenleaf says, "Love is an undefinable term, and its manifestations are both subtle and infinite. It has only one absolute condition: unlimited liability!" Although it might run counter to our traditional notion of American capitalism, employees should be encouraged to act as if they "own the place"; it is a sign of love, and it is a prerequisite for establishing a positive climate for change.

Assessing a Need

The next step in the integrated change process is the needs assessment. Unfortunately, this step is often ignored. Many educational leaders become enamored of one educational reform or another and try to implement it whether or not there is an identified and agreed upon need. Reforms, such as the whole language approach to reading, cooperative learning, block scheduling, interdisciplinary curricula, distance learning, and even site-based management, have been adopted arbitrarily by misguided educational administrators. When implemented without a needs assessment, or at lease an after-the-fact needs assessment, these changes are destined to failure. Both critical theory and the Ignatian vision call on us to be inclusive and empowering in the process of establishing a need. Faculty and staff input is essential for success.

Ordinarily, a needs assessment calls for a review of existing data and may require some surveying of clients and other appropriate reference groups. There is always a certain risk in a needs assessment. In the process of uncovering needs, one might also raise expectations that all of the respondent's concerns will be addressed. Fundamental to effecting change is priority setting and focus; thus, not all needs can be met immediately. Resources are in short supply, and difficult, sometimes painful decisions have to be made about which from an array of crucial needs requires attention. Three reference groups are especially important to the needs assessment and the change process: students and parents, professional staff, and educational policy makers. Oftentimes, it is the students and/or parents who are left out of the process. Leaving them out, of course, has distribution of power implications and is a violation of the principles of critical theory and the Ignatian vision.

Data about students are readily available in the records a typical school generates and maintains. Standardized test scores, attendance records, free or reduced-price lunch recipients, analyses of students with disabilities, transportation reports, and a host of other official and unofficial sources serve as basic data sources when it comes time to develop a profile of the students in the school or school district. Informal discussions with colleagues, other professionals, and the students and parents themselves are another source of information. Student focus groups and systematic observation by both teachers and administrators are still other ways of assessing whether there is a need for change in the school.

Use of community and parent surveys can be very helpful to the school leader, as can community advisory groups. Such surveys are invaluable in determining parent and community expectations and attitudes and perceptions of the educational needs of the community's young people. The diverse nature of most communities requires that in any survey care needs to be taken that the necessary degree of randomness exists. Concern for complete information and diversity of opinion should also be reflected in the composition of advisory groups.

Another source of information regarding the needs of the school is the professional staff. They can be helpful with regard to instructional and curricular needs and can offer specific observations about the nature of the student body. Staff surveys or any of a number of rational problem-solving processes are useful in needs assessments. Using some of these methods in combination can be effective. For example, a faculty meeting can be used to brainstorm the strengths and weaknesses of the institution. The information could then be summarized and items generated for a survey to determine the perceived intensity and importance of the issues identified. The nominal group technique or the Delphi technique can then be used.

Central office personnel, local and state board members, state department of educational, legislators, the federal Department of Education, education advocacy groups, accrediting groups, and other such entities are example of educational policy makers. They also should be consulted to identify the needs of the educational institution. Lastly, the reports of accrediting associations, such as the Middle States Association, Phi Beta Kappa, and the American Association of Colleges and Schools of Business (AACSB) can be valuable tools for assessing the needs of an institution.

Creating a Sense of Urgency

Because our natural instinct is to resist change, to effect a needed change, a sense of alarm or urgency often must be created. To overcome our innate sense of inertia, the dire consequences of remaining in the status quo need to be articulated. There are a number of ways to create a sense of urgency, including citing comparable data and projected enrollment declines. But in creating a sense of urgency, the change agent must be aware that individuals and groups are often moved by dissimilar forces. In other words, what might cause a sense of urgency in one person might not do so in another.

Creating a sense of urgency or stress can have both functional and dysfunctional outcomes. Whether stress takes a constructive or destructive course in influenced by the sociocultural context in which the stress occurs, because differences tend to exaggerate barriers and reduce the likelihood of conflict resolution. The issues involved also will affect the likely outcomes. Whether the individuals or groups have cooperative, individualistic, or competitive orientations toward stress will affect the outcomes, as well.

Effective educational administrators learn how to create functional conflict and manage dysfunctional conflict. They develop and practice techniques for diagnosing the causes and nature of stress and transform it into a productive force that fosters needed change in the institution. Many universities, for example, have healthy competition among their schools (Business College, College of Arts and Sciences, College of Education, etc.) for recruitment of the most qualified students. This is an example of functional sense of urgency or stress.

One can see, then, that some stress is beneficial. It can encourage organizational innovation, creativity, and adaptation. For example, a number of nonpublic school systems, and even some public ones, allow schools within the system to compete the same students. This "open enrollment" or "public school choice" policy often spawns innovation and change in marketing techniques and, more important, in curriculum and instruction. In these cases, creating a sense of urgency can result in more employee enthusiasm and better decision making. The challenge is to be able to create a sense of urgency without allowing it to become dysfunctional. This means that the change agent must know the stages of stress and when to intervene. In addition, if we adhere to the Ignatian concept of *cura personalis* (care of the person), we have an obligation to avoid creating dysfunctional stress in our colleagues.

Assessing Favorable and Opposing Forces

Accurate assessment of the forces that affect proposed reform is possibly the most important step in the integrated change process. Correctly identifying the forces that favor the reform and those that oppose it is crucial to effective implementation of the change. Further, the interventions chosen to neutralize the forces against change and enhance the forces in favor of it are instrumental to its eventual success.

The forces resistant to change can be considerable. These forces range from simple ignorance of an individual to the complex vested interests of our own institutions' members. As the comic strip character Pogo phrased it, "We have met the enemy and he is us."

The forces resistant to change are an important part of the organization's environment or climate. They must be diagnosed, understood, and taken into account in the targeting process and in selecting a change strategy. The environment harboring the forces of resistance is typically not social or technical but sociotechnical. A sociotechnical interpretation of environment refers to the behavior of individuals as it is shaped by the interaction of technical characteristics such as instructional equipment, physical layout of the school, activity schedules, and social characteristics, such as norms, informal groups, power centers, and the like.

According to Richard Carlson, a major organizational feature that contributes to resistance to change is the domestication of public schools and other educational institutions. A domesticated organization has many properties of the monopoly: it does not have to compete for resources, except in a very limited area; it has a steady flow of clients; and its survival is guaranteed. Although private schools and colleges do not possess all of these characteristics in the way that public schools do, many of the teachers view their institutions in this way. One often hears the college professor or the private school teacher proclaim in the light of declining enrollments, "That's the administration's problem."

Because these institutions are domesticated organizations, they do not face the problems of private organizations that make it necessary to build major change mechanisms into their structures. Change capability permits private organizations to make the necessary modification in production and product continually to hold their share of the market and expand it if possible. The domestication of the school builds in a layer of protective insulation that cannot be penetrated easily. Thus, to effect change in a domesticated organization becomes a greater challenge.

An interesting example of this type of organizational behavior was part of California's omnibus educational reform bill of 1983, which was intended to increase instructional time in the classroom. A comparative study had shown that California's students received two and a half weeks' less instructional time than the national average. The bill offered financial incentives to districts to meet the target of 180 days a year and 240 minutes a day at a cost of $250 million annually for the first 3 years. The average high school needed to add four days to its school year and six minutes each day to qualify for the incentive award of $75 per pupil. The average elementary school needed to add four days for a $55-per-pupil-per-day-bonus.

In light of a potential contract violation and teachers' resistance to increased instructional time without increased compensation, districts found creative ways to lengthen the school day and year without increasing instructional time. Some districts added 1 minute to each passing period between classes, which could add up to 900 minutes or about eighteen 50-minute classes. Other schools extended homeroom periods by 5 minutes each day, totaling 900 minutes per year. Others added an extra recess to the school day. Some schools did add one or two minutes of instructional time to each class. When considering educational change in a domesticated organization, therefore, the result is not always the desired outcome.

Goodwin Watson points out that during the process of effecting change, perceived resistance moves through a four-stage cycle. He describes the arrival of a reform in these terms: "In the early stage, when only a few pioneer thinkers take the reform seriously, resistance appears massive and undifferentiated. 'Everyone' knows better; 'No one in his right mind' could advocate the change. Proponents are labeled crack-pots or visionaries."

In the second stage, some support becomes evident, the pro and con forces become visible, and the lines of battle are drawn. In the third stage the battle is engaged "as resistance becomes mobilized to crush the upstart proposal." The supporters of the change are often surprised and frequently overwhelmed by the opposition's tenacity. Survival of the innovation depends on developing a base of power to overcome the opposition.

If the supporters of change are victorious in the third stage, the fourth stage is characterized by support flowing to the newly arrived reform. "The persisting resistance is, at this stage, seen as a stubborn, hidebound, cantankerous nuisance. For a time, the danger of a counter-swing of the pendulum remains real." The cycle begins anew when another effort toward change occurs.

Force-Field Analysis

To understand the changing forces that affect a change, we can use an analytical technique called *force-field analysis*, which views a problem as a product of forces working in different, often opposite directions. An organization, or any of its subsystems, maintains the status quo when the sum of opposing forces is zero. When forces in one direction exceed forces in the opposite one, the organization or subsystem moves in the direction of the greater forces. For example, if forces for change exceed forces against change, then change is likely to occur.

To move the educational institution toward a different desired state requires increasing the forces for change in that direction, decreasing the forces against change in that direction, or both. Generally, reducing resistance forces creates less tension in the system and fewer unanticipated consequences than increasing forces for change. Suppose your institutional was moving from homogenous to heterogenous grouping. Reducing the resistances to the changes created by the introduction of heterogenous grouping increases the likelihood of the changeover. When the administrators and staff no longer resist change, the present state moves closer to the desired state.

Consider again our example of heterogenous grouping. Moving from homogenous grouping in the form of tracking to the more egalitarian heterogenous grouping is bound to encounter resistance. What are the opposing forces that one can anticipate? Certainly, some of the teaching staff will be against the change because it will entail more small-group instruction and adapting their lesson plans to a variety of ability levels. On the contrary, what are the forces in favor of change? Once again, one can anticipate that certain of the faculty, especially the critical pedagogues, will favor the more egalitarian approach that is embodied in het-

erogeneous grouping. A savvy administrator will be able to apply interventions that would neutralize the opposition and mobilize the forces in
favor of this change. Using force-field analysis in a systematic way can
be very helpful in bringing about desired change.

Changes in the organization's environment, such as new laws or regulations, rapidly increasing competition, or an unpredictable rate of in-
flation, might require the organization to implement new structures or
reward systems. New programs resulting from the availability of improved technology; changes in competition in education; or unusual requirements of the new generation of students, such as inclusion or
mainstreaming, can also affect the institution.

Finally, reduced productivity and effectiveness, product quality, satisfaction, commitment, or increased turnover or absenteeism might require
for changes in intra- or international relations. One or two specific events
external to the institution frequently precipitate the change. For example,
the publication of *A Nation at Risk* in the 1980s caused a flurry of educational reforms that continue to this day. The events at Columbine High
School are another example of how an external event can effect change in
your own institution.

Forces known as *resistance forces* counteract the forces for change.
Administrators might resist changes to their routines and supervisory activities; they might also be unwilling to relinquish their decision making
authority. Superintendents may be unwilling to allocate the resources
required to change the culture. Identifying and then reducing resistance
forces might be essential to making an individual or group receptive to
change.

Forces against a change often reside within the institution and stem
from rigid organizational structures and individual thinking. Specific
forces against change include employees' distrust of the change agent,
fear of change, desire to maintain power, and complacency; lack of resources to support the change; conflicts between individual and organizational goals; and organizational inertia against changing the status quo.
These forces frequently combine into significant resistance to change.

Resistance results from a variety of factors. First, it occurs when a
change ignores the needs, attitudes, and beliefs on an organization's members. If teachers, for example, have high security needs, they might see as
threatening the increased attention to distance learning. Second, individuals resist change when they lack specific information about the change;

they might not know when, how, or why it is occurring. Third, individuals might not perceive a need for change; they might feel that their organization is operating effectively and efficiently. In these cases change often is neither voluntary nor requested by organization members. Fourth, organization members frequently have a we-they mentality that causes them to view the change agent as their enemy, particularly when change is imposed by representatives outside of the immediate work site. Fifth, members might view change as a threat to the prestige and security of the institution. They might perceive the change in procedures or policies as a commentary that their performance is inadequate. Sixth, employees might perceive the change as a threat to their expertise, status, or security. Introduction of a new computer-aided instructional system, for example, might cause teachers to feel that they lack sufficient knowledge to perform their jobs; revision of an organization's structure might challenge their relative status in the organization; introduction of a new reward system might threaten their feelings of job security. For effective change to occur, the change agent must confront each of these factors and overcome the resulting resistance. It helps a great deal if the change agent has engendered a sense of *mutual trust and respect* among his or her colleagues before the effort to effect change begins.

The implications of structural functionalism, critical theory, and the Ignatian tradition on dealing with the resistance to change are many. The use of force-field analysis recommended here to facilitate the change process implies a structural functionalist view of the educational administration. We are assuming that by using this model, we will have a better change of effecting successful change. This implies that there is a systematic, rational method of arriving at a positive result, even when dealing with the unpredictability of human nature.

As we discussed earlier, many administrators might deal with opposing forces with equal force. Human nature provokes many of us "to fight fire with fire." As critical pedagogues and Ignation humanists, however, we concern ourselves with sharing power and influence, not with eliminating it. Thus, is the process of applying force-field analysis, we must be careful to use compelling argument rather than coercion to neutralize opposing forces. Likewise, when we are developing and selecting alternatives, we must be careful to make the process inclusionary rather than exclusionary. Participative decision making needs to be employed, and group decision making should be the rule rather than the exception. More about this in the next section.

The principles prescribed by the critical theory and the Ignatian tradition would require that in the process of addressing the resistant forces to change, we be careful to *inspire* our colleagues, but not *manipulate* them. Not only do our overall goals have to be laudable, but also the *means* by which we reach those goals must be likewise. So, in utilizing the structural functionalist strategies suggested here, we must continually be concerned with the equitable distribution of power, the need to be other centered rather than self-centered, the mindless perpetuation of the dominant culture, the care of the person, and solidarity with the underserved. If we view our leadership behavior under these lenses, we argue that a culture of mutual trust and respect will be developed and needed change will be more readily accepted.

Developing and Selecting Alternatives

Although the already-mentioned steps in the integrated change process are being addressed, the change agent should establish a committee or task force of "believers" to begin developing alternatives that would address the perceived need for change. Ideally, a deliberative consideration of the various alternatives should be undertaken, and the most cost-efficient and effective alternative should be chosen. All too often, however, "the powers that be" have chosen the alternative already and the change agent is expected simply to implement it. Of course, "the powers that be" in this instance, would certainly not have been utilizing the principles espoused here if they determined the change by fiat. In these instances, however, the change agent should at the very least be free to adapt the reform to meet local needs.

Another phenomenon that sometimes occurs during this phase of the change process is the tendency to *satisfice*, or choose the alternative that offends the fewest individuals and/or groups, rather than choosing the best alternative. *Satisficing* is a term coined by Herbert Simon, a Nobel Prize winner in economics, who was critical of the so-called rational model of decision making, which indicates that decision makers develop and analyze all of the possible alternatives and select the best one available. Dr. Simon was apparently an early devotee of critical theory.

According to Simon, at a certain point in the decision-making process, rather than the best-possible alternative being chosen, in the interest of efficiency the decision maker will *satisfice*, or sacrifice the optimal for a solution or alternative that is satisfactory or good enough. For example, if a school is trying to decide between the traditional phonics-approach versus the whole-language approach to teaching reading, the change agent(s) may satisfice and choose an *integrated* model that combines the best aspects of both the phonics and whole-language approaches. Thus, the change agent may sacrifice the optimal solution for one that satisfies the greatest number of constituencies.

In a similar approach to selecting an alternative, the model known as *decision making by objection* prompts decision makers not to seek an optimal solution to a problem, but to choose a course of action that does not have a high probability of making matters worse. The decision makers first produce a rough description of an acceptable resolution of the situation. Then, they propose a course of action, accompanied by a description of the positive outcomes of the action. Objections to the action are raised, further delimiting the problem and defining an acceptable resolution. The decision makers repeat this process, creating a series of courses of action, each one having fewer objections than the previous one. Finally, the most acceptable alternative evolves. On the surface, this approach seems to violate the magis principle, but Ignatius tells us that where the greatest good is not attainable, the greater good is sometimes acceptable.

Once the force-field analysis described earlier has been completed, it is time to generate alternatives that could be implemented to address the identified need effectively. Generally, a small committee representing as many of the institution's constituencies as appropriate should be established. The members of the committee should be those who are advocates of change with possibly a nay-sayer or two included as "devil's advocates." In preparation for their work, committee members should be provided with the latest research findings regarding the reform being considered and be encouraged to make themselves aware of successful uses of the alternatives being considered. The so-called *best practices approach* can be effective in identifying possible alternatives and convincing staff members of the reform's efficacy. The alternative that is finally chosen should be the one that best fits the local needs and should be selected according to its (1) rationale, (2) proven effectiveness, (3) resource requirements, (4) distinctive qualities, (5) mission appropriateness, and (6) cost/benefits.

The next logical question that the structural functionalist might ask is how can change agents overcome barriers, reduce, biases, and make more effective decisions regarding the selection of the appropriate reform alternative? At least three techniques can improve the alternative development and selection process: (1) brainstorming, (2) the nominal group technique, and (3) the Delphi technique.

Groups of individuals use brainstorming to generate many alternatives for consideration in the selection process. In brainstorming, the group lists as many alternatives as possible without evaluating the feasibility of any alternative. For example, if a cost-reduction program is needed in a school district to offset continuing budget deficits, the change agent might be charged with listing all of the ways of reducing costs in a school system. The absence of evaluation encourages group members to generate rather than defend ideas. Then, after ideas have been generated, they are evaluated, and selections are made. Although brainstorming can result in many shallow and useless ideas, it can also motivate members to offer new and innovative ideas. It works best when individuals have a common view of what constitutes a good idea, but it is more difficult to use when specialized knowledge or complex implementation is required. Because most educational reforms are complex in nature, brainstorming can only be used effectively in a limited number of cases and as part of the alternative generation process, rather than as the alternative selection process.

The nominal group technique is a structured group meeting that helps resolve differences in group opinion by having individuals generate and then rank-order a series of ideas in the problem-solving, alternative generation, or decision-making stage of a planning process. A group of individuals is presented with a stated problem. Each person individually offers alternative solutions in writing. The group then shares the solutions and lists them on a chart, as in brainstorming. Group members discuss and clarity the ideas, then they rank and vote their preference for the various ideas. If the group has not reached an agreement, they repeat the ranking and voting procedure until the group reaches some agreement.

The size of the group and the diverse expertise of its members increase the usefulness of the nominal group technique. It encourages each group member to think individually and offer ideas about the content of a proposal, and then directs group discussion. It moves the group toward problem resolution by systematically focusing on top-ranked ideas and eliminating less-valued ones. The nominal group technique also encourages continued exploration of the issues, provides a forum for the expression of minority viewpoints, gives individuals some time to think about the issues before offering solutions, and provides a mechanism for reaching a decision expediently through the ranking-voting procedure. It fosters creativity by allowing extensive individual input into the process. Strong personality types dominate the group less often because of the opportunity for systematic input by all group members. It encourages innovation, limits conflict, emphasizes equal participation by all members, helps generate consensus, and incorporates the preferences of individuals in decision-making choices. However, unless the change agent is trained in the use of this technique, it is more prudent to use an organizational consultant trained in these techniques to act as a facilitator.

The Delphi technique structures group communication by dealing with a complex problem in four phases: (1) exploration of the subject by individuals, (2) reaching understanding of the group's view of the issues, (3) sharing and evaluating any reasons for differences, and (4) final evaluation of all information. In the conventional Delphi, a small group designs a questionnaire, which is completed by a larger respondent group; the results are then tabulated and used in developing a revised questionnaire, which is again completed by the larger group. Thus, the results of the original polling are fed back to the respondent group to use in subsequent responses. This procedure is repeated until the issues are narrowed, responses are focused, or consensus is reached. In another format, a computer summarizes the results, thus replacing the small group. Such group decision support systems have increased the focus on the task or problem, the depth of analysis, communication about the task and clarifying information and conclusions, effort expended by the group, widespread participation of group members, and consensus reaching.

Delphi is very helpful in a variety of circumstances. First, if the decision makers cannot apply precise analytical techniques to solving the problem, but prefer to use subjective judgments on a collective basis, Delphi can provide input from a large number of respondents. Second, if the individuals involved have failed to communicate effectively in the past, the Delphi procedures offer a systematic method for ensuring that their opinions are presented. Third, the Delphi does not require face-to-face interaction, so it succeeds when the group is too large for such a direct exchange. Fourth, when time and cost prevent frequent group meetings or when additional pre-meeting communication between group members increases the efficiency of the meeting held, the Delphi technique offers significant value for decision making. Fifth, the Delphi can overcome situations where individuals disagree strongly or where anonymity of views must be maintained to protect group members. Finally, the Delphi technique reduces the likelihood of groupthink; it prevents one or more members from dominating by their numbers or strength of personality.

On another issue related to developing alternatives, we often hear about the alleged virtue of bottom-up versus top-down strategies for generating educational reforms. In fact, utilizing the principles of critical theory and the Ignatian vision would prompt us to prefer the bottom-up approach. Thus, it is the minority view is that top-down strategies are more effective. The fact of the matter is that neither of these strategies is maximally effective in isolation. Rather, coordinating top-down and bottom-up strategies for educational reform is most effective.

Small- and large-scale studies of top-down strategies have demonstrated consistently that local implementation fails in the vast majority of cases. The best-known study of voluntary adoption of top-down movements is the Rand Change Agent study conducted by Berman and McLaughlin and associates. They investigated federally sponsored educational programs adopted in 293 sites and found that, even though adoption was voluntary, districts often took on change projects for opportunistic rather than substantial reasons.

On a more sweeping scale, Sarason argues that billions of dollars have been spent to top-down reforms with little to show for it. Sarason observes that such reform efforts do have an implicit theory of change: Change can come about by proclaiming new policies, or by legislation, or by new performance standards, or by creating a shape-up-or-ship-out ambiance, or all of the preceding. It is a conception that in principle is similar to how you go about creating and improving an assembly line—that is, what it means to those who work on the assembly line is of secondary significance, if it has any significance at all. The workers will change.

In short, centralized reform mandates have a poor track record as instruments for educational improvement. This failure has led some to conclude that only decentralized, locally driven reform can succeed. Site-based management, or giving more decision-making power to the local level, is currently the most prominent manifestation of this focus. So far, however, the claim of superiority of grassroots initiatives is primarily theoretical. In reviewing evidence on site-based management in

The New Meaning Educational Change, one can conclude that restructuring reforms that involved decision making by schools might have altered governance procedures, but they do not affect the teaching-learning process in any significant way.

The evidence that bottom-up strategies are no more effective than top-down ones continues to mount (Educational Administration, Robert Palestini, Scarecrow Press, 1999) Taylor and Teddlie draw similar conclusions in their study of the extent of classroom change in "a district widely acclaimed as a model of restructuring." They examined classrooms in thirty-three schools (sixteen from pilot schools that had established site-based management programs and seventeen from nonpilot schools in the same district). They did find that teachers in the pilot schools reported higher levels of participation in decision making, but they found no differences in teaching strategies (teacher-directed instruction and low student involvement dominated in both sets of cases). Further, there was little evidence of teacher–teacher collaboration. Extensive collaboration was reported in only two of the thirty-three schools, and both were nonpilot schools. Taylor and Teddlie observe: "Teachers in this study did not alter their practice... Increasing their participation in decision making did not overcome norms of autonomy so that teachers would feel empowered to collaborate with their colleagues." In sum, then, decentralized initiatives do not fare any better than centralized reforms.

A number of educational researchers have concluded that organizations, including schools, that underwent successful revitalization followed a particular sequence in which individual, small group, and informal behavior began to change first (bottom-up, if you will), which, in turn, was reinforced and further propelled by changes in formal design and procedures (structures, personnel practices, compensation systems, etc.) in the organization (top-down). Both local and central levels can be active and influential at all phases. These studies and my own experience have led me to promote an integrated change process that involves both top-down and bottom-up strategies that operate simultaneously in effectively implemented reform.

Top-down strategies result in conflict, or superficial compliance, or both. Expecting local units to flourish through laissez-fare decentralization leads to drift, narrowness, or inertia. Combined strategies that capitalize on the central office's strengths (to provide direction, incentives, networking, and monitoring) and the local institution's capacities (to learn, create, respond, and contribute) are more likely to achieve greater overall effectiveness. Such systems also have greater accountability, given that the need to obtain political support for ideas is built into their pattern of interaction.

Simultaneous top-down/bottom-up strategies are essential because dynamically complex societies are full of surprises. Only the negotiated capacity and strengths of the entire school community are capable of promoting school improvement while retaining the capacity to learn from new patterns, whether anticipated or not. Finally, one level cannot wait for the other level to act. Systems do not change by themselves; individuals and groups change systems. Breakthroughs occur when productive connections amass, creating growing pressure for systems to change. The more that top-down and bottom-up forces are coordinated, the more likely that complex systems will move toward greater effectiveness.

Promoting a Sense of Ownership

It is a truism is education, and in other fields as well, that if a change or reform is to be implemented successfully, it must have the support of the faculty and staff. Consequently, we often hear managers suggest that a new program does not have a chance of succeeding unless the employees take ownership of it. Most of us agree with the common sense of this assertion. But how does a leader effectively promote employee ownership? Let us suggest four steps that embody critical theory and the Ignatian vision as a beginning:

- *Respect people*. As we have indicated earlier, this starts with appreciating the diverse gifts that individuals bring to your organization. The key is to dwell on the strengths of your coworkers, rather than on their weaknesses. This does not mean that disciplinary action, or even dismissal, will never become necessary. It does mean, however, that we should focus on the formative aspect of the employee evaluation process before we engage in the summative part. Leaders are obligated to develop colleagues' skills and place them in situations that will maximize their potential for success.

- *Let belief guide policy and practice.* We spoke earlier of developing a culture of civility in an institution. If there is an environment of mutual respect and trust, the institution will flourish. Leaders need to let their belief or value systems guide their behavior. Style is merely a consequence of what we believe and what is in our hearts.

- *Recognize the need for covenants.* Contractual agreements cover such things as salary, fringe benefits, and working conditions. They are part of organization life, and there is a legitimate need for them. But in today's educational institutions, where the best people working in our schools are similar to volunteers, we need covenantal relationships. Our best workers might choose their employers. They usually choose the institution where they work based on reasons less tangible than salaries and fringe benefits. They do not need contracts; they need covenants. Covenantal relationships enable educational institutions to be civil, hospitable, and are understanding of individuals' differences and unique natures. They allow administrators to recognize that treating everyone equally is not necessarily treating everyone fairly. Sometimes exceptions need to be made, and certain individuals need to be treated in special ways. Otherwise, the dominant culture will continue to prevail to the detriment of diverse views.

- *Understand that culture counts more than structure.* An educational institution recently went through a particularly traumatic time when the credibility of the administration was questioned by the faculty and staff. Various organizational consultants were interviewed to facilitate a healing process. Most of the consultants spoke of making the necessary structural changes to create a culture of trust. The consultant who was hired, however, began with the attitude that organizational structure has nothing to do with trust. Interpersonal relations based on mutual respect and an atmosphere of goodwill are what create a culture of trust. Would you rather work as part of a school with an outstanding reputation or work as part of a group of outstanding individuals? Many times, these two characteristics are found in the same institution, but if one had to make a choice, my suspicion is that most people would opt to work with outstanding individuals.

So, it all starts with trust. These are exciting times in education. Revolutionary steps are being taken to restructure schools and rethink the teaching–learning process. Empowerment, total quality management, the use of technology, and strategic planning are becoming the norm in education. However, although these reforms have the potential to influence education in significantly positive ways, they must be based on a strong foundation to achieve their full potential.

Achieving educational effectiveness is an incremental, sequential improvement process. This process begins by building a sense of security within each individual so that he or she can be flexible in adapting to changes within education. Addressing only skills or techniques, such as communication, motivation, negotiation, or empowerment, is ineffective when individuals in an organization do not trust its systems, themselves, or each other. An institution's resources are wasted when invested only in training programs that assist administrators in mastering quick-fix techniques that at best attempt to manipulate and at worst reinforce mistrust.

The challenge is to transform relationships based on insecurity, adversarialism, and politics to those based on mutual trust. Trust is the beginning of effectiveness and forms the foundation of a principle-centered learning environment that emphasizes strengths and devises innovative methods to minimize weaknesses. The transformation process requires an internal locus of control that emphasizes individual responsibility and accountability for change and for promoting effectiveness. Of course, we argue that this "transformation" can be greatly facilitated by adopting the tenets of critical theory and the Ignatian tradition.

If one is expected to create a sense of trust and to engender employee ownership of a change or reform, the change agent needs to be seen as making effective *decisions*. The administrative and organizational theory literature is in agreement about the two most important factors to be considered in determining the decision style that will produce the most effective decisions. Although Vroom and Yetton's model includes the additional dimension of shared goals and conflict possibility, the two key elements are the *quality* and the *acceptance* of the decision.

The two key elements are quality, or the likelihood of one decision being more rational than another, and acceptance, or the extent to which acceptance or commitment on the part of subordinates is crucial to effective implementation of the decision. For example, if a new law is passed regarding the inclusion of special education students, and the quality of the decision (to promulgate it and include it in the catalog) is more important than the acceptance. Therefore, the appropriate decision style is *command*. That is, the administrator alone decides to promulgate it and include it in the catalog. In this case, there is no need for participative decision making. On the other hand, if acceptance is more important than quality, or if the quality and acceptance are both important, as in the development of a new teacher evaluation instrument, the proper decision style is *consensus*. Finally, if neither the quality nor the acceptance is important, such as deciding what color to paint the school lockers, *convenience* is the applicable style.

In addition to evaluating the quality and acceptance of a decision, one can assess how well it meets the criterion of ethical fairness and justice. Here is another instance where critical theory and the Ignatian vision come into play. Consider, for example, a disastrous decrease in standardized test scores in a high school. Top administrators are faced with the dilemma of whether to risk public outrage and the possible transfer of significant numbers of students or to gloss over the situation.

Administrators and staff can assess whether the decisions they make are ethical by applying personal moral codes or society's codes of values; they can apply philosophical views of ethical behavior; or they can assess the potential harmful consequences of behaviors to certain constituencies. One way of thinking about ethical decision making suggests that a person who makes a moral decision first must recognize the moral issue of whether a person's actions can hurt or help others; second, make a moral judgment; third, decide to attach greater priority to moral concerns than financial or other concerns, or establish their moral intent; and, finally, act on the moral concerns of the situation by engaging in moral behavior. In conclusion, therefore, by combining the components of effective decision making with the characteristics of an ethical decision, the change agent can accomplish two important points: increase employee ownership of change, and build a culture of trust and respect.

Another issue that is important in developing "ownership" in the change process is the idea of empowerment. Empowering employees can have a motivating and energizing effect on their performance. Ironically, in the first wave of educational reforms in the 1980s teachers were identified as the problem. More recently, however, they have been identified as the solution. Critics of the early reforms argued that increasing state-mandated educational standards and the prescribed content and form of schooling were too rigid to produce learners who can think critically, synthesize, and create new information.

The 1990s saw reform reports that brought a new focus to the challenges of improving American education. A bottom-up approach to reform was common among the most influential of these reports, which were produced by The Holmes Group, The Carnegie Forum, and The National Governors' Association.

The reports stressed that teachers have been assigned one of society's most difficult tasks but have not been given the authority to resolve them. Effective teaching and learning consists of a complex mix of intellect, spontaneity, insight, personal understanding, love, and patience. Rules, especially those imposed from afar, constrain the learning process rather than release it. The second wave of reform reports differed from the first by arguing that the restructuring should "empower teachers rather than manage them."

According to Thomas Sergiovanni and John Moore, empowerment is not the same as acknowledging the defacto discretion that already exists in the classroom. It is a deliberate effort to provide principals and teachers with the room, right, responsibility, and resources to make sensible decisions and informed professional judgments that reflect their circumstances. In effect, it gives basic education teachers the same type of academic freedom that those in higher education have.

This effort calls for enhancing the professional status of teachers by providing them with more autonomy, training, trust, and collegial opportunities to carry out their tasks—that is, not to treat teachers like factory workers who are told what to do, how to do it, and when to do it. The effectiveness of this task-oriented approach is also being questioned in industry, by the way. The concept of empowerment has become a force in education, not only with teachers, but also with other educational personnel. Every school should be given the freedom and flexibility to respond creatively to its educational objectives and, above all, to meet the needs of its students. This approach engenders employee ownership and helps bring about change more effectively. It also coincides with the principles of critical theory and the Ignatian vision.

Providing Staff Development

Very often, staff development, an essential part of the change process, is neglected or overlooked completely. Many educational reforms have failed because of an enthusiastic but ill-advised leader who has tried to implement a change before engaging in staff development. Sometimes, even when staff development is provided, it has been ineffective. Negative responses to organized efforts in the name of staff development are the result of a history of poor experiences with activities that have taken place in the name of in-service training. However well-intended such activities might have been, too frequently they have not addressed the needs of the individual or the institution, the nature of adult learners, the time and effort required, and the importance of staff development to the ultimate success of any change or reform.

Staff development is a form of human resources development; a process that uses developmental practices to bring about higher quality, greater productivity, and more satisfaction among employees as organization members. It is a function of both an individual's knowledge, skills, and attitudes, and the policies, structure, and management practices that make up the system in which the employee works. In a school setting, the ultimate goal of human resource development is to produce the highest-quality instruction and service to the students.

The most important resource in an institution is its staff. When the staff's thinking is congruent with organizational needs, and when the staff is well-trained, adaptive, and motivated, effective schools result. To achieve this goal requires attention to the various ways in which human potential can be realized and to the variety of needs that any particular person and group might have at any particular stage of development.

The implications of critical theory and the Ignatian vision for staff development are widespread. In particular, Ignatius' concept of *cura personalis* is particularly applicable to staff development. Providing adequate and effective staff development enables individuals to reach their potential; it enables them to succeed. What better way is there to ensure *cura personalis* than to provide a means for individuals to better actualize their potential? Effective staff development helps place individuals in such a position, and in doing so, manifests the Ignatian ideal of care of the person.

Operationalizing Change

Action follows identification of target forces for and against change; development of, selection of, and implementation of intervention strategies; and the determination of a staff development plan. At this point, we operationalize the change, or give form to our vision. Although careful preparation for change increases the chances of success, it does not guarantee effective action. Placing the plan in operation requires establishment of the organizational structure that will best suit the change, and development of an assessment process to determine if the change is remaining on course. Briefing sessions, special seminars, or other means of information dissemination must permeate the change effort. Operationalizing the change must include procedures for keeping all participants informed about the change activities and its effects.

The use of a broad-based steering committee to oversee the change can increase its likelihood of success. Such broad-based input is also in the critical theory and Ignatian traditions. This group, composed of representatives of all areas of the institution (external and internal), can advise on program budget and organizational policies and priorities. It is helpful if the same task force is active throughout the change process in that it guarantees needed continuity.

Further, the dynamic nature of organizational systems calls for flexibility in action. All efforts must include contingency plans for unanticipated cost, consequences, or resistance. A strong commitment to the change by top leaders can buffer change efforts from these difficulties and ensure the transfer of needed resources to the action plan.

Managing large-scale organizational change might require a more elaborate approach. The process includes at least four components: (1) pattern breaking, (2) experimenting, (3) visioning, and (4) bonding and attunement.

Pattern breaking involves freeing the system from structures, processes, and functions that are no longer useful. An organization can be open to new options if it can relinquish approaches that no longer work, or experience a *paradigm shift*.

Experimenting by generating new patterns encourages flexibility and yields new options. Training small groups of administrators to institute teamwork illustrates this element. To experiment, organizations must have a philosophy and mechanisms in place that encourage innovation and creativity, and discourage coercion and fear of failure.

Visioning activities, such as building shared meaning throughout the institution and using the current mission statement, generate support for and commitment to the planned changes.

In the last component, *bonding and attunement*, management attempts to integrate all facets of the institutional change to move members toward the new way of action by focusing them on important tasks and generating constructive interpersonal relationships.

To operationalize a reform properly, the change agent needs to be keenly aware of the existing culture and the structure of the institution, and what form of organizational structure will best facilitate successful implementation of the change. For ease of operation, the various schools of thought regarding organizational structure can be grouped into three types of organizational theory, namely, *classical organization theory, social systems theory,* and *open system theory.* We related these theories to critical theory and the Ignatian vision in the previous chapter, but here we discuss them in the context of the process of change.

The classical theorists believe that an application of bureaucratic structure and processes or organizational control will promote rational, efficient, and disciplined behavior, making possible achievement of well-defined goals. Efficiency, then, is achieved by arranging positions within an organization according to hierarchy and jurisdiction, and by placing power at the top of a clear chain of command. Scientific procedures also are used to determine the best way of performing a task, and then rules are formulated that require workers to perform in a prescribed manner. Experts are hired for defined roles and are grouped according to task specialization. Using rationally defined structures and processes such as these, a scientifically ordered flow of work can be carried out with maximum efficiency.

The conceptual model distilled from classical theory had a great impact on the practice and study of organizational life. It quickly spilled over the boundaries of industry and was incorporated into management practice in all sectors of society, including educational institutions. In fact, it is currently the dominant structural theory utilized in education. Thus, the tendency is to operationalize a change within the context of a classical structure. The obvious question is whether the classical structure lends its self effectively to all of the current reform movements? Critical theorists and humanists would answer that question with a resounding, "No!"

Social Systems Theory   Within the classical theory framework, the individual worker was conceived of as an object, a part of the bureaucratic machine. Preparing the work environment for maximizing labor efficiency was not unlike applying precepts from the physical sciences to the human domain of work. As Elton Mayo found in the Hawthorne Works' studies the impact of social-psychological variables within a worker group was significant. The discovery that workers could control the production process to a considerable degree, independent of the demands of management, shattered many of the precepts central to classical theory. A new era of organization theory, and one more in tune with critical theory and the Ignatian vision, had arrived. This domain of thought is sometimes referred to as *social systems theory.*

Classical management theory taught that the needs of the organization and the needs of the worker coincided—if the company prospered, the worker would prosper, as well. However, as an awareness of the basic differences between the needs of the individual and the needs of the organization grew, and as worker groups became more sophisticated in manipulating the production process, management technology gave birth to social systems theory and its approaches as a means of reducing conflict. The argument went that by being considerate, using democratic procedures whenever possible, and maintaining open lines of communication, management and workers could talk over their respective problems and resolve them in a friendly, congenial way.

Not unlike the classical theory of the previous generation, the human relations orientation to the problems of managerial control quickly spread to other sectors of society, including education. The social upheaval caused by the Depression and the turmoil of World War II created a receptive climate for this new administrative theory. Enthusiasm for the human relations orientation dampened considerable after the 1950s, however, because many worker organizations came to view it as just another management tactic designed to exploit workers.

The study of behavior in social-system settings intensified, however, and a greater sophistication developed about how and why group members behave as they do under given conditions. In time, a natural social systems orientation to the analysis of behavior evolved in the literature as an alternative to the rational systems approach. The natural social systems orientation attempts to take into account how people behave in organizations rather than how they should behave.

The conceptual perspective of the natural social-systems model suggests that an organization consists of a collection of groups (social systems) that collaborate to achieve system goals on some occasions and, on other occasions, that cooperate to accomplish the goals of their own groups. Coalitions among subgroups within an organization (e.g., English teachers, history teachers, and biology teachers) form to provide power cases on which action can be taken (e.g., "Let's all vote to reject writing behavioral objectives."). Within the social-systems framework, the study of formal and informal power is one of several critical variables used to identify and analyze the processes of organizational governance.

Open System Theory   During the 1960s, another strand of thought developed that originated in the new technostructure of society. The earlier two traditions of classical and social systems theory tend to view organizational life as a closed system—that is, as isolated from the surrounding environment. *Open system theory* sees an organization as a set of interrelated parts that interact with the environment. It receives inputs, such as human and material resources, values, community expectations, and societal demands; transforms them thorough a production process (e.g., classroom activities); and exports the product (e.g., graduates, new knowledge, revised value sets) into the environment (e.g., businesses, the military, homes and colleges) with value added. The organization receives a return (e.g., community financial support in the form of school taxes or tuition) for its efforts so that it can survive and prosper and begin the cycle over again.

Within the systems theory context, the organization is perceived as consisting of cycles of events that interlock through exporting and importing with other organizations, which also are made up of cycles of events. Management is very complex because leadership has almost no control over the shifting conditions in the environment (e.g., new laws, demographic shifts, political climate, market for graduates) on the input or the output side of the equation. Control of the production process is also complex because the various subsystems of the organization (e.g., athletic department or minority group students) also are shaped by event cycles that are programmed by values, expectations, traditions, and vested interests. Changing these internal subgroups and their event cycles is difficult. The administrator attempts to stream the cycles together so that minimum conflict and inefficiency is generated.

Through the perspective of open-system theory, a new logic on issues of organizational governance has emerged. It emphasizes the relationship of the organization with its surrounding environment, and thus places a premium on planning and programming of events that cannot be controlled directly. The key to making an open-system work effectively and efficiently is its ability to gather, process, and use information. In a school, the facility with which a need is discovered, a goal is established, and resources are coalesced to meet the need that determines the effectiveness and efficiency of that school. This characteristic of the institution is particularly important if change is to take place effectively.

Contingency Theory   In recent years, a view of organization development has surfaced that treats each organization, and even entities within the organization, as unique. For centuries, this orientation has been at the core of practitioner behavior but has been seen as an anomaly, reflective of inefficiency or unpreparedness (managing by the seat of your pants), and thus was overlooked by management scientists. Currently, the changing situational character of management is now coming to be understood as a key to the management process itself.

Many management scholars and practitioners would now agree with the observation that *contingency theory* is perhaps the most powerful current and future trend in organization development. At this stage of development, however, contingency theory is not really a theory. Rather, it is a conceptual tool that facilitates our understanding of the situational flow of events and alternate organizational and individual responses to that flow. Thus, as a conceptual tool, contingency theory does not possess the holistic character of the three major models discussed earlier. In many ways, contingency theory can be thought of as a subset of open system theory because it is through open system theory that we come to understand the dynamic flows of events, personnel, and resources that take place in organizations. It is also helpful for understanding the process of change, and the need for the educational institution undergoing change to have facets of all three mainstream organizational structures. It is equally important that the change agent be aware of the organizational structure impact on whether the reform is ultimately successfully implemented.

Critical theory and the Ignatian vision would suggest that aspects of the social systems theory be utilized wherever possible. However, contingency theory would suggest that the best aspects of all of the structural theories be utilized in appropriate situations. Nevertheless, once the organizational structure is in place, the next step in operationalizing the change is to devise and implement a plan of action. The reform project should be separated into a series of activities, with the complex activities being subdivided into elements or events, the completion of which will conclude the activity. Clearly defined responsibilities should be assigned and accepted. Before proceeding, there is need to establish realistic target dates, develop the project calendar, and put into place a monitoring and evaluation process. Project planning computer software is of great assistance in organizing and managing large projects.

EVALUATING CHANGE

The next step in the integrated change process is the evaluation of the change. Authentic assessment is a topical issue in education these days. Many are questioning exactly how to assess performance most accurately, effectively, and fairly. After generations of focusing on program inputs, stressing program outcomes as an authentic measure of a program's effectiveness are gaining in popularity. The emphasis on outcomes should be applied to evaluation of a change or reform.

The change agent(s) should collect data about the nature and effectiveness of the change. The results of the evaluation indicate whether the change process is complete, or a return to an earlier stage should occur. The criteria for success should be specified in advance of a change effort. These criteria can be culturally linked and varied; they also should be closely related to the goals of the reform. If ineffective outcomes result from the introduction of site-based management, for example, the process should return to an earlier stage, such as assessment, to determine if the institution is really in need of it, and the school community has been properly prepared.

One process for evaluating the effectiveness of a change or reform is to consider participants' affective reactions, learning, behavior changes and performance changes.

Affective reactions are the participants' attitudes or disposition toward the reform. Questionnaires and interviews can be used to collect this information. Obviously, the change agent(s) is looking for development of a positive attitude toward the change. If it has been operationalized successfully, positive attitudes should prevail.

Learning refers to the participants' understanding of the change and the acquisition of new knowledge and skills as a result of its successful implementation. In the case of introducing cooperative learning techniques in the classroom, for example, did the participants develop an understanding of the principles of cooperative learning, and do they demonstrate the skills needed to implement it properly in the classroom? Classroom observations are one way of assessing whether appropriate learning has taken place. If the staff-development phase of the integrated change process has been implemented properly, appropriate learning should be apparent.

Behavioral changes include *participants'* actions in the workplace. Do they interact appropriately with colleagues and others? The following behavioral changes might occur as a result of an effectively implemented change:

- *Communicating openly.* Sharing intentions, motives, needs, feelings, and observations. Asking for and giving feedback that is descriptive rather than judgmental and specific rather than general. Using active listening techniques, including paraphrasing, summarizing, asking for clarification, and checking out the observation of one's external behavior and attitude. Using assertive communication techniques, rather than being nonassertive or aggressive.
- *Collaborating.* Discussing, planning, and revising the goals of the reform jointly and cooperatively. Using participative decision-making techniques, while avoiding arbitrary and unilateral decisions. Expanding influence skills so that compelling arguments for one's point of view can be made, rather than making decisions by fiat.
- *Taking responsibility.* Being a self-starter and not depending on constant direction. Taking the initiative to develop innovative and creative ways of performing one's duties. Streamlining the organization or department activities to promote operating efficiency.
- *Maintaining a shared vision.* Developing and communicating a clear philosophy, along with goals and objectives. Having and telling a

story, a shared history that gives meaning to the institution's activities. Creating rituals and ceremonies to reestablish and remember values.

- *Solving problems effectively.* Defining problems in a nonadversarial way so that they may be resolved from a win–win perspective rather than win–lose. Perceiving and projecting problems as challenges rather than obstacles. Using group problem-solving techniques where applicable.

- *Respecting/supporting.* Using the various motivational theories to generate enthusiasm and give affirmation to and support for desired behavior. Dwelling on an individual's strengths, rather than on his or her weaknesses. Giving individuals the benefit of the doubt and not being judgmental. Exhibiting ethical behavior and treating everyone fairly. In other words, displaying the outcomes of practicing critical theory and the Ignatian vision.

- *Processing/facilitating interactions.* Clarifying meeting goals and purposes. Reserving time at the end of meeting to critique what was done well/poorly, what facilitated making the decision or performing the task (a colleague of mine ends every meeting by asking each individual, "What did you learn today?"). While this can be annoying if overdone, it is an effective example of processing/facilitating interactive behavior.

- *Inquiring and experimenting.* Using an analytical approach to problem solving. In the process, looking for new and creative ways of addressing an issue. Frequently examining and questioning the existing structure and culture to be certain they maximize the institution's goals.

The following are common behavior changes that educational *leaders* exhibit when a change or reform has been operationalized properly:

- *Generating participation.* Involving other people when they have the necessary expertise, when the decision must be high quality, and when it also requires high acceptance. Relaxing traditional lines of command and empowering others to make decisions. Assuming a delegating, coaching style rather than a directive, task-oriented style.

- *Leading with vision.* Continually articulating the institution's mission, goals, and objectives. Providing feedback mechanisms whereby faculty and staff own the institutions' goals. Revising the institution's mission and the leader's personal vision when necessary.

- *Functioning strategically.* Ariticulating underlying causes, interdependencies, and long-range consequences and acting accordingly. Acting in an institutional mode, rather than a territorial one. Developing strategies and tactics to operationalize the institution's mission and goals. Developing among the faculty and staff the knowledge and skills required to meet future objectives.

- *Promoting information flow.* Communicating clearly the elements necessary to make the change effective. Being clear about expectations, commitments, and needs. Establishing multiple channels of communication and using the appropriate one under existing circumstances. Establishing the proper chain of command for the various types of communication. For example, external communication ordinarily should follow a formal chain of command, while internal communication might follow a less formal, matrix line. Enhancing mechanisms for feedback.

- *Developing others.* Here is where critical theory and the Ignatian once again apply. Teaching needed skills and preparing others within the institution to replace those whom may leave. Rewarding desired behavior and delegating to those who prove ready and capable of increased responsibility. Providing opportunities for and building on employees' success. Adapting one's leadership style to the readiness level of the follower(s).

In evaluating the effectiveness of an institutional reform and the process leading to the change, an institution may address the following questions:

- How did the institution determine the knowledge and skills necessary to implement the reform, and what type of staff development program was used to bring about the desired results?
- What were the conditions—economic, political, and demographic—of the external environment at the time of the reform?
- Did the conditions in the external environment have an effect on the success of the reform?
- How much has the institution's internal environment changed, and has it had an effect on the effectiveness of the reform?

- What are the primary technologies necessary to implement the reform?
- Is the division of labor appropriate to implement the change.
- What is the prevailing norm of the institution regarding improvement efforts?
- How comprehensive and consistent with current organization theory were the guiding assumptions and models used in implementing the reform?
- Were the purposes and need to implement the reform clear and accepted?
- Was a change process established, and were all of the steps used and integrated?
- Were the appropriate change agents identified and empowered?
- How explicit and detailed were the plans?
- What were the intended outcomes of the program, and what were the actual outcomes?
- How were the outcomes assessed?

The answers to these questions will enable the evaluator to assess whether the reform attained its objectives and, if it did not, determine the possible reasons.

INSTITUTIONALIZING CHANGE

Provided that the evaluation process shows that the reform has been effective, the change then should become institutionalized—that is, the changed processes should be established as permanent ways of operating. Otherwise, when the current change agent(s) leaves, the change may not be perpetuated. Ideally, the reform should become part of the organizational culture. It is in this way that a legacy is created from which future generations of students, parents, faculty, and staff can benefit. The results of a failure to institutionalize a reform are often seen at the state and federal Department of Education levels. How many times have we seen a governor or president set an educational agenda, only to have it scuttle and replaced with a different agenda by the subsequent administration? If a successful change is to prevail over time, it must be institutionalized.

Thus, action must extend beyond short-term changes for real organizational improvement to take place. Enculturating the change must be a significant goal of the integrated change process. How, for example, does a reform like site-based management become a permanent part of the governance structure of a school? Certainly, the way the activities are performed in moving from the first to the last step in the integrated change process will influence the permanency of the change. Accurate targeting of forces influencing change, followed by careful selection of change agents and intervention strategies, and concluding with effective action, contributes to long-range improvement.

In addition, mechanisms for continual monitoring of the changes must be developed and instituted. Permanent committees or task forces to observe ongoing implementation and outcomes can serve the monitoring functions. Formulation of new institutional policies and procedures based on the reform can encourage its continuation. Most important, however, is a commitment to the reform by the great majority of the school community. This community's commitment will expedite the reform's institutionalization.

Educational leaders, therefore, must build learning communities, ones that emphasize ongoing adaptability and self-generation, thereby emphasizing coping and looking at the world creatively. Peter Senge says, "Leaders in learning organizations are responsible for building organizations where people are continually expanding their capabilities to shape their future—that is, leaders are responsible for learning." Where better to implement Senge's ideas regarding a learning community than in an educational institution?

Another way of institutionalizing a reform is by encouraging development of *heroes* who embody the institution's vision and *tribal storytellers* who promulgate it. We often hear individuals in various organizations describe a colleague as "an institution around here." Heroes such as these do more to establish the organizational culture of an institution than any manual or policies and procedures handbook ever written. The senior faculty member who is recognized and respected for his or her knowledge and human treatment of students is an invaluable asset to an educational institution. This person is a symbol of the institution's character. The presence of these heroes sustains the reputation of the institution and allows the work force to feel good about itself and about the place where they work. The deeds and accomplishments of these heroes need to be promulgated to become part of the institution's folklore.

The deeds of these heroes usually are perpetuated by an organization's tribal storytellers, individuals who know the history of the institution and relate it through stories of its former and current heroes. An effective leader encourages the tribal storytellers, knowing that they are serving an invaluable service. They work at the process of institutional renewal, they allow the institution to improve continuously, they preserve and revitalize the values of the institution, and they mitigate the tendency of institutions, especially educational institutions, to become bureaucratic. Every institution has its heroes and storytellers. It is the educational leader's function to see to it that things like manuals and handbooks do not replace them.

One caveat regarding these heroes and storytellers, however, is that they can also perpetuate the status quo and thus be a force against change. The key is to let them know first of an implementing change. If informed at the outset and convinced of the reform's efficacy, the heroes and storytellers can be among the change agent's most valuable assets throughout the process, especially during the institutionalization phase. Cultivation of heroes and storytellers needs to take place early in the process if they are to be an asset by the end of the process. This is yet another indication of the importance of considering this process as integrated, rather than step by step.

CASE STUDY 10.1: TRINITY HIGH SCHOOL

TRINITY HIGH SCHOOL

Trinity High school, a comprehensive HS with a faculty of 210 and a multicultural student body of over 3,000 students, is headed by an administrative staff composed of a principal and two vice principals. In the past, Trinity was a part of a region known as the Central East Region of District Seven. Communication would filter from the superintendent to the deputy superintendent for school operations to the associate superintendent for curriculum to the regional superintendents who would then filter information to the principals. The principals would then disseminate information to department heads and school staff. This communication structure represents the classical chain of command. Communication was transmitted from central office through clearly defined channels and each employee understood the sanctity of the chain of command. In 1994, when David Beck was recruited as superintendent of schools, he mapped out a broad plan for change that affected the traditional hierarchical structure. The regions became clusters and the district superintendents became cluster leaders. Each cluster provides leadership and support for reform in small school groupings K–12. Each high school and its feeder schools form a cluster. The centralized bureaucracy shrank and clusters were given greater authority to support efforts of schools to plan improvements. The cluster office for the Trinity Cluster is now located in the basement of Trinity High School. This set the stage for ongoing conflict between the principal, Fran Tarkington, and the Cluster Leader, Rita Moreno.

FRAN TARKINGTON

For the past four years, Fran has been the principal of Trinity High School. He spent twenty-five years in the school system at Martin Luther King High School. He was a former gym teacher who worked his way up from physical education department head to vice principal and then to principal. Martin Luther King, unlike Trinity was a very traditional setting where reforms, such as small learning communities, the Coalition of Essential Schools, or teachers conducting classroom research, were unheard of. He entered Trinity totally unprepared for the level of activism evident in his faculty. He adopted a laissez faire style of supervision and left the day-to-day running of the curricular program to department heads and small learning community coordinators. He held weekly meetings with the school leadership teams and insisted that all ideas about curricular change or school activities be submitted to him for formal approval prior to a discussion with the general faculty. This arrangement worked well for most of the staff that enjoyed the level of autonomy afforded under Mr. Tarkington's leadership. He honored the diverse cultures in the building by establishing a "Multicultural Hall of Flags" in the main entranceway to honor the home countries of the school's incredibly diverse student population. He decorated the school with banners reading "I am determined to succeed" and distributed pens with the same logo to any student he encountered in the hall. Teachers and students were satisfied with the symbolic leadership exercised by Mr. Tarkington. The school does not have a Home and School Association, nor does it have a Pupil Support Committee. Both of these structures are necessary features of school communities under David Beck's "Children Achieving" Agenda.

RITA MORENO

Rita, a former principal of an elementary school in the Cluster, became Cluster Leader in 1995. She entered with definite ideas for the reform of teaching and learning at the high school. She had heard of Mr. Tarkington's laissez-faire leadership style and she was determined to provide a different kind of leadership. She initially adopted a human relations approach and presented herself as a collegial leader. She held meetings with school administrators, department heads, small learning community leaders, the custodians, and NTAs. She called numerous meetings and engaged teachers and other staff members in professional development opportunities that often included conferences that took teachers out of the classroom, often for two or more days. Rita often failed to notify the principal of meetings she scheduled with "his" staff and a few times he was stuck with trying to secure substitute coverage for teachers away on "school business" without his knowledge. When it came to the principal, Rita traded collegiality for autocracy. She became quite autocratic in her directives to the principal. She chastised him for not having a Home and School Association and for not having a Pupil Support Committee.

Rita undertook the difficult task of motivating staff to take risks and set new directions for the school without the aid of the principal. She faced the resistance and skepticism of teachers who saw her as an elementary person with no understanding of the high school and the anger of a principal who felt alienated by new communication structures that often ignored him.

Rita's political savvy brought the Cluster and Beck's "Children Achieving" Program millions of dollars. She brought together a grant writing team that secured the Trinity Cluster's IBM Reinventing Education Grant. This brought 2 million dollars of equipment and technical support to the Cluster. Rita proved herself to be a real "operator" to quote "Bolman and

Deal." Teachers from Trinity and Central Middle School and Clara Barton Elementary received computers in the classroom, as well as professional development funded by IBM to integrate technology into the classroom. Teachers received correspondence from the Cluster and IBM regarding training and meetings at the IBM training center in New Jersey. Several of the participating teachers who held other leadership roles in the school were often scheduled for Cluster meetings at the same time the principal scheduled a pupil support committee or Home and School development meeting. Often the principal's meetings were canceled to accommodate the Cluster meetings. Eventually, Mr. Tarkington started to countermand Cluster invitations to "his" teachers. His shouts, "I am still your boss" echoes in the ears of many. His parting words to Rita and the Cluster staff were ADIOS, SENORITAS!!!

SUMMARY

Edwards Deming said that healthy organizations are ones that are continually improving. Continuous improvement assumes change. Therefore, if an educational leader is to be effective, he or she must become an agent of change.

Mastering the change process requires a leader to know and understand the steps involved in planning a successful transformation in an organization. If the change can take place in an atmosphere of mutual trust and respect, its chances for success are maximized.

A common model for effecting change is to access the organization to ascertain the need for change, to diagnose the forces that influence change, and to implement the change by maximizing the forces in favor of the change and minimizing the forces opposing the change.

Once the change is made, a thorough evaluation of its effectiveness precedes the final step of institutionalizing the change, which ensures its continuation—even after the change agent is no longer present.

The key step in the process is the diagnosing of the forces influencing change. A useful technique in assessing these factors is called *force-field analysis*. This technique allows one to determine the forces in favor and those opposed to change and to plan interventions that would mobilize the forces in favor of change and mitigate the forces opposing change.

If one can effectively orchestrate this step of the process, the desired change will most likely occur. In many ways, successfully affecting the process of change necessitates the collective use of all of an administrator's abilities and skills. It can be seen as the culminating activity of an effective administrator and leader.

NOTES

1. D. A. Kolb and A. L. Frohman, An Organization Development Approach to Consulting, *Sloan Management Review* (Fall 1970): 51–65.

2. W. K. Hoy and A. E. Wollfolk, Socialization of Student Teachers: Annual Meeting of the American Educational Research Association (1989), San Francisco.

3. R. H. Kilmann, M. J. Saxton, and R. Serpa, *Gaining Control of the Corporate Culture* (San Francisco, Jossey-Bass, 1985).

4. This technique is based on an early work in the field, K. Lewin, *Field Theory in Social Science* (New York: Harper & Row, 1951).

5. K. Albrecht, *Organization Development: A Total Systems Approach to Positive Change in Any Business Organization* (Englewood Cliffs, N.J.: Prentice-Hall, 1983).

6. W. L. French, A Checklist for Organizing and Implementing an OD Effort, in *Organization Development: Theory, Practice, and Research*, ed. W. L. French, C. H. Bell, Jr., and R. A. Zawacki (Dallas: Business Publications, 1978).

7. L. P. White and K. C. Wooten, Ethical Dilemmas in Various Stages of Organizational Development, *Academy of Management Review* 8, no. 2 (1983): 690–697.

8. R. H. Kilmann, T. J. Covin, and Associates, eds., *Corporate Transformation: Revitalizing Organizations for a Competitive World* (San Francisco: Jossey-Bass, 1988).

9. R. Beckhard, The Executive Management of Transformational Change, in *Corporate Transformation*, ed. Kilmann et al.

10. This model is drawn from D. L. Kirkpatrick, Four Steps to Measuring Training Effectiveness, *Personnel Administrator* 28 (November 1983): 19–25.

11. P. M. Senge, The Leader's New Work: Building Learning Organizations, *Sloan Management Review* (Fall 1990): 7–23.

11

LEADING WITH HEART

Do unto others what you would have them do unto you.

—The Golden Rule

How the leader utilizes the concepts contained in the preceding chapters of this book depends largely on his or her philosophy of life regarding how human beings behave in the workplace. The two extremes of the continuum might be described as those leaders who believe that human beings are basically lazy and will do the very least that they need to do to "get by" in the workplace. Or those who believe that people are basically industrious and, if given the choice, would opt for doing a quality job. I believe that today's most effective leaders hold the latter view. I agree with Max DePree, owner and CEO of the highly successful Herman Miller Furniture Company. Writing in his book *Leadership Is an Art*, he says that a leader's function is to "liberate people to do what is required of them in the most effective and humane way possible."[1] Instead of catching people doing something wrong, our goal as enlightened leaders is to catch them doing something right. I would suggest, therefore, that in addition to a rational approach to leadership, a truly enlightened leader leads with heart.

Too often, leaders underestimate the skills and qualities of their followers. I remember Bill Faries, the chief custodian at a high school at which I was assistant principal in the mid-1970s. Bill's mother, with whom he had been extraordinarily close, had passed away after a long illness. The school was religiously affiliated and the school community went "all out" in its remembrance of Bill's mother. We held a religious service in which almost 3,000 members of the school community participated. Bill, of course, was very grateful. As a token of his gratitude he gave the school a 6-by-8-foot knitted quilt that he had personally sewn. From that point on, I did not know if Bill was a custodian who was a quilt weaver, or a quilt weaver who was a custodian. The point is that it took the death of his mother for me and others to realize how truly talented our custodian was. So, our effectiveness as leaders begins with an understanding of the diversity of people's gifts, talents, and skills. When we think about the variety of gifts that people bring to organizations and institutions, we see that leading with heart lies in cultivating, liberating, and enabling those gifts.

LEADERSHIP DEFINED

The first responsibility of a leader is to define reality through a vision. The last is to say thank you. In between, the leader must become the servant of the servants. Being a leader means having the opportunity to make a meaningful difference in the lives of those who allow leaders to lead. This summarizes what I call leading with heart. In a nutshell, leaders don't inflict pain; they bear pain.

Whether one is a successful leader can be determined by looking at the followers. Are they reaching their potential? Are they learning? Are they able to change without bitterness? Are they able to achieve the institution's goals and objectives? Can they manage conflict among themselves? Where the answers to these questions is an emphatic "yes" is where an effective leader resides.

I prefer to think about leadership in terms of what the gospel writer Luke calls, the "one who serves." The leader owes something to the institution he or she leads. The leader is seen in this context as steward rather than owner or proprietor. Leading with heart requires the leader to think about his or her stewardship in terms of legacy, direction, effectiveness, and values.

Legacy

Too many of today's leaders are interested only in immediate results that bolster their career goals. Long-range goals are left to their successors. I believe that this approach fosters autocratic leadership, which oftentimes produces short-term results but militates against creativity and its long-term benefits. In effect, this approach is the antithesis of leading with heart.

On the contrary, leaders should build a long-lasting legacy of accomplishment that is institutionalized for posterity. They owe their institutions and their followers a healthy existence and the relationships and reputation that enables continuity of that healthy existence. Leaders are also responsible for future leadership. They need to identify, develop, and nurture future leaders to carry on the legacy.

Values

Along with being responsible for providing future leaders, leaders owe the individuals in their institutions certain other legacies. Leaders need to be concerned with the institutional value system that determines the principles and standards that guide the practices of those in the organization. Leaders need to model their value systems so that the individuals in the organization can learn to transmit these values to their colleagues and to future employees. In a civilized institution, we see good manners, respect for people, and an appreciation of the way in which we serve one another. A humane, sensitive, and thoughtful leader will transmit his or her value system through his or her daily behavior. This, I believe, is what Peter Senge refers to as a "learning organization."[2]

Direction

Leaders are obliged to provide and maintain direction by developing a vision. We made the point earlier that effective leaders must leave their organizations with a legacy. Part of this legacy should be a sense of progress or momentum. An educational administrator, for instance, should imbue his or her institution with a sense on continuous progress; a sense of constant improvement. Improvement and momentum come from a clear vision of what the institution ought to be, from a well-planned strategy to achieve that vision, and from carefully developed and articulated directions and plans that allow everyone to participate and be personally accountable for achieving those plans.

Effectiveness

Leaders are also responsible for effectiveness by being enablers. They need to enable others to reach their potential both personally and institutionally. I believe that the most effective ways of enabling one's colleagues is through participative decision making. It begins with believing in the potential of people; believing in their diversity of gifts. Leaders must realize that to maximize their own power and effectiveness, they need to empower others. Leaders are responsible for setting and attaining the goals in their organizations. Empowering or enabling others to help achieve those goals enhances the leader's chances of attaining the goals, ultimately enhancing the leader's effectiveness. Paradoxically, giving up power really amounts to gaining power.

Employee Owners

We often hear managers suggest that a new program does not have a chance of succeeding unless the employees take "ownership" of the program. Most of us agree to the common sense of such an assertion. But how does a leader promote employee ownership? Let me suggest four steps as a beginning. I am certain that you can think of several more.

1. *Respect people.* As we have indicated earlier, this starts with appreciating the diverse gifts that individuals bring to your institution. The key is to dwell on the strengths of your coworkers, rather than on their weaknesses. Try to turn their weaknesses into strengths. This does not mean that disciplinary action or even dismissal will never become necessary. What it does mean, however, is that we should focus on the formative aspect of the employee evaluation process before we engage in the summative part.

2. *Let belief guide policy and practice.* We spoke earlier of developing a culture of civility in your institution. If there is an environment of mutual respect and trust, I believe that the organization

will flourish. Leaders need to let their belief or value system guide their behavior. Style is merely a consequence of what we believe and what is in our hearts.

3. *Recognize the need for covenants.* Contractual agreements cover such things as salary, fringe benefits, and working conditions. They are part of organizational life and there is a legitimate need for them. But in today's organizations, especially educational institutions, where the best people working for these institutions are like volunteers, we need covenantal relationships. Our best workers choose their employers. They usually choose the institution where they work based on reasons less tangible than salaries and fringe benefits. They do not need contracts; they need covenants.

   Covenantal relationships enable educational institutions to be civil, hospitable, and understanding of individuals' differences and unique charisms. They allow administrators to recognize that treating everyone equally is not necessarily treating everyone equitably and fairly.

4. *Understand that culture counts more than structure.* An educational institution that I have been associated with recently went through a particularly traumatic time when the credibility of the administration was questioned by the faculty and staff. Various organizational consultants were interviewed to facilitate a "healing" process. Most of the consultants spoke of making the necessary structural changes to create a culture of trust. We finally hired a consultant whose attitude was that organizational structure has nothing to do with trust. Interpersonal relations based on mutual respect and an atmosphere of good will is what creates a culture of trust. Would you rather work as part of a school with an outstanding reputation or work as part of a group of outstanding individuals? Many times, these two characteristics go together, but if one had to make a choice, I believe that most people would opt to work with outstanding individuals.

IT STARTS WITH TRUST AND SENSITIVITY (HEART)

These are exciting times in education. Revolutionary steps are being taken to restructure schools and rethink the teaching-learning process.

The concepts of empowerment, total quality management, the use of technology, and strategic planning are becoming the norm. However, although these activities have the potential to influence education in significantly positive ways, they must be based upon a strong foundation to achieve their full potential.

Achieving educational effectiveness is an incremental, sequential improvement process. This improvement process begins by building a sense of security within each individual so that he or she can be flexible in adapting to changes within education. Addressing only skills or techniques, such as communication, motivation, negotiation, or empowerment, is ineffective when individuals in an organization do not trust its systems, themselves, or each other. An institution's resources are wasted when invested only in training programs that assist administrators in mastering quick-fix techniques that at best attempt to manipulate and at worst reinforce mistrust.

The challenge is to transform relationships based on insecurity, adversarialism, and politics to those based on mutual trust. Trust is the beginning of effectiveness and forms the foundation of a principle-centered learning environment that places emphasis upon strengths and devises innovative methods to minimize weaknesses. The transformation process requires an internal locus of control that emphasizes individual responsibility and accountability for change and for promoting effectiveness.

TEAMWORK

For many of us, there exists a dichotomy between how we see ourselves as persons and how we see ourselves as workers. We began chapter 1 of this book with the words of a Zen Buddhist:

> The master in the art of living makes little distinction
> between his work and his play, his labor and his leisure,
> his mind and his body, his education and his recreation,
> his love and his religion. He hardly knows which is which.
> He simply pursues his vision of excellence in whatever he does, leaving others to decide whether he is working or playing. To him he is always doing both.

Work can be and should be productive, rewarding, enriching, fulfill-ing, and joyful. Work is one of our greatest privileges, and it is up to leaders to make certain that work is everything that it can and should be.

One way to think of work is to think of how a philosopher would lead an organization, rather than how a businessman or businesswoman would lead an organization. Plato's "Republic" speaks of the "philosopher-king," where the king would rule with the philosopher's ideals and values.

Paramount among the ideals that leaders need to recognize in lead-ing an organization is the notion of teamwork and the valuing of each in-dividual's contribution to the final product. The synergy produced by an effective team is greater than the sum of its parts.

The foundation of the team is the recognition that each member needs every other member and no individual can be successful without the co-operation of others. As a young boy, I was a very enthusiastic baseball fan. My favorite player was the Hall of Fame pitcher Robin Roberts of the Philadelphia Phillies. During the early 1950s, his fastball dominated the National League. My uncle, who took me to my first ballgame, explained that opposing batters were so intimidated by Roberts's fastball that they were automatic "outs" even before they got to the plate. My uncle claimed that Robin Roberts was unstoppable. Even as a young boy, I in-tuitively knew that no one was unstoppable by himself. I said to my un-cle that I knew how to stop Robin Roberts. "Make me his catcher."

EMPLOYEES AS VOLUNTEERS

Our institutions will not amount to anything without the people who make them what they are. And the individuals most influential in mak-ing institutions what they are, are essentially volunteers. Our very best employees can work anywhere they please. So, in a sense, they volun-teer to work where they do. As leaders, we would do far better if we looked upon and treated our employees as volunteers. We made the point earlier that we should treat our employees as if we had a covenan-tal relationship rather than a contractual relationship with them.

Alexander Solzhenitsyn, speaking to the 1978 graduating class of Har-vard College, said this about legalistic relationships: "a society based on the letter of the law and never reaching any higher, fails to take advantage of the full range of human possibilities. The letter of the law is too cold and formal to have a beneficial influence on society. Whenever the tissue of life is woven of legalistic relationships, this creates an atmosphere of spiritual mediocrity that paralyzes men's noblest impulses." And later: "After a certain level of the problem has been reached, legalistic thinking induces paralysis; it prevents one from seeing the scale and the meaning of events."[3]

Covenantal relationships, on the other hand, induce freedom, not paralysis. As the noted psychiatrist William Glasser explains, "coercion only produces mediocrity; love or a sense of belonging produces excellence."[4] Our goal as leaders is to encourage a covenantal relationship of love, warmth, and personal chemistry among our employee volunteers. Shared ideals, shared goals, shared respect, a sense of integrity, a sense of quality, a sense of advocacy, a sense of caring, these are the basis of an organization's covenant with its employees.

THE VALUE OF HEROES

Leading with heart requires that an organization has its share of heroes, both present and past. We have often heard individuals in various organizations say that so and so is an "institution" around here. Heroes such as these do more to establish the organizational culture of an institution than any manual or policies and procedures handbook ever could. The senior faculty member who is recognized and respected for his or her knowledge as well as his or her humane treatment of students is a valuable asset to an educational institution. He or she is a symbol of what the institution stands for. It is the presence of these heroes that sustains the reputation of the institution and allows the workforce to feel good about itself and about where it works. The deeds and accomplishments of these heroes need to be promulgated and need to become part of the folklore of the institution.

The deeds of these heroes are usually perpetuated by the "tribal storytellers" in an organization.[5] These individuals know the history of the organization and relate it through stories of its former and present heroes. An effective leader encourages the tribal storytellers, knowing that they are serving an invaluable role in an organization. They work at the process of institutional renewal. They allow the institution to continuously improve. They preserve and revitalize the values of the institution. They mitigate the tendency of institutions, especially educational institutions, to become bureaucratic. These concerns are concerns of everyone in the institution, but they are the special province of the tribal storyteller. Every institution has heroes and storytellers. It is the leader's job to see to it that things like manuals and handbooks don't replace them.

EMPLOYEE OWNERS

If an educational institution is to be successful, everyone in it needs to feel that he or she "owns the place." "This is not the school district's school; it is not the school board's school; it is my school." Taking ownership is a sign of one's love for an institution. In his book *Servant Leadership*, Robert Greenleaf says, "Love is an undefinable term, and its manifestations are both subtle and infinite. It has only one absolute condition: unlimited liability!"[6] Although it might run counter to our traditional notion of American capitalism, employees should be encouraged to act as if they own the place. It is a sign of love.

THE SIGNS OF HEARTLESSNESS

Up to now, we have dwelled on the characteristics of a healthy organization. In contrast, here are some of the signs that an organization is suffering from a lack of heart:

- when there is a tendency to merely "go through the motions"
- when a dark tension exists among key individuals
- when a cynical attitude prevails among employees
- when finding time to celebrate accomplishments becomes impossible
- when stories and storytellers cease
- when there is the view that one person's gain needs to be at another's expense

- when mutual trust and respect erode
- when leaders accumulate power rather than distribute it
- when attainment of short-term goals becomes detrimental to the acquisition of long-term goals
- when individuals abide by the letter of the law, but not its spirit
- when people treat students or customers as impositions
- when the accidents become more important than the substance
- when a loss of grace, style, and civility occurs
- when leaders use coercion to motivate employees
- when administrators dwell on individuals' weaknesses rather than strengths
- when individual turf is protected to the detriment of institutional goals
- when diversity and individual charisms are not respected
- when communication is only one way
- when employees feel exploited and manipulated
- when arrogance spawns top-down decision making
- when leaders prefer to be served rather than to serve

EDUCATIONAL ADMINISTRATION AS A MORAL SCIENCE

Here we address how an educational administrator should be educated and trained for such a position. Traditionally, there has been only one answer: Practicing and future administrators should study educational administration in order to learn the scientific basis for decision making and to understand the scientific research that underlies proper administration. Universities train future administrators with texts that stress the scientific research done on administrative behavior, review various studies of teacher and student performance, and provide a few techniques for accomplishing educational goals. Such approaches instill a reverence for the scientific method, but an unfortunate disregard for any humanistic and critical development of the art of administration.

We are suggesting a different approach. Although there is certainly an important place for scientific research in supporting empirically supported administrative behavior, we suggest that educational administrators also be *critical humanists*. Humanists appreciate the usual and unusual events of our lives and engage in an effort to develop, challenge, and liberate human souls. They are critical because they are educators and are therefore not satisfied with the status quo; rather, they hope to change individuals and institutions for the better and to improve social conditions for all. We argue that an *administrative* science be reconstructed as a *moral* science. An administrative science can be empirical, but it also must incorporate hermeneutic (the science of interpreting and understanding others) and critical dimensions. Social science has increasingly recognized that it must be informed by moral questions. The paradigm of natural science does not always apply when dealing with human issues. As a moral science, the science of administration is concerned with the resolution of moral dilemmas. A critical and a literary model of administration helps to provide us with the necessary context and understanding wherein such dilemmas can be wisely resolved, and we can truly actualize our potentials as administrators and leaders.

One's proclivity to be a critical humanist oftentimes depends on one's philosophy on how human beings behave in the workplace. The two extremes of the continuum might be described as those leaders who believe that human beings are basically lazy and will do the very least that they need to do to "get by" in the workplace. And those who believe that people are basically industrious and, if given the choice, would opt for doing the "right thing." We believe that today's most effective leaders hold the latter view. It is worth reiterating what was said in chapter 1, that we agree with Max DePree, owner and CEO of the highly successful Herman Miller Furniture Company. Writing in his book *Leadership Is an Art*, DePree argues that a leader's function is the "liberate people to do what is required of them in the most effective and humane way possible." Instead of catching people doing something *wrong*, our goal as enlightened leaders is to catch them doing something *right*. Such behavior is reflective of a leader who is in the humanist, if not also in the critical, tradition.

The Humanist Tradition

The first responsibility of a leader is to define reality through a vision. The last is to say "thank you." In between, the leader must become the servant of the servants. Being a leader means having the opportunity to make a meaningful difference in the lives of those who allow leaders to lead. This summarizes what it means to be an administrator and leader in the humanist tradition.

Whether one is a successful leader can be determined by looking at one's followers. Are they reaching their potentials? Are they learning? Are they able to change without bitterness? Are they able to achieve the institution's goals and objectives? Can they mange conflict among themselves? Do they have an internal locus of control? Are they concerned with the social implications of educational policy? Where the answer to these questions is an emphatic "yes" is where an effective and humanist leader resides.

We prefer to think about administration in terms of what the gospel writer Luke calls the "one who serves." The leader owes something to the institution he or she leads. The leader is seen in this context as steward rather than owner or proprietor. Administration as a moral science requires the leader to think about his or her stewardship in terms of legacy, values, direction, and effectiveness.

Too many of today's administrators are interested only in immediate results that bolster their career goals. Long-range goals are left to their successors. We believe that this approach fosters autocratic leadership, which often produces short-term results but militates against creativity and its long-term benefits. In effect, this approach is the antithesis of leading humanely. On the contrary, leaders should build a long-lasting legacy of accomplishment that is institutionalized for posterity. They owe their institutions and their followers a healthy existence and the relationships and reputation that enable continuity of that healthy existence. Educational administrators are also responsible for future leadership. They need to identify, develop, and nurture future leaders to carry on the legacy.

Along with being responsible for providing future leaders, administrators owe the individuals in their institutions certain other legacies. Leaders need to be concerned with the institutional value system that determines the principles and standards that guide the practices of those in the organization. Administrators need to model their value systems so that the individuals in the organization can learn to transmit these values to their colleagues and to future employees. In a civilized institution, we see good manner, respect for people, and an appreciation of the way in which we serve one another. Humane, sensitive, and thoughtful leaders will transmit their value systems through their daily behavior.

Administrators are obliged to provide and maintain direction by developing a vision. We made the point earlier that effective leaders must leave their organizations with a legacy. Part of this legacy should be a sense of progress or momentum. An educational administrator, for instance, should imbue his or her institution with a sense of continuous progress—a sense of constant improvement. Improvement and momentum come from a clear vision of what the institution ought to be, from a well-planned strategy to achieve that vision, and from carefully developed and articulated directions and plans that allow everyone to participate and be personally accountable for achieving those plans. Here is where functionalism and critical humanism intertwine. An institution cannot be humane if it is in chaos. It needs to be effectively and efficiently operated.

Leaders are also responsible for effectiveness by being enablers. They need to enable others to reach their potential both personally and institutionally. We believe that the most effective ways of enabling one's colleagues is through participative decision making. It begins with believing in the potential of people, believing in their diversity of gifts. Leaders must realize that to maximize their own power and effectiveness, they need to empower others. Leaders are responsible for setting and attaining the goals in their organizations. Empowering or enabling others to help achieve those goals enhances the leader's chances of attaining the goals, ultimately enhancing the leader's effectiveness. Paradoxically, giving up power really amounts to gaining power.

The Critical Tradition

A post-positivist leader combines the *humanist* tradition with *critical* theory. Dissatisfaction with current administrative approaches for examining social life stems from administrations' inability to deal with questions of value and morality and its inability to fulfill its promise. For example, Griffiths criticizes orthodox theories because they "ignore the presence of unions and fail to account for the scarcity of women and minorities in top administrative positions." Ericson and Elelttt ask, "Why had educational research had so few real implication for educational policy?" and answer that an empiricist research program modeled on the natural sciences fails to address issues of understanding and interpretation. This failure precludes researchers from reaching a genuine understanding of the human condition. It is time, they argue, to treat educational research as a moral science. The science of administration can also be a moral one, a critically moral one.

The term *moral* is being used here in its cultural, professional, spiritual, and ethical sense, not in a religious sense. The moral side of administration has to do with the *dilemmas* that face us in education. All educators face three areas of dilemmas: control, curriculum, and societal. Control dilemmas involve the resolution of classroom management and control issues, particularly the issue of who is in charge and to what degree. Control dilemmas center around four questions: (1) Do you treat the child as a student, focusing narrowly on cognitive goals, or as a whole person, focusing more broadly on intellectual, aesthetic, social, and physical dimensions? (2) Who controls classroom time? In some classrooms, children are given latitude in scheduling their activities; in others, class activities follow a strict and mandatory schedule. (3) Who controls operations or what larger context of what it means to be human and how we resolve the inevitable goes on in the classroom? (4) Who controls the standards and defines success and failure?

Similar dilemmas occur in the curricular domain and relate to whether the curriculum is considered as received, public knowledge, or whether it is considered private, individualized knowledge, of the type achieved through discoveries and experiments. These curricular difficulties also depend on whether one conceives of the child as customer or as an individual.

The customer receives professional services generated from a body of knowledge, whereas the individual receives personal services generated from his or her particular needs and context.

A final set of dilemmas has to do with what children bring to school and how they are to be treated once there. One concerns the distribution of teacher resources. Should one focus more resources on the less talented, in order to bring them up to standards, or on the more talented, in order for them to reach their full potential? The same question arises in regard to the distribution of justice. Should classroom rules be applied uniformly without regard to the differing circumstances of each child, or should family background, economic factors, and other socio-logical influences be considered? Should a teacher stress a common culture or ethnic differences and subculture consciousness?

Much of teaching involves resolving such dilemmas by making a variety of decisions throughout the school day. Such decisions can be made, however, in a *reflective* or an *unreflective* manner. An unreflective manner means simply teaching as one was taught, without giving consideration to available alternatives. A reflective approach involves and examination of the widest array of alternatives. Thus, reflective teaching suggests that dilemmas need not be simply resolved but can be transformed so that a higher level of teaching expertise is reached.

This same logic can be applied to administration. Administration involves the resolution of various dilemmas, that is, the making of moral decisions. One set of dilemmas involves control. How much participation can teachers have in the administration of the school? How much participation can parents and students have? Who evaluates and for what purpose? Is the role of administration collegial or authority centered? The area of the curriculum brings up similar questions. Is the school oriented to basic skills, advanced skills, social skills, or all three? Should the curricula be teacher made or national, state, or system mandated? Should student evaluation be based on teacher assessment or standardized tests? What is authentic assessment? Finally, an additional set of dilemmas pertains to the idea of schooling in society. Should the schools be oriented to ameliorate the apparent deficits that some students bring with them, or should they see different cultures and groups as strengths? Should schools be seen as agents of change, oriented to the creation of a more just society, or as socializers who adapt the young to the current social structure?

Oftentimes, these questions are answered unreflectively and simply resolved on an "as needed" basis. This approach often resolves the dilemma, but does not foster a real *transformation* in one's self, role, or institution. If administration and leadership encompasses transformation, and we would argue that it should, then an additional lens to structural functionalism must be found through which these questions can be viewed. We suggest that the additional lens be in the form of critical humanism and the Ignatian vision. In this context, then, administrative leadership can be viewed as a moral science.

THE IGNATIAN VISION

More than 450 years ago, Ignatius of Loyola, a young priest born to a Spanish aristocratic family, founded the Society of Jesus, the Jesuits, and wrote his seminal book, *The Spiritual Exercises.*[7] In this book, he suggested a "way of life" and a "way of looking at things" that has been propagated by his religious community and his other followers for almost five centuries. His principles have been utilized in a variety of ways. They have been used as an aid in developing one's own spiritual life; they have been used to formulate a way of learning that has become the curriculum and instructional method employed in the sixty high schools and the twenty-eight Jesuit colleges and universities in the United States; and, they have been used to develop one's own administrative style. Together, these principles comprise the *Ignatian vision.*

There are five Ignatian principles that we wish to explore here as a foundation for developing an administrative philosophy and leadership style: (1) Ignatius' concept of the *magis,* or the "more." (2) The implications of his notion of *cura personalis,* or "care of the person." (3) The process of *inquiry* or *discernment.* (4) The development of *men and women for others.* (5) And service to the *underserved* and marginalized, or his concept of *social justice.*

At the core of the Ignatian vision is the concept of the *magis,* or the "more." Ignatius spent the greater part of his life seeking perfection in all areas of his personal, spiritual, and professional life. He was never satisfied with the status quo. He was constantly seeking to improve his own spiritual life, as well as his secular life as leader of a growing religious community. He was an advocate of "continuous improvement" long before it became a corporate slogan, and long before people like Edwards Deming used it to develop his Total Quality Management approach to management, and long before Japan used it to revolutionize its economy after World War II.

The idea of constantly seeking "the more" implies change. The magis is a movement away from the status quo; and moving away from the status quo defines change. The Ignatian vision requires individuals and institutions to embrace the process of change as a vehicle for personal and institutional improvement. For his followers, frontiers and boundaries are not obstacles or ends, but new challenges to be faced, new opportunities to be welcomed. Thus, change needs to become a way of life. Ignatius further implores his followers to "be the change that you expect in others." In other words, we are called to model desired behavior—to live out our values, to be of ever fuller service to our communities, and to aspire to the more universal good. Ignatius had no patience with mediocrity. He constantly strove for the greater good.

The magis principle, then, can be described as the main norm in the selection of information and the interpretation of it. Every real alternative for choice must be conducive to the advancement toward perfection. When some aspect a particular alternative is *more* conducive to reaching perfection than other alternatives, we have reason to choose that alternative. In the last chapter, we spoke of the "dilemmas" that educators face during every working day. The magis principle is a "way of seeing" that can help us in selecting the better alternative.

At first hearing, the magis principle might sound rigid and frightening. It is absolute, and Ignatius is unyielding in applying it, but not rigid. On the one hand, he sees it as the expression of our love of humanity, which inexorably seeks to fill all of us with a desire to not be content with what is less good for us. On the other hand, he sees that humanity not only has its particular gifts, but also has its limitations and different stages of growth. If making a choice that, in the abstract, would be more humane than it would be in the concrete, that choice would not be seen as adhering to the magis principle. For example, tracking students according to ability can be seen as humane in the abstract, but in the concrete can be dehumanizing. Ignatius would advise us to focus on the concrete in resolving this *dilemma.*

In every case, then, accepting and living by the magis principle is an expression of our love of humanity. So, whatever the object for choice, the measure of our love of neighbor will be the fundamental satisfaction we will find in choosing and acting by the magis principle. Whatever one chooses by this principle, no matter how undesirable in some other respect, will always be what one would most want as a moral and ethical member of the human race.

Closely related to the principle of the magis is the Ignatian principle of *inquiry* and *discernment.* In his writings, he urges us to challenge the status quo through the methods of inquiry and discernment. This is very similar to one of the tenants of critical theory. In fact, the Ignatian vision and critical theory share a number of norms.

To Ignatius, the need to enter into inquiry and discernment is to determine God's will. However, this process is of value for the purely *secular* purpose of deciding on which "horn of a dilemma" one should come down. To aid us in utilizing inquiry and discernment as useful tools in challenging the status quo and determining the right choice to be made, Ignatius suggests that the ideal disposition for inquiry and discernment is humility. The disposition of humility is especially helpful when, despite one's best efforts, the evidence that one alternative is more conducive to the betterment of society is not compelling. When the discerner cannot find evidence to show that one alternative is more conducive to the common good, Ignatius calls for a judgment in favor of what more assimilates the discerner's life to the life of poverty and humiliation. Thus, when the *greatest* good cannot readily be determined, the *greater* good is more easily discerned in position of humility. These are very demanding standards, but they are consistent with the magis principle and the tenets of critical humanism.

In addition to the magis principle norm, taking account of what has just been said and of what was said earlier about the norm of humility as a disposition for seeking the greater good, the relationship of the greater good norm to the greatest good norm can be clarified. The latter is absolute, overriding, and always primary. The greater good norm is secondary; it can never, in any choice, have equal weight with the first magis principle; it can never justify a choice of actual poverty and humiliation over riches and honors if the latter are seen to be more for the service of humanity in a particular situation for choice, with all its concrete circumstances, including the agent's responsibilities to others and his or her own stage of psychological and spiritual development. In other words, if being financially successful allows one to better serve the poor and underserved, that would be preferred to actually poverty.

Ignatius presents us with several other supplemental norms for facing our "dilemmas." In choices that directly affect the individual person and the underserved or marginalized, especially the poor, Ignatius urges us to give preference to those in need. This brings us to his next guiding principle, *cura personalis* (care of the person).

Another of Ignatius' important and enduring principles is his notion that, despite the primacy of the common good, the need to care for the individual person should never be lost. From the very beginning, the *cura personalis* principle has been included in the mission statement of virtually every high school and college founded by the Jesuits. It also impacts the method of instruction suggested for all Jesuit schools in the *Ratio Studiorum,* or the "course of study" in these institutions. All Jesuit educational institutions are to foster what we now refer to as a "constructivist" classroom, where the student is an active participant in the learning process. This contrasts with the "transmission" method of instruction where the teacher is paramount, and the student is a passive participant in the process. In the Ignatian vision, the care of the person is a requirement not only on a personal needs basis, but also on a "whole person" basis, which would, of course, include classroom education.

This principle also has implications for how we conduct ourselves as educational administrators. Ignatius calls us to value the gifts and charisms of our colleagues and to address any deficiencies that they might have and turn them into strengths. For example, during the employee evaluation process, Ignatius would urge us to focus of the formative stage of the evaluation far more than on the summative stage. This would be one small way of applying *cura personalis* theory to practice.

The fourth principle that we wish to consider is the Ignatian concept of service. Once again, this principle has been propagated from the very outset. The expressed goal of virtually every Jesuit institution is "to develop men and women for others." Jesuit institutions are called on to create a culture of service as one way of ensuring that the students, faculty and staffs of these institutions reflect the educational, civic and spiritual values of the Ignatian vision.

Institutions following the Ignatian tradition of service to others have done so through community services programs and, more recently, service learning. Service to the community provides students with a means of helping others, a way to put their value system into action, and a tangible way to assist local communities. Although these were valuable benefits, there was no formal integration of the service experience into the curriculum and no formal introspection concerning the impact of service on the individual. During the last ten years, there has been a movement toward creating a more intentional academic relationship. Service has evolved from a modest student activity into an exciting pedagogical opportunity. In the past, service was viewed as a co-curricular activity; today, it plays an integral role in the learning process.

Because many institutions are situated in an urban setting, service gives them a chance to share resources with surrounding communities and allows for reciprocal relationships to form between the university and local residents. Immersion into different cultures—economic, racial, educational, social, and religious—is the vehicle by which students make connections. Working side by side with people of varying backgrounds significantly impacts the students, forcing them outside of their comfort zones and into the gritty reality of how others live. Through reflection, these students have the opportunity to integrate these powerful experiences into their lives, opening their eyes and hearts to the larger questions of social justice. Peter-Hans Kolvenbach, the superior general of the Jesuit order, in his At Santa Clara University of the occasion of their Sesquicentennial address on justice in American Jesuit universities in October 2000, used the words of Pope John Paul II to challenge Jesuit educators to "educate the whole person of solidarity for the real world," not only through concepts learned in the classroom, but also by contact with real people.

Upon assuming the position of superior general in 1973 and echoing the words of Ignatius, Pedro Arrupe declared "our prime educational objective must be to form men and women for others; men and women who will live not for themselves but for others." In this inaugural address, upon being named Superior General in Rome, Italy, in the spirit of these words, the service learning movement has legitimized the educational benefit of all experiential activity. The term *service learning* means different things to different people, and debates on service learning have been around for decades, running the gamut from unstructured "programmatic opportunities" to structured "educational philosophies." At Ignatian institutions, service learning is a bridge that connects faculty, staff, and students with community partners and their agency needs. It connects academic and student life views about the educational value of experiential learning. It also connects students' textbooks to human reality; and their minds and hearts with values and action. The programs are built on key components of service learning, including integration into the curriculum, a reciprocal relationship between the community agency and student, and structured time for reflection, which is very much related to the Ignatian principle of *discernment* discussed earlier.

Participation in service by high school and college students, whether as a co-curricular or a course-based experience, correlates to where they are in their developmental process. Service work allows students to explore their skills and limitations, to find what excites and energizes them, to put their values into action, and to use their talents to benefit others, to discover who they are and who they want to become. By encouraging students to reflect on their service, these institutions assist in this self-discovery. The reflection can take many forms: an informal chat, a facilitated group discussion, written dialogue, journal entries, reaction papers, or in-class presentations on articles. By integrating the service experience through critical reflection, the student develops self-knowledge of the communities in which he or she lives, and knowledge about the world that surrounds them. It is only after the unfolding of this service-based knowledge that the students are able to synthesize what they have learned into their lives. Through this reflection, the faculty members also have an opportunity to learn from and about their students. Teachers witness the change and growth of the students first hand. In short, "service to others" changes lives.

The implications of "service to others" for administration are clear. Not only can educational administrators enhance their effectiveness by including the idea of service to others in their curricula, but also by modeling it in their personal and professional lives. The concept of administrators becoming the "servant of the servants" is what we have in mind here. Servant leaders do not inflict pain, they bear pain, and they treat their employees as "volunteers," a concept that we explore more fully later.

The Ignatian concept of "service" leads into his notion of solidarity with the underserved (poor) and marginalized and his principle of *social justice*. We begin with an attempt to achieve some measure of clarity on the nature and role of social justice in the Ignatian vision. According to some, Ignatius defined justice in both a narrow and wide sense. In the *narrow* sense, it is "justice among men and women" that is involved. In this case, it is a matter of "clear obligations" among "members of the human family." The application of this kind of justice would include not only the rendering of material goods, but also immaterial goods, such as "reputation, dignity, the possibility of exercising freedom."

Many of his followers also believe Ignatius defined justice in a *wider* sense "where situations are encountered which are humanly intolerable and demand a remedy." Here, the situations might be a product of "explicitly unjust acts" caused by "clearly identified people" who cannot be obliged to correct the injustices, yet the dignity of the human person requires that justice be restored; or they might be caused by nonidentifiable people. It is precisely within the structural forces of inequality in society where injustice of this second type is found, where injustice is "institutionalized," that is, built into economic, social, and political structures, both national and international, and where people are suffering from poverty and hunger, from the unjust distribution of wealth, resources, and power. The critical theorists, of whom we spoke earlier, would likely concur with this wider definition of social justice.

It is almost certain that Ignatius did not only concern himself with injustices that were purely economic. He often cites injustices about "threats to human life and it quality," "racial and political discrimination," and loss of respect for the "rights of individuals or groups." When one adds to these the "vast range of injustices" enumerated in this writings, one sees that the Ignatian vision understands its mission of justice to include "the widest possible view of justice," involving every area where there is attack on human rights. We can conclude, therefore, that although Ignatius was to some degree concerned about commutative justice (right relationships between private persons and groups) and distributive justice (the obligations of the state to render to the individual what is his or her due), he is most concerned about what is generally called today *social justice*, or "justice of the common good." Such justice is comprehensive, and includes the above strict legal rights and duties, but is more concerned about the natural rights and duties of individuals, families, communities, and the community of nations toward one another as members of the common family of human beings. Every form of justice is included in and presupposed by social justice, but with social justice, it is the social nature of the person that is emphasized, as well as the social significance of all earthly goods, the purpose of which is to aid all members of the human community to attain their dignity as human beings. Many of Ignatius' followers believe that this dignity is being undermined in our world today, and their main efforts are aimed toward restoring that dignity.

In the pursuit of social justice, Ignatius calls on his followers to be "in solidarity with the poor." The next logical question might then be, who

are the poor? The poor are usually thought to be those who are economically deprived and politically oppressed. Thus, we can conclude
that the promotion of justice means to work to overcome the oppres-
sions or injustices that make the poor poor. The fallacy here, however, is
that the poor are not necessarily oppressed or suffering injustice, and so
Ignatius argues that our obligation toward the poor must be understood
to be linking "inhuman levels or poverty and injustice and not be understood to be concerned with the "lot of those possessing only modest
resources," even though those of modest means are often poor and oppressed. So, we conclude that the poor include those "wrongfully" im-
poverished or dispossessed.

An extended definition of the poor, one that Ignatius would espouse,
would include any of the following types of people.

First are those who are economically deprived and socially marginalized and oppressed, especially, but not limited to, those with whom one
has immediate contact and is in a position to positively effect.

The second group includes the "poor in spirit." That is, those who lack
a value system or an ethical and moral sense.

The third group includes those who are emotionally poor, those who
have psychological and emotional shortcomings and are in need of
comfort.

In defining the poor in the broadest way, Ignatius exhorts us to un-
dertake social change in our role as leader; to do what we can do to bring
an end to inequality, oppression, and injustice. Once again, we can see
the close connection between the Ignation principles of social justice
and the main tenets of critical theory.

IMPLICATIONS FOR ADMINISTRATION

Each of the principles of the Ignatian vision noted earlier has a variety
of implications for educational administrators. The *magis* principle has
implications for administrators in that it calls for us to continually be
seeking perfection in all that we do. In effect, this means that we must
seek to continually improve. And, because improvement implies
change, we need to be champions of needed change in our institutions.
This means that we have to model a tolerance for change and embrace

not only our own change initiatives, but also those in other parts of the organization. An in-depth application of the Ignatian vision to the process of change is discussed later.

The principle of *cura personalis* has additional implications. To practice the Ignatian vision, one must treat people with dignity under all circumstances. *Cura personalis* also requires us to extend ourselves in offering individual attention and attending to the needs of all those in whom we come in contact. Being sensitive to the individual's unique needs is particularly required. Many times in our efforts to treat people equally, we fail to treat them fairly and equitably. Certain individuals have greater needs than others, and many times these needs require exceptions to made on their behalf. For example, if an adult student does not hand in an assignment on time, but the tardiness is due to the fact that he or she is going through some personal trauma at the moment, the principle of *cura personalis* calls on us to make an exception in this case. It likely that many would consider such an exception to be unfair to those who made the effort to complete the assignment in a timely manner or, that we cannot possibly be sensitive to the special needs of all of our students and colleagues. However, as long as the exception is made for anyone in the same circumstances, Ignatius would not perceive this exception as being unfair. In fact, the exception would be expected if one is practicing the principle of care of the person.

The Ignatian process of *discernment* requires educational administrators to be reflective practitioners. It calls on us to be introspective regarding our administrative and leadership behavior. We are asked to reflect on the ramifications of our decisions, especially in light of their cumulative effect on the equitable distribution of power and on the marginalized individuals and groups in our communities. In effect, the principle of discernment galvanizes the other principles embodied in the Ignatian vision. During the discernment process, we are asked to reflect upon how our planned behavior will manifest the *magis* principle, *cura personalis*, and service to the community, especially the underserved, marginalized, and oppressed.

The development of men and women for others requires one to have his or her own sense of service toward those with whom the leader interacts, and that one also develops this spirit of service in others. The concept of "servant leadership" requires us to encourage others toward a life and career of service and to assume the position of being the "servant of the servants." Ignatius thinks about leadership in terms of what the gospel writer Luke calls the "one who serves." The leader owes something to the institution he or she leads. The leader is seen in this context as steward rather than owner or proprietor.

The implications of Ignatius' notion of social justice are myriad for the administrator. Being concerned about the marginalized among our constituencies is required. We are called to be sensitive to those individuals and groups that do not share equitably in the distribution of power and influence. Participative decision making and collaborative behavior is encouraged among administrators imbued with the Ignatian tradition. Equitable representation of all segments of the school community should be provided whenever feasible. Leadership behavior such as this will ensure that the dominant culture is not perpetuated to the detriment of the minority culture, rendering the minorities powerless.

CASE STUDY 11.1: MERCY ACADEMY

Mercy Academy (MA) is a private school for children in preschool through grade eight that is owned and operated by a religious congregation. The board of directors for MA consists of the five members of the leadership team for the religious congregation of the regional community. The principal and vice principal are directly accountable to them.

In addition to principal and vice principal, the administrative team for the school consists of the treasurer, the director of admissions, the director of religious education, the director of development and alumni relations, and the director of public relations. This team is supported by an administrative assistant and two school secretaries.

An advisory board also provides support to the administrators of the school. In the past, this board was jointly shared with Waldron Academy, the girls' high school that is on the same campus with MA. This board was in existence for the last nine years, serving both schools. As of November, this board ceased to exist in that structure, and both schools are now in the process of forming their own advisory board. The board consists of the following committees: executive, education, finance, development, public relations, and building and facilities. Members of the board may be directly related to the school, such as parents both past and present, or they may have been graduates of the school. They may also have been invited to serve on the board because their area of expertise is such that the administration can benefit from their ideas and perspectives.

The leadership mode for this school is definitely not classical. The roles of the principal and the vice principal at MA are not clearly defined. Both share the responsibility for the leadership of the school. Therefore, I do not discuss only the principal as the head of the school, but myself as well.

In some areas, we have taken on responsibilities because that is where our interests lie, or because we have a "gift" for it, or because neither one of us wants to do it but we know that someone has to. But we do not have formal job descriptions and we share most of the duties that go along with running a school. And for the most part, parents, teachers, and students know that they can approach either of us with a question or concern and they will get an appropriate response. This works well for us because we work well together. Neither one of us is particularly fond of the bureaucratic approach, but we can deal successfully with the bureaucracy when we need to. We both tend to be more interested in human relations and group dynamics. This should become clear when I talk about the culture of MA and the changes we've made within the school over the last six years.

When you talk about the organizational theory for this school, I would say that we follow the contingency approach. Certainly, we are classical in the sense that we have a number of administrators, coordinators, and department heads.

We also subscribe to the social system when you consider all the celebrations that we share as a faculty and staff. Many of these are school related, such as celebrations for the completion of Middle States work or our strategic planning. We also celebrate milestones; for example, we have a dinner for faculty/staff and their spouses or guests to celebrate their fifth, tenth, fifteenth, and twentieth years at MA. We include a celebration of birthdays at every faculty meeting or inservice day that we can share together. We don't limit our celebrations to school-related ones. We always come together to celebrate engagements, weddings, births, and so on. This year, we happened to have eight members of our faculty and staff who will mark twenty-five years of married life. So, we planned a Saturday night liturgy and reception where we can join together to celebrate this special occasion in their lives. We always try to recognize the accomplishments of our faculty and staff by publicizing within our school any awards that they receive. Because of a very generous donation from a graduate, we are able to recognize an exemplary teacher each year at our closing luncheon and provide him or her with a plaque and $500 check.

There are also many times when the Open System is evident within the school community. We believe very strongly that we all need to work together to make the most of what we have. In addition to the advisory board, we also have a very active parent/teacher cooperative. (I think that the fact that we call it a "cooperative" instead of the more traditional "organization" or "association" speaks to the value we place on working together—cooperatively.) We also encourage and support teachers and staff members who work together in teams within the school.

The leadership theory that best describes the administrators at MA would probably be transformational. Part of the reason that I choose this theory has to do with the circumstances surrounding our appointments, the way we became its leaders, and what we did as such.

Six years ago, the principal came to MA. At that time, I was hired as the vice principal, after having been there for seven years. The principal came with the experience of being principal in two other schools, whereas I had the experience of being a teacher and the director of admissions in this school. I knew what needed to be changed in the school. Because she was "new" and not known, it was easy for people to accept change because one expects change when the leaders change. I believe that you are able to have changes seem more acceptable if you are able to use personal charisma to present your ideas. Fortunately, we were taking a school that was already a very good school and making it better. We had just completed our Middle States evaluation so we knew what we needed to do, and the school community was ready for us to do it. It was relatively easy for us to be "agents of change." We had an action plan to implement, which we accomplished over the last five years. This spring and summer, we worked with our board, our teachers and administrative team, and our parents on a new two-year strategic plan. Both of these plans have given form to our vision for the school. We have communicated this vision to the larger community and we have institutionalized the changes that have occurred.

Although I think that the faculty and staff were willing to accept and implement change initially because it was expected, to continually make changes you need to motivate them. To explain the motivation theories that we practice at MA, I use as examples one content model and one process model.

The content model would be Maslow's Hierarchy of Needs. We meet as many of their needs as we can. We provide a safe, secure environment and a salary that is greater than one that they would receive in other private schools. Although our salary scale is not on par with public school districts, we do provide perks such as coffee and donuts/Danish/bagels each morning and a full hot lunch that many teachers say is so substantial that it serves as their main meal of the day. We make every effort to treat teachers as the professionals that they are. We have teachers and staff members who come to school because they want to, not have to. We do not limit personal days or sick days in our contracts. We have many teachers who are parents and we recognize that this is their first priority. If they have a sick child at home, then they need to be home with him or her. They don't need to call in saying that they themselves are sick. We try to be understanding of the problems in their personal lives. We help them to feel loved and appreciated for the gifts and talents that they have. We recognize their accomplishments. We encourage and financially support their professional development through courses, workshops, and in-service opportunities. We provide them with substitutes who are teachers so that they can take advantage of these opportunities and not have to worry that their students are just doing busywork for the day. Through their professional development we know that they are reaching their potential. We try to recognize and encourage them to work to that potential. We have "promoted" teachers to leadership roles either in administration or as coordinators for different curriculum areas.

The process model that we implement is the Goal-Setting Theory. Each year, we have teachers set goals and we work with them to develop those goals over the course of the year. Their evaluation at the end of the year reflects their success at reaching their goals, although many times these goals are in-process from one year to the next. Some years, we ask them to set goals in relation to a schoolwide theme. For example, this year, since we presented our strategic plan to the total faculty and staff in September, we then had teachers set their personal goals around the implementation of the strategic plan goals for the school. As we do our formal observations in the classrooms, we've asked teachers to demonstrate, where possible, how they are implementing these goals.

For communication within the school community, we take many approaches. Certainly, when necessary, we use classical, top-down, one-way communication. We use a variety of means to accomplish this. In school, we begin each day with announcements on the public address system. We use this method to convey information that is pertinent and relevant for faculty, staff, and students for that day. While we are primarily responsible for the information that is relayed at this time, frequently teachers or staff members have information to convey as well. We also have the daily sheet, which is written communication that is distributed each day to all faculty and staff members. On this, we can include information that is not necessary for students to hear or know. This sheet also lists the names of any students who are absent that day. Because this communication is hand-delivered by students to each teacher, we do not include anything of a confidential nature. To relay this kind of information, we use a memo or letter that is put into each person's mailbox in the faculty mailroom. Each Thursday, we send home to each family a brown communication envelope that contains information related to school activities. We also include in this envelope newsletters or discussion topics that will help parents learn parenting skills. Because most parents receive only on-the-job training as parents, we have found disseminating this information to be helpful to them.

We also use the open systems for communication that requires two-way interaction. In school, this is accomplished through the use of grade meetings. We have three classes of each grade. One of the things that I found frustrating as a teacher at WMA was the inability to meet with my grade partners on a regular basis. At that time, we had a schedule that gave us some days with two free periods and other days with none. Grade partners were almost never free at the same time. One of the first changes we made was to reschedule "specials" classes for the same period each day for all three grade partners. That way, they can meet each day, if necessary. Now, we also have one day each week where either the principal or vice principal meets with the three teachers in each grade to address any concerns in that grade. This is a tremendous help for planning, for us to know what is happening in each grade, and for teachers to know what is happening in their grade partner's room.

For questions or concerns of a schoolwide nature, we discuss these at our monthly faculty meetings or in-service days. The week before these meetings, the committee that plans the meeting invites teachers to add agenda items that they would like to communicate to everyone or that they would like to have everyone discuss at the meeting. About three or four years ago, we started recording and distributing the minutes of these meetings to ensure that the decisions that were reached were clearly understood by all present, and even those who were unable to be a part of the meeting. After discussions where a consensus has not been reached, we send out a survey to get feedback from teachers after they have had time to reflect and digest what has been said. That information is then conveyed to everyone. For times when we need to make decisions between faculty meetings, we have used the survey format to get a sense of what teachers and staff members think about a particular issue.

We have monthly meetings of the parent–teacher cooperative, where we also invite parents to add agenda items that they would like to see addressed. Because we are not a neighborhood school and it's harder to get parents to come out for a meeting on a week night, a relatively small group of parents tends to be present for these meetings. Therefore, for topics that we want to get a broader outlook, we send home a questionnaire/survey to all parents for feedback. These have been especially helpful when we need a parent's perspective. For example, a few years ago we wanted to change our school uniform. At that time, parents were ordering from and dealing with four different vendors. We had one company for the boys' school uniform, one for the girls' winter uniform, another for their spring/fall uniform, and a different company for the boys' and girls' gym uniforms. Because we wanted to change the uniform, we thought we ought to make parents' lives simpler by only having to deal with one company. When we asked parents in the survey about possible uniform changes, we also asked about their experiences dealing with the different uniform vendors. We suspected that their perspective would be different than ours. Their input was valuable in our selection of one company to service the entire school. We also sent home an end-of-the-year survey each spring to get an overview of the year's programs and activities from a parent's perspective. We have found that although parents might not always agree with everything we do, they are pleased to be asked for their opinion. In one of our fall letters in the communication envelope, we highlight changes that were instituted based on the information we received in these surveys.

The principal happens to be very nonconfrontational. I tend to want to jump right in and fix things that I perceive as broken. What I have learned by watching the avoidance tactics is that sometimes the problem goes away or doesn't seem as great with the passing of time. This doesn't necessarily mean that you never have to deal with it, but that sometimes when it surfaces again, you have a different perspective on the situation.

At MA, we use all the different styles of dealing with conflicts. The most frequently used style is probably collaborating. Given the structure of communication within the school, and the ability that we have to meet together in grade teams or as a total faculty, we solve most conflicts collaboratively. In fact, when we interview and consider hiring new teachers, we have as a part of the process, a meeting between the candidate and the teachers that he or she will be working with. During these meetings, I serve as the facilitator and the observer to see how the candidate and the other teachers interact. I pay particular attention to the manner in which they respond to differences of opinions. We have found that this is a good indicator of how they will collaborate in the future. After the new teacher is hired, it's interesting to see the way in which these teams of teachers compromise, compete, and accommodate each other.

The last topic that I would like to discuss is strategic planning. After completing our last five-year plan, we began the process of forming a new two-year plan in the spring of this year. We started with a vision statement that was drafted by our advisory board. This statement flowed from our mission, and was presented to our total faculty and staff for review and to see if there was anything that needed to be added or deleted. Once this vision statement was in final form, the administrative team met to determine the committees that were needed to make this vision a reality. We then brainstormed for members of each committee. These members included an administrator, two or three teachers, and three or four parents. We met with all the members of this planning process and presented the vision statement to them. As a total group, we set goals that supported the vision. Over the course of the summer, the committees met to set specific goals and objectives. They also worked on strategies to implement these goals and objectives, and they determined how they would assess their progress over the next two years. We met again as a total group to share the work of each committee. The strategic plan was then presented by the teachers on the committees to the total faculty at our meeting before school reopened. It was also presented by the parents on the committees to the parent body at our back-to-school meeting in September. The feedback that we received from all parties was very positive.

SUMMARY

We began this book by suggesting that leaders are made, not born. We posited that if one could master the skills involved in effective leadership, one could become a successful administrator. In this chapter, however, we make the assertion that learning the skills involved in effective leadership is only part of the story. Leadership is as much an art, a belief, a condition of the heart, as it is a set of skills. A truly successful leader, therefore, is one who leads with both the *mind* and the *heart.*

NOTES

1. Max DePree, *Leadership is an Art* (New York: Dell Publishing, 1989), 27.

2. Peter M. Senge, *The Fifth Dimension: The Art and Practice of the Learning Organization* (New York: Doubleday, 1990).

3. Alexander Solzhenitsyn, *A World Split Apart* (New York: Harper and Row, 1978), 17–19.

4. William Glasser, *Control Theory, A New Explanation of How We Control Our Lives* (New York: Harper and Row, 1984).

5. Lee Bolman and Terrence Deal, *Reframing Organizations, Artistry, Choice, and Leadership* (San Francisco: Jossey-Bass, 1991).

6. DePree, *Leadership is an Art*, 12.

12

ORGANIZATIONAL DIAGNOSIS

Science can only ascertain what is, but not what should be, and outside of its domain value judgments of all kinds remain necessary.

—Albert Einstein

In this chapter, we draw together the concepts discussed in the earlier chapters and use them in an integrated fashion to engage in an organizational diagnosis that will evaluate the institutional health of an educational entity. An organizational diagnosis requires the educational administrator to systematically analyze the various aspects of the educational institution. Periodic review and analysis of the structure, culture, leadership, motivation, communication, conflict management, process of change, strategic plan, decision making, and the distribution of power in an institution needs to take place if the institution is to remain viable.

THE DIAGNOSTIC CHECKLIST

Organizational Structure

- Is there appropriate division of labor and is it flexible?
- Is the division of labor conducive to reaching organizational goals?

- Is the structure of the organization well designed?
- Do work groups operate effectively?
- Are the best aspects of the classical, social, and open systems' organizational structures present?
- Does the organization's structure respond to the environmental contingencies?

Organizational Culture

- Does the organization exhibit a culture of mutual trust and respect?
- Do perceptual distortions proliferate?
- Does the workforce exhibit an internal locus of control?
- Is the institution a learning organization?
- Are the various learning styles being addressed in the management process?
- What beliefs and values do the individuals in the organization have?
- How do these beliefs and values influence individual attitudes?
- What functional and dysfunctional behaviors result from the individuals' attitudes?

Leadership

- Do the administrators display the necessary behaviors required for effective leadership?
- Do the leaders encourage the appropriate amount of participation in decision making?
- Does the leadership adapt to the task and the maturity level of the followers?
- Do transformational leaders exist?
- Do they operate in all four frames of organizational leadership?

Motivation

- Do the rewards satisfy the variety of individual needs?
- Are rewards both internal and external?

- Are they applied equitably and consistently?
- Do individuals value the rewards they receive?
- Do they perceive that their efforts correlate with performance?
- Do individuals set goals as a source of motivation?
- Are the rewards and incentives effective in motivating desired behaviors?

Communication

- How effective is the communication process?
- Is the correct communication style utilized under the proper conditions?
- What barriers to communication exist?
- Does communication include feedback where appropriate?
- Is there a climate of mutual trust and respect?
- Are active listening and other techniques that improve the communication process used?
- Do individuals use assertive, nonassertive, or aggressive communication?

Conflict Management

- Is the conflict in the organization functional or dysfunctional?
- Are there mechanisms for effectively managing conflict and stress?
- Do the mechanisms reflect the situational nature of conflict resolution?
- Are avoidance, compromise, competition, accommodation, and collaboration utilized in the appropriate situations?

Change Process

- Are the steps of the rational change model implemented?
- Is a force-field analysis used during the change process?
- Are appropriate change agents identified?
- Are intervention strategies appropriate for the situation?
- Do mechanisms exist for institutionalizing the change?

Strategic Planning

- Does a strategic plan exist?
- Does it begin with a vision statement?
- Are the goals and objectives clear and measurable?
- Is the planning process ongoing?

Decision Making

- What type of decisions are being made?
- Do organizational members make high-quality, accepted, and ethical decisions?
- Do decision makers follow the basic process of decision making?
- Is the group appropriately involved in decision making?
- What barriers are there to effective decision making?
- What techniques are being used to overcome these barriers?

Power and Negotiation

- Who has power in the organization?
- From what sources does the power emanate?
- Is power appropriately shared?
- What type of negotiations occur in the school district or educational institution?
- Do the negotiations tend to be distributive or integrative?
- What degree of preparation takes place?
- Is the contract language understood by the administrators?
- Is provision made for the proper administration of the contract?

Leading with Heart

- Is there a climate of trust and respect in this organization?
- Are decisions made and conflicts resolved collaboratively?
- Is communication primarily from the open self?
- Is there evidence of a social and/or open systems organizational structure?
- Is there relatedness as well as task behavior exhibited by the leaders?

THE HEART SMART ORGANIZATIONAL
DIAGNOSIS MODEL

Just as there are vital signs in measuring individual health, we believe that there are vital signs in measuring the organizational institutions. This survey will help us to determine those vital signs. The purpose of the Heart Smart Organizational Diagnosis Questionnaire, therefore, is to provide feedback data for intensive diagnostic efforts. Use of the questionnaire, either by itself or in conjunction with other information-collecting techniques such as systematic observation or interviewing, will provide the data needed for identifying strengths and weaknesses in the functioning of an educational institution or a school system.

A meaningful diagnostic effort must be based on a theory or model of organizational development. This makes action research possible as it facilitates problem identification, which is essential to determining the proper functioning of an organization. The model suggested here establishes a systematic approach for analyzing relationships among the variables that influence how an organization is managed. It provides for assessment of ten areas of formal and informal activity: structure, culture, leadership, motivation, communications, decision making, conflict resolution, goal setting and planning, power distribution, and attitude toward change. The outer circle in the figure 12.1

Structure
How is this institution organized?

Conflict Resolution
Is this institution functional or
dysfunctional?

Culture
What values and beliefs are important here?

Goal Setting & Planning
Are the goals clear, accepted and
operationalized

Leadership
How effectively are the boxes kept in balance?

INTERNAL
Power Distribution
Aare the faculty and staff empowered?

ENVIRONMENT
Motivation
Are the rewards and incentives effective?

Attitude
Is this institution continually improving?

Communication
Is the messagebeing transmitted clearly?

Decision Making
How and by whom are decisions being made?

EXTERNAL ENVIRONMENT

EXTERNAL ENVIRONMENT

Figure 12.1. The heart smart wheel

represents an organizational boundary for diagnosis. This boundary demarcates the functioning of the internal and external environments. Because the underlying organizational theory upon which this survey is based is an open system model, it is essential that influences from both the internal and external environment be considered for the analysis to be complete.

The Heart Smart Organizational Diagnosis Questionnaire

Please think of your present work environment and indicate the degree to which you agree or disagree with each of the following statements. A "1" is *Disagree Strongly* and a "7" is *Agree Strongly*.

Agree Strongly	Agree	Agree Slightly	Neither Agree Nor Disagree	Disagree Slightly	Disagree	Disagree Strongly
1	2	3	4	5	6	7

1. The manner in which the tasks in this institution are divided is a logical one.
2. The relationships among coworkers are harmonious.
3. This institution's leadership efforts result in its fulfillment of its purposes.
4. My work at this institution offers me an opportunity to grow as a person.
5. I can always talk to someone at work if I have a work-related problem.
6. The faculty actively participate in decisions.
7. There is little evidence of unresolved conflict in this institution.
8. There is a strong fit between this institution's mission and my own values.
9. The faculty and staff are represented on most committees and task forces.
10. Staff development routinely accompanies any significant changes that occur in this institution.

11. The manner in which the tasks in this institution are distributed is fair.
12. Older faculty's opinions are valued.
13. The administrators display the behaviors required for effective leadership.
14. The rewards and incentives here are both internal and external.
15. There is open and direct communication among all levels of this institution.
16. Participative decision making is fostered at this institution.
17. What little conflict that exists at this institution is not dysfunctional.
18. Representatives of all segments of the school community participate in the strategic planning process.
19. The faculty and staff have an appropriate voice in the operation of this institution.
20. This institution is not resistant to constructive change.
21. The division of labor in this organization helps its efforts to reach its goals.
22. I feel valued by this institution.
23. The administration encourages an appropriate amount of participation in decision making.
24. Faculty and staff members are often recognized for special achievements.
25. There are no significant barriers to effective communication at this institution.
26. When the *acceptance* of a decision is important, a group decision-making model is used.

Agree Strongly	Agree	Agree Slightly	Neither Agree Nor Disagree	Disagree Slightly	Disagree	Disagree Strongly
1	2	3	4	5	6	7

27. There are mechanisms at this institution to effectively manage conflict and stress.
28. Most of the employees understand the mission and goals of this institution.

29. The faculty and staff feel empowered to make their own decisions regarding their daily work.
30. Tolerance toward change is modeled by the administration of this institution.
31. The various grade level teachers and departments work well together.
32. Differences among people are accepted.
33. The leadership is able to generate continuous improvement in the institution.
34. My ideas are encouraged, recognized, and used.
35. Communication is carried out in a nonaggressive style.
36. In general, the decision-making process is an effective one.
37. Conflicts are usually resolved before they become dysfunctional.
38. For the most part, the employees of this institution feel an "ownership" of its goals.
39. The faculty and staff are encouraged to be creative in their work.
40. When changes are made they do so within a rational process.
41. This institution's organizational design responds well to changes in the internal and external environment
42. The teaching and the nonteaching staffs get along with one another.
43. The leadership of this institution espouses a clear educational vision.
44. The goals and objectives for the year are mutually developed by the faculty and the administration.
45. I believe that my opinions and ideas are listened to.
46. Usually, a collaborative style of decision making is utilized at this institution.
47. A collaborative approach to conflict resolution is ordinarily used.
48. This institution has a clear educational vision.
49. The faculty and staff can express their opinions without fear of retribution.
50. I feel confident that I will have an opportunity for input if a significant change were to take place in this institution.

Agree Strongly	Agree	Agree Slightly	Neither Agree Nor Disagree	Disagree Slightly	Disagree	Disagree Strongly
1	2	3	4	5	6	7

51. This institution is "people oriented."
52. Administrators and faculty have mutual respect for one another.
53. Administrators give people the freedom to do their job.
54. The rewards and incentives in this institution are designed to satisfy a variety of individual needs.
55. The opportunity for feedback is always available in the communications process.
56. Group decision-making techniques, like brainstorming and group surveys, are sometimes used in the decision-making process.
57. Conflicts are oftentimes prevented by early intervention.
58. This institution has a strategic plan for the future.
59. Most administrators here use the power of persuasion rather than the power of coercion.
60. This institution is committed to continually improving through the process of change.
61. This institution does not adhere to a strict chain of command.
62. This institution exhibits grace, style, and civility.
63. The administrators model desired behavior.
64. At this institution, employees are not normally coerced into doing things.
65. I have the information that I need to do a good job.
66. I can constructively challenge the decisions in this institution.
67. A process to resolve work-related grievances is available.
68. There is an ongoing planning process at this institution.
69. The faculty and staff have input into the operation of this institution through a collective bargaining unit or through a faculty governance body.
70. The policies, procedures, and programs of this institution are periodically reviewed.

Heart Smart Scoring Sheet

Instructions: Transfer the numbers you circled on the questionnaire to the blanks below. Add each column and divide each sum by seven. This will give you comparable scores for each of the ten areas.

Structure	Culture/Heart	Leadership	Motivation
1 _____	2 _____	3 _____	4 _____
11 _____	12 _____	13 _____	14 _____
21 _____	22 _____	23 _____	24 _____
31 _____	32 _____	33 _____	34 _____
41 _____	42 _____	43 _____	44 _____
51 _____	52 _____	53 _____	54 _____
61 _____	62 _____	63 _____	64 _____
Total			
_____	_____	_____	_____
Average			
_____	_____	_____	_____

Communication	Decision Making	Conflict Resolution	Goal Setting/ Planning
5 _____	6 _____	7 _____	8 _____
15 _____	16 _____	17 _____	18 _____
25 _____	26 _____	27 _____	28 _____
35 _____	36 _____	37 _____	38 _____
45 _____	46 _____	47 _____	48 _____
55 _____	56 _____	57 _____	58 _____
65 _____	66 _____	67 _____	68 _____
Total			
_____	_____	_____	_____
Average			
_____	_____	_____	_____

Power Distribution   Attitude toward Change

  9 _____   10 _____
 19 _____   20 _____
 29 _____   30 _____
 39 _____   40 _____
 49 _____   50 _____
 59 _____   60 _____
 69 _____   70 _____

Total

_____   _____

Average

_____   _____

The Heart Smart Organizational Diagnosis Interpretation Sheet

Instructions: Transfer your average scores from the scoring sheet to the appropriate boxes in figure 12.1. Then study the background information and interpretation suggestions that follow.

Background

The Heart Smart Organizational Diagnosis Questionnaire is a survey-feedback instrument designed to collect data on organizational functioning. It measures the perceptions of persons in an organization to determine areas of activity that would benefit from an organizational development effort. It can be used as the sole data-collection technique or in conjunction with other techniques (interview, observation, etc.). The instrument and the model reflect a systematic approach for analyzing relationships among variables that influence how an organization is managed. Using the Heart Smart Organizational Diagnosis Questionnaire is the first step in determining appropriate interventions for organizational change efforts.

Interpretation and Diagnosis

A crucial consideration is the diagnosis based upon data interpretation. The simplest diagnosis would be to assess the amount of variance for each of the ten variables in relation to a score of 4, which is the neutral point. Scores *below* 4 would indicate a *problem* with organizational functioning. The closer the score is to 1, the more severe the problem would be. Scores *above* 4 indicate the *lack of a problem*, with a score of 7 indicating optimum functioning.

Another diagnostic approach follows the same guidelines of assessment in relation to the neutral point (score) of 4. The score of each of the seventy items on the questionnaire can be reviewed to produce more exacting information on problematic areas. Thus, diagnosis would be more precise. For example, suppose that the average score on item number 8 is 1.4. This would indicate not only a problem in organizational purpose or goal setting, but also a more specific problem in that there is a gap between organizational and individual goals. This more precise diagnostic effort is likely to lead to a more appropriate intervention in the organization than the generalized diagnostic approach described in the preceding paragraph.

Appropriate diagnosis must address the relationships between the boxes to determine the interconnectedness of problems. For example, if there is a problem with *communication,* could it be that the organizational *structure* does not foster effective communication? This might be the case of the average score on item 25 was well below 4 (2.5 or lower) and all the items on organizational *structure* (1, 11, 21, 31, 41, 51, 61) averaged above 5.5.

CASE STUDY 12.1: MERCHANTVILLE SCHOOL SYSTEM

It was past midnight as Anne Forsythe closed the garage door, collected her notes from the car, and entered the house. The lights were off downstairs, but she was pleased to see the light from her husband's reading lamp as she tiptoed upstairs.

"Thank goodness Hank's awake," she thought. "I felt guilty dashing out tonight leaving instructions with Jason about dinner. Why did I ever get involved with this school board? Now, if I can just get Hank to not insist on my rehashing tonight's meeting, perhaps I can unwind."

Anne, a tall, attractive woman, had worked for ten years as a legal secretary before "retiring" to raise a family. Her husband, a lawyer, had taken a real interest in having Anne maintain her interest in the law and now, after almost nine years of night school, she looked forward to completing a law degree this spring. With their oldest child in college and Jason leaving in the fall, Anne was determined to get out and find a full-time job.

"I agreed a year ago to serve on our local school board," she said, "as a first step to using my education to do more than ferry around four-foot-high people in station wagons. I had no ides, however, how much time it would take and, worse, how much time was wasted on politics and on the wrong issues."

THE MERCHANTVILLE SCHOOL SYSTEM

Merchantville, Ohio, is a suburb of Cleveland, with a population of 32,000. Its board of education consists of nine members, who serve for three-year terms with a turnover of three members per year. For many years, Merchantville had been one of the most popular suburban communities because of the reputation of the school system. Real estate commands a 10 to 20 percent higher price than in neighboring communities, and while these other communities rose up in arms over spiraling school costs, Merchantville's residents supported systems budgets. One of the reasons for Merchantville's excellent reputation has been its superintendent of schools, John Newland. With more than 40 years experience as an educator and administrator, Newland has acquired national recognition among educational administrators. During his eighteen years in Merchantville, he has maintained excellent relations with both the professional staff and the community.

Although his critics consider him more of a salesman and politician than an educator, they had little basis for faulting his results until four years ago. At that time, a bond issue for a new elementary school was presented to the voters. The proposal stirred up much controversy because of debate on where to situate the new building, and the board of education worked long hours to deal with the many problems that arose.

Citizen groups organized, took sides, and for the first time many who moved to Merchantville because of its schools got involved.

Before this time, the board met twice a month, except for the last two months of the year, when teacher evaluation and budget reviews increased the number of meetings to four, or even five a month. During the eighteen months of controversy surrounding the new building, the board was required to meet at numerous hearings and citizen-sponsored "cottage parties." During this same period, legislative changes led to recognition of the Merchantville's Teacher Association as a legal bargaining unit—a union. Given Merchantville's reputation, teacher union officials from all over the state sought to "help" its teachers. At that time, the Merchantville Board of Education considered hiring a professional to negotiate with their teachers. Their decision not to do so was based on a promise from the Teachers Association that they would not use state union help if the board didn't use outsiders either. As a result, the board negotiating team (three members) frequently meets two or three nights a week for several months to bring about a contract agreement.

JOHN NEWLAND

During that eighteen-month period four years ago (Newland said), the whole character of the board and their perception of their role changed. In the past, being a board member was an honor and required little work. Running the system was left to the professionals. During that period, everything changed. Meetings ran past midnight and were frequently called for Saturday, as well as two or three meetings, "cottage parties," and hearings on weeknights. There was a great deal to be done, but it took more time than it should because the board wasn't used to doing it.

We had two elections during that period, and with the growing awareness in the community of how much work was involved, the traditional board types wouldn't run. Instead, we got a lot of candidates who were liberal thinkers and not only supported education but also thought they knew more about it than the professionals. As a result, our board is now about evenly divided into two groups. The first are those who realize they have a full-time staff to run the system and should get involved only on board policy matters. The second group feels the professionals are too traditional and slow to change, and thus want to get into the details of running the system. I could keep this group out of my hair when they were busy with the new building and negotiations, but now these things have settled down and they don't have enough to do. They want all kinds of citizens, teachers, and board committees to get into every aspect of the system. Believe me, it will be a disaster if they get control of the board. I've seen these well-intentioned, frustrated "educators" ruin a school district before.

In my 40 years, I have beaten back some such efforts and left communities where I couldn't. With less than five years until retirement, however, I don't feel like fighting and have no intention of moving.

THE "CURRENT SOCIAL ISSUES" COURSE

A year and a half ago, two high school teachers approached the new principal with a proposal for an experimental course. One, an older man, was a long-service history teacher; the other, a young woman, was a non-tenured member of the English department. They asked the principal to permit them to team-teach a new elective course on current social issues. Their idea was to combine readings from history and English literature with current-events topics.

Dan Kneep, the high school principal, said, "I liked the idea, particularly when they told me they would teach the course twice in the first year and ask for only one course credit each. In this way, they were bearing the extra cost of team-teaching.

"If the course was successful, I told them we would consider making this a permanent elective and provide for its staffing. As an experimental course, with no extra cost, I figured I could approve it on my own. Because I'm new and lack tenure, however, I thought that I would play it safe, so I checked with the two department chairmen involved. The chairman of the history department was skeptical but, given the stature of his senior colleague in history who proposed it, he raised no objection. The chairman of the English department indicated that she thought it a good idea and so I approved it."

The course was offered in the spring of last year and again in the fall and this spring. Although the number of students was small at first, the class had to be closed at 30 both terms this year. When the two teachers requested that Kneep approve the course as a permanent elective, he did so. Formal approval of a permanent course requires approval by the superintendent after review by the director of curriculum, Jesse Lake.

THE DIRECTOR OF CURRICULUM'S REPORT

Jesse Lake is the second in command in the Merchantville school system. He had earned his doctorate in education and had taught for fifteen years before becoming superintendent of a small school district. Though successful as superintendent, Lake did not like the administrative work and the politics and accepted his present post at Merchantville nine years ago.

"I thoroughly enjoy working for Dr. Newland (Lake said), and I respect him as an educator and as a person. He knows how to pick good staff people and get the best out of them. Mine is a difficult job in many districts. Technically, I am a staff person and have no line of authority over teachers and principals. Although I am legally responsible for the district in the superintendent's absence, he is the boss. In many school systems, the assistant superintendent is regarded as a flunky or staff nuisance. Thanks to John, I have considerable influence here.

I think it's a crime to see him badgered by some segments of the community and some of the new-breed board members. They come in with half-baked ideas by the bushel and no real sense of their implications. Then they try to shove them down our throats, and by the time it is clear that they won't work, the instigators have left the board and start pestering the planning board or police commissioner."

Lake has reviewed Kneep's request for the new course to be made a permanent elective and recommends it be rejected. In his report, he states:

... my opinions are based on my own experience plus interviews with all parties. I have carefully reviewed the course syllabus and find insufficient evidence of intellectual or methodological substance to justify its place in our curriculum.

Although there is no doubt that this is a popular course with the students, this popularity cannot be linked to intellectual stimulation. Rather, it is a function of their interest in what they call "relevant" issues. It is my belief that today's young people use the term "relevant" to apply to any issue that is sufficiently topical and debatable to lead them to believe that their hastily considered opinions are worth accepting as truths.

The proposed course would cater to only a relatively small number of select students, whereas the school would be better served by innovations that affect most, if not all, students. The quality of our instruction (and our general reputation) is judged by the scores our students make in national tests, and this course would contribute little toward that end. If it were an effort to bring up the lowest percentile of those scores, it would derive stronger support.

Finally, I am certain that this course's popularity is directly traceable to the pedagogical skill of the two teachers involved. I strongly recommend that these skills be applied to existing courses whose proven value to the curriculum deserves their talents. I have discussed this matter with the two department chairman and they both support my recommendation.

ANNE FORSYTHE

"Well, what great matters of state kept you so late tonight?" Hank asked as Anne dropped wearily in a chair.

"I was hoping you wouldn't ask," she replied. "We got a petition tonight signed by several hundred students and parents protesting our decision to drop some courses. Frankly, I didn't even know we had this course, let alone that we were dropping it."

"What is the course about?" Hank asked.

"I haven't the foggiest idea. We spent three hours debating the procedure for approving courses and whether the board should get involved in this kind of issue at all. The board was split right down the middle. Four members made it clear that they feel Lake is too traditional and that Newland is not interested in getting involved in curriculum issues. They want the board involved in curriculum changes. Another four were split between those who sort of agree with the others and those who disagree and think that Lake is right. These four, however, agree that it is wrong for the board to deal with this kind of issue because it opens the way for more and more board involvement in the day to day running of the system. I am certain that had we voted, we would have had a four-four tie."

"Aren't there nine members?" Hank asked.

"Yes," said Anne, "and I'm the ninth. I haven't even passed the bar exam and I feel like a judge. I feel pulled two ways. I agree that Lake is too traditional and slow to change and that Newland won't rock the boat unless we push him. But I don't want the board having to battle with that seasoned old campaigner. Even if we won, we would not know what to do to run the system and we certainly can't fire John."

"Well, how will you vote?"

"I hope I won't have to. John postponed a formal vote and indicated that he would review the recommendation. If he comes in tomorrow night and reverses himself to support the course, we will probably be off the hook. If he doesn't, then I will have to make up my mind. Apparently, the high school principal is wavering in his support. He is new enough to not know what is 'right' but savvy enough to know he is likely to get caught in the middle. Lake is highly regarded by Newland and by most of the teachers. Some of the newer ones get a bit impatient with him, but almost everyone respects him. Well, let's get some sleep."

SANDRA SAVAS

"You can't imagine how surprised and let down, and then mad, I was when Mr. Lake and Mr. Newland vetoed out current school issues course." Sandra Savas sighed. "That course is a great way of capturing student interest and making their school work relevant to the exciting events going on every day. Why the top brass is slapping us down instead of urging us on I just don't understand."

The course had been given on an experimental basis by Sandra Savas and Martin Reis. The enthusiastic response by both students and teachers led to a request that the course be made a regular elective.

Savas came to Merchantville High School as an English teacher two years ago. Because of her strong record in both academic studies and student affairs at Smith College, school officials were pleased when she accepted their offer. Savas has become a popular teacher. She also became immediately active in the county teachers' association, and especially in a workshop concerned with making the study of English more appealing to high school students. In fact, the current social issue experiment was one of the projects fully discussed in the workshop this year.

Martin Reis, who team-taught the social issues course with Savas, is an untypical history teacher. During his fifteen years at Merchantville, he had frequently given special sections of course for bright students, and worked on outside projects with students he felt were motivated to move into college-level studies. He expects and usually gets a lot of work from his students. The joint venture with Savas was quite in character, and the precedent of previous successful ventures contributed to the prompt endorsement of the experimental course by the chairmen of the history and English departments.

THE OUTCOME

Department chairmen in the Merchantville High School have a rather ambiguous position. They are regular teachers, usually with long service at Merchantville, who are asked to "coordinate materials in various courses, assist newly hired teachers, and advise the school principal on personnel matters." Department chairmen are usually given a little relief from teaching because of their duties as chairmen. In a formal sense, however, all teachers report to the principal.

The principal, Dan Kneep, is the administrative head of the school. He has an assistant principal for student counseling and a director of physical education; so he is expected to give much of his time to academic matters. Under the superintendent of schools are building and grounds, personnel, and financial divisions, which serve all the schools in the local system.

From typical day-to-day contracts, the history and English department chairmen have learned about the current social issues course experiment and the formal proposal. Over the years, the history chairman has become quite relaxed about Reis's ventures: He commented to Dan Kneep, "Reis soaks up some juvenile restlessness in a very constructive manner, and since most of his special sections come in the senior year—like this latest one on Social Issues—they don't upset our regular work."

The English department chairman likes Savas's enthusiasm but has explained to her, "We're under pressure to show up well on the state and national achievements tests. There is a lot of public outcry about students not knowing how to spell or write an English sentence, and a school like ours can't afford to be low on the lists."

Savas's response was, "We give more, not less, written work in the social issues course, and I watch the quality of work very closely. I'll guarantee that students in the course have scores well above the average for our senior class. And what's more important, those students will remember the value of clear, clean convincing statements because they see its importance in what they read and in the action reports we ask them to write. Let me show you some—or all—of the reports turned in last Friday."

After further discussion, the English department chairman suggested that Savas and Reis submit a request for switching the course from experimental to regular status. Dan Kneep talked about the proposal with both of the sponsors, complimented them on their initiative, and said he would recommend that the school board approve it.

Six weeks later, word came that "the need to focus resources on higher-priority objectives prevents approval of the suggested course at this time."

"What a shocker that was," said Savas. "I had assumed that with Kneep's endorsement, we were all set. Before taking this Merchantville job, I asked whether teachers had freedom in designing at least some of their own courses. I was assured that 'the school is run on a decentralized basis, because we realize learning depends on the interaction between each teacher and individual students.' And until this turndown, that seemed to be the way it worked."

Savas and Reis talked about what to do next. Reis said, "We just haven't made a clear case. My impression is that plenty of support exists in Merchantville for a course like this, at least as an elective. Because we preach democracy, why don't we let the students and maybe the parents decide whether this is the kind of education they want? We might be wrong ourselves." "O.K.," responded Savas. "I know several students well enough to get their candid opinion, "I'll ask them what they think."

SUMMARY

We have explored a number of concepts in organizational development in the first eleven chapters of this book. In this chapter, we integrate these concepts in the analysis of an organization and how effectively it is functioning. In diagnosing the organizational effectiveness of a school or school system, for example, we have suggested that the leader systematically analyze each of the components of an effective organization. We suggested a series of questions to be asked regarding the structure, culture, leadership, motivation, communication, conflict management process, change process, strategic planning process, decision-making process, the distribution of power in an organization, and whether the leaders in the organization are leading with heart.

By systematically analyzing these components, the educational administrator can ascertain the strengths and weaknesses in a school or school system. The weaknesses identified can be addressed and the organizational health of the school system can be improved in the process. We've concluded this chapter by referring to an organizational diagnosis model that might help the administrator facilitate the process. It is imperative that a newly appointed administrator engage in this process. In addition, periodic organizational analysis and diagnosis is characteristic of effective leadership.

THE DIAGNOSTIC APPROACH

AN INTRODUCTION TO THE CASE-STUDY METHOD

A case study is a written description of a problem or situation requiring analysis and decision. Most cases depict real situations and are based on site visits. In some instances, the data are disguised, and, infrequently, cases are fictional. Typically, a case focuses on a single incident or problem. Cases are not intended to be comprehensive or exhaustive; indeed, most cases are "snapshots" of a particular situation within a complex environment.

The purpose of the case method is to develop and enhance skills in:

- analysis of problems
- decision making
- planning

Normally, this is achieved by efforts to integrate theory and practice and to build on the experiences of participants. The case method allows participants to learn from one another as well as from the material and from faculty members. Because of this, the case method is an especially effective pedagogy for those with experience.

Because it describes reality, case study might be frustrating. "Real life" is ambiguous, and cases reflect that reality. The case method places participants in the role of decision makers, asking them to distinguish pertinent from peripheral facts, to identify central problems among several issues competing for attention, and to formulate policy recommendations. In the case method, participants are obliged to deal with such data as are available: a "right" answer or "correct" solution is rarely apparent. Differences among participants and faculty members typically arise, and conflicting recommendations emerge as participants with varied perspectives, experience, and professional responsibilities consider the case.

The preparation of a case for class varies with the background, concerns, and natural interests of participants. In general, however, preparing for class discussion involves these steps:

- reading the case carefully to establish the facts,
- determining the decisions that need to be made,
- considering the consequences of decisions, and articulating priorities and alternatives,
- developing recommendations and making decisions.

A helpful next step in preparing a case is to meet with a small group to review data, compare analyses, and suggest strategies.

The differences that emerge through discussion add richness and dimension to consideration of the issues. The faculty member's role is to involve many participants in presenting and defending their analyses and recommendations. The faculty member moderates discussion calling on participants, guiding the discussion, asking questions, and synthesizing comments. Discussion is intended to develop and test the nature and implications of alternate solutions.

Diagnosis is an important skill for effective educational administrators. The diagnostic approach to organizational development and problem solving is proposed as an effective way of analyzing case studies. This approach includes four phases: (1) description, (2) diagnosis, (3) prescription, and (4) action.

DESCRIPTION

Phase 1, description, is simply that: a reporting of concrete aspects of or events in a specific situation without any attempt to explain the reasons for the events or to make inferences about a person's motives or purposes.

The process of simple description is much more difficult than it looks: Sometimes, it is not easy to separate facts from assumptions. Most of us have little practice in making such a separation. Yet, effective diagnosis and understanding of the situation depend on a valid and factual description of it. The better we can describe situations, the better we will understand them.

How can we obtain information that allows us to describe events, behaviors, and attitudes accurately? Administrators and organizational developers primarily use four methods for collecting data about situations they face or analyze: direct observation, questionnaires, interviews, and written documents. Each of these methods helps us to report events, not to diagnose their causes or effects. Together, these methods help us validate our perceptions of the events.

DIAGNOSIS

The next phase, diagnosis, attempts to explain the reasons for, or causes of, the behaviors and attitudes described. This book offered a number of theories that people studying organizational behavior have developed to explain why events such as these occur. You can then use these theories to diagnose the situations or problems that exist. You can apply them in sequence and test whether they help you understand the situation better. Once you know and understand the theories, you can choose the most appropriate ones to use in diagnosis.

In this book, we take a specific approach to diagnosis: We assume that events, behaviors, and attitudes that occur in institutions typically have more than one cause and that it is important to try to understand the cause as fully as possible. The more completely we understand the cause, the more appropriately we will act in problem-solving situations.

PRESCRIPTION

Phase 3, prescription, involves identifying, reviewing, evaluating, and then deciding on a desired course of action for particular circumstances and based on the foregoing diagnosis. Prescription is the first part of translating diagnosis, or your understanding of a situation, into action. Educational administrators must act in problem situations and other organizational situations; they do not have the luxury of simply understanding them, although understanding alone can have value and relevance also. In the prescription phase the administrator must propose ways of correcting the problems identified in the diagnosis phase.

Most problem situations have no single correct response, in part because the problems are complex. Thus, we would begin the prescription phase by proposing multiple solutions to diagnosed problems. We might recommend redesigning work, modifying the reward system, or ensuring direct communication as ways of addressing motivation problems, for example. We might propose organizational restructuring, defining the goals, or the introduction of new responsibilities as ways of dealing with conflict between groups.

In this book, you have been asked to suggest solutions to problems, to develop specific courses of action for different situations. You are then asked to evaluate the solutions proposed in terms of the models and theories discussed, and to test whether the recommended changes should result in the desired outcomes.

You should consider as many reasonable, feasible, and practical alternative solutions to each problem or behavioral concern diagnosed as possible. Evaluate these alternatives and their effectiveness by using the relevant theoretical models to predict the outcomes of the various approaches. Determine the advantages and disadvantages or each alternative. Then select the alternative with the relatively fewest disadvantages and highest number of advantages.

ACTION

The final phase, action, is the implementation of the solutions you propose. Often, we know the correct solution, but cannot apply it. Action might involve testing the prescription in a limited part of the educational institution. Pilot programs are frequently used to implement change in institutions in measured, observable ways.

Action involves a careful scrutiny of all individuals and other systems in the organization to plan for the impact of the changes. It means determining what resistances to change exist and planning strategies and activities to overcome them. Implementing staffing or policy changes might require the introduction of new education programs; new resources might be necessary to support the new programs. The effects of action could have a domino effect throughout the institution.

In this book, you have been given opportunities to test your ideas to see how they work in different problem situations. You can act as an administrator would act in a given situation. You will then have the opportunity to evaluate these actions and consider ways of improving leadership behavior. And so the cycle may start again. As part of the evaluation, you will describe your own and others' behavior and attitudes. Then, you can diagnose the reasons the behavior succeeded or failed, offer new prescriptions, and once more act.

PORTFOLIOS

Accumulating a portfolio of examples of one's achievements and progress toward becoming an accomplished professional is a popular exercise in education these days. It is thought to be a more authentic way of accessing an individual's performance and progress than the more traditional forms of assessment like pencil-and-paper tests. The diagnostic approach suggested in this book lends itself very nicely to accumulating an impressive portfolio of one's ability to effectively analyze situations and suggest alternatives for improvement.

The reader might wish to include in his or her portfolio each case analysis that he or she completes. The completed portfolio can be presented during an interview for an administration position as an indication of the applicant's ability to be an effective educational manager and leader. An example of case history in which the diagnostic approach has been applied follows this discussion. A collection of analyzed case studies such as this can constitute an impressive portfolio for potential administrators and leaders.

●II

AN ONLINE COURSE SYLLABUS: ADMINISTRATION, ORGANIZATIONAL CULTURE, AND PLANNED CHANGE (EDU 4505)

Dr. Robert H. Palestini

TABLE OF CONTENTS

After completing the course, the student should be able to demonstrate the following competencies and be able to:

1. Outline the diagnostic approach to analyzing an organization like a school or school system and identify the basic elements of an organizational system.

2. Identify the major historical perspectives of organizational thought and utilize them in analyzing an organization's strengths and weaknesses.

3. Understand the systems framework and use it to analyze an organization.

4. Describe the processes of perception, attribution, and learning within an organization.

5. Identify the major motivational theories and reward systems.

6. Describe the evolution of leadership theory and practice.

7. Develop an effective process of communication in an organization.

8. Identify the steps in the decision making and change processes.

9. Understand the various methods of resolving conflict in an organization.

10. Develop a plan to improve organizational effectiveness.

11. Develop the use of organizational and interpersonal skills related to living in a multicultural society.

12. Diagnose the strengths and weaknesses of an organization and develop and implement the changes necessary to improve the functioning of the organization (engage in organizational development).

Level One: What content (facts, details, concepts, terminology) will students need to be familiar with in your course?

- Historical perspectives of organizational development
- The various types of organizational structures
- The components of an organization's culture
- The various theories of leadership
- The various theories of motivation
- The steps in an effective communication process
- The methods of resolving conflict in an organization
- The steps in the strategic-planning process
- The steps in the decision-making process
- How power is exerted in an organization
- The steps in the process of change
- The need for the human touch in educational administration

Students will need to learn the following procedures, techniques, or methods:

Level Two: What procedures, techniques, or methods will they need to learn?

- How to accurately diagnose the strengths and weaknesses of an organization and prescribe ways of addressing the weaknesses in order to improve the organization (the organization development process).
- Acquire the knowledge and skills to be able to effect change or improvement in an organization.

Students will be expected to master the following higher-order thinking skills:

Level Three: What higher-order thinking skills (processes, strategies) do you want students to develop in this course?

- The process of diagnosing an organization's weaknesses and prescribing corrective measures
- The process of strategic planning for change
- The change process as it affects the organizational structure, culture, leadership, communication, motivation, power structure, decision making, and conflict management

Please reflect on your thinking about the evidence you will need to observe to determine if students have mastered the competencies in your course.

- Students will demonstrate their competencies in the one-page case study analysis that is required for each of the topics addressed in the course.
- They will also demonstrate their competencies in the classroom discussions surrounding the case studies.
- Finally, they will demonstrate their competencies in developing and analyzing their own case study.

In Worksheet 1, you identified the strategic knowledge students need to learn in your course. For the purposes of the CADE workshop, we will build our competencies around this strategic knowledge. Now consider the following question, how will you know that students have mastered or achieved a particular competency?

Competencies: List the strategic knowledge you want students to develop in your course (refer to worksheet 1–level 3).

Evidence: Identify the evidence (student thinking or behavior) that will indicate students have mastered these competencies. Include specific abilities involved in the competency, artifacts students can develop as a result of mastering the competency, and characteristics of student behavior that indicate mastery.

- Diagnosing an organization's strengths and weaknesses.
- Prescribing corrective measures.
- Mastering the strategic planning process.
- Mastering the process of change.
- Applying organizational theory to practice.

- Accurately analyzing a series of case studies whereby the student is able to correctly identify the strengths and weaknesses of the organization in the case study and identify ways of building on the strengths and correcting the weaknesses.
- Developing a strategic plan that would operationalize the suggestions and recommendations made in the case study.
- Develop a plan for bringing about the changes needed to improve the organization.
- Provide evidence of implementing the planned change successfully.

Please reflect on the "thinking" skills that are used by various levels of expertise

- Experts are able to use higher-order thinking skills, such as analysis, understanding, generalization, summarizing, and prescribing.
- Recent graduates will also use these higher-order thinking skills.
- Novices might reflect higher-order thinking skills, but might not be able to apply them because they do not have the content knowledge required.

Assessment	Analysis
Identify one of your level-3 competencies and then describe the assessment that will provide the evidence you identified in Worksheet 2 for that competency.	Diagnosing an organization's strengths and weaknesses.

Prompting Questions:	Expert	Recent Graduate	Novice to the Program
What are the strategies or processes an expert, a recent graduate, or a novice will use to approach or solve this problem?	An expert would run through the 10 or so important facets of an organization and analyze whether the organization reflects acceptable practices in these areas.	A recent graduate would go through the same process as the expert, but would not have the experience to know exactly how to address the deficiencies identified.	A novice would literally not know where to start.
What features of the problem or situation will they focus on?	Experts would focus on the organizational structure, culture, leadership, motivation, decision making, planning, conflict management, distribution of power, communication, and the process of change in the organization.	Recent graduates will consider the same areas, but would not have the experience to understand the nuances involved.	Novices would only be able to identify a few of these areas on which to focus.

What will they take into consideration as they attempt the problem?	Experts will take into consideration all of the above facets of an organization.	Recent graduates will also take into consideration all of the above facets.	Novices would only take a few of the facets listed into consideration.
What content will be necessary tools for them to reach a solution or make a decision?	Experts would need to know the basic facets or dimensions of an organization.	Recent graduates would also need to know the basic facets of an organization.	Novices would have to have the same content knowledge as experts and recent graduates to reach a solution. Because they do not yet have this content knowledge, they will not be able to effectively reach a solution.
What actions or behaviors would exhibit the ability to think analytically with respect to this problem?	Experts would be able to analyze a case study and correctly determine the strengths and weaknesses of an organization.	Recent Graduates would be able to analyze a case study and correctly determine the strengths and weaknesses of an organization.	Novices would most likely not be able to correctly determine the strengths and weaknesses in the case study.

To complete this worksheet, you must identify an assessment in which you will see the evidence of student mastery of a competency. Identify the competency, then choose a typical "problem" situation in your discipline: case study, argumentative essay, journal entry) that assesses the competency. Next, describe, to the best of your ability, the behaviors or characteristics of the thinking process of an expert, a recent graduate, and a novice if they were given the assessment. Use the questions at the left to guide your thinking.

Please reflect on your thinking about the course outline; you need to support the competencies you will teach in your online course.

ADMINISTRATION, ORGANIZATIONAL CULTURE & PLANNED CHANGE

Spring 2004

Dr. Robert Palestini

Course Description

This course is rooted in the diagnostic approach: describing, understanding, and explaining behavior in organizations, especially schools and school systems. It considers various methods for managing and influencing human behavior. The key components or subsystems of administration are reviewed, including: management theories, decision making, communications, leadership, organizational structures, and change processes. Individual and group behavior is examined with emphasis placed on motivational techniques, reward systems, performance assessment, and conflict management. Readings, case studies, and exercises are utilized.

Course Assignments

Student assessments will include class participation, case-study discussions, case-study analyses for each class session, and a final case study development and analysis.

Grading Policy

Grades will be assigned according to the grade policy in the graduate catalog. The following assignments will be used in the grading process:

Case Study Analyses	60%
Class Participation	10%
Final Case Study	30%

Required Text

Palestini, Robert H. *Educational Administration: Leading with Mind and Heart*, 2nd edition. Lanham, Md.: Scarecrow Press, 2004.

Session One: Introduction to Organizational Development
Description of Session:

Course introduction
Introduction of instructor
Introduction of students
Review syllabus
Course objectives
Introduction to competencies (what students will take away from the
    course)
Course schedule
Explain blackboard and other technology issues
Diagnosis of a case study

Competencies

Understanding the overall goals of the course.
Understanding the process of diagnosing a case study.

Evidence of Mastery

Students will be able to articulate the goals of the course.
Students will be able to analyze a case study by diagnosing the orga-
    nization's strengths and weaknesses and prescribing interventions
    to correct the weaknesses.

Assignments

Submit a one-page analysis of the case study on organizational structure.
Read the chapter of the text entitled, Organizational Structure.
Be prepared to discuss the case study on organizational structure in the
next class session.

Resources

Read Chapters 1 & 2 in *Educational Administration: Leading with Mind and Heart.*

Session Two: Organizational Structure
Description of Session

This session is designed to expose students to the various facets of organizational structure. Being aware of the organizational structure of a school or school system is the first step in effective school administration. It is the administrator's means of "knowing the territory." In this session, the various theories of organizational structure will be discussed and explored.

Competencies Involved

After completing the readings and activities in this session, the student will be able to:

- Cite reasons why an understanding of organizational structure is important to school administration.
- Identify, compare, and contrast the major periods and perspectives in the history of organizational thought.
- Comment on the way contingency theory addresses the shortcomings of previous theories of organizational structure.
- Engage in the process of analyzing and diagnosing the effectiveness of an institution's organizational structure and prescribing measures to change and improve it.

Evidence of Mastery

The students will be able to accurately analyze and diagnose a case study and determine the structural strengths and weaknesses of the organization and suggest interventions to address the weaknesses.

Assignments

Students are required to submit a one-page analysis of an assigned case study on organizational structure.

Resources

Students are required to read the chapter on organizational structure in *Educational Administration: Leading with Mind and Heart*. They are also required to research and read one supplementary journal article on organizational structure and submit a copy of the article with their case study analysis.

Session Three: Organizational Culture
Description of Session

In addition to organizational structure, the other half of "knowing the territory" for the school administrator is to be aware of the organizational behavior or culture of a school. Organizational culture is composed of the shared beliefs, expectations, values, and norms of conduct of its members. In any organization, the informal culture interacts with the formal organizational structure and control system to produce a generally clear understanding of the "way things are done around here." Even more than the forces of bureaucracy, the organization's culture is the glue that binds people together. It is through this culture that our images of reality are shaped, often in an unconscious manner.

Competencies Involved

After completing the readings and activities in this session, the student will be able to:

- Describe school culture and its relationship to team performance.
- Describe the process of perception and show how perceptual biases influence effective action.

- Describe the process of attribution and illustrate the way attributional biases influence effective action.
- Differentiate among and identify the factors of three models of learning.
- Illustrate the process of attitude formation and cite two strategies for influencing attitudes.
- Describe ways of assessing attitudes in schools.
- Engage in the process of analyzing and diagnosing the effectiveness of an institution's organizational culture and prescribing measures to change and improve it.

Evidence of Mastery

The students will be able to accurately analyze and diagnose a case study and determine the strengths and weaknesses of the organizational culture and suggest interventions to address the weaknesses.

Assignments

Students are required to submit a one-page analysis of an assigned case study on organizational culture.

Resources

Students are required to read the chapter on organization culture in *Educational Administration: Leading with Mind and Heart.* They are also required to research and read one supplementary journal article on organizational culture and submit a copy of the article with their case study analysis.

The viewing of the video *Prima Donnas* with a follow-up discussion will be part of this session.

The Gregoric Leaning Style Inventory and the Personal Profile System Survey are administered in this session.

Session Four: Leadership Theory
Description of Session

Leadership is offered as a solution for most of the problems of organizations everywhere. Schools will work, we are told, if principals provide strong instructional leadership. Around the world, administrators and managers say that their organizations would thrive if only senior management provided strategy, vision, and real leadership. Though the call for leadership is universal, there is much less clarity about what the term means.

Historically, researchers in this field have searched for the one best leadership style that would be most effective. Current thought is that there is no one best style. Rather, a combination of styles depending on the situation the leaders finds himself or herself in has been found to be more effective. To understand the evolution of leadership-theory thought, we will take a historical approach and trace the progress of leadership theory, beginning with the trait perspective of leadership and moving to the more current contingency theories of leadership.

Competencies Involved

After completing this session, the student will be able to:

- Show how trait theories contributed to our understanding of effective leadership.
- Show how the behavioral perspective of leadership contributed to our understanding of leadership.
- Describe the early situational theories and their implications for effective leadership.
- Offer a prescription for becoming a transformational leader.
- Offer a strategy for effective educational leadership, given a knowledge of the school's culture.
- Engage in the process of analyzing and diagnosing the effectiveness of the leadership styles present within an institution and prescribe ways of improving it.

Evidence of Mastery

Students will be required to analyze a case study dealing with leadership and diagnose the leadership strengths and weaknesses of the institution in the case study and suggest interventions that would address the leadership weaknesses.

Assignments

Students will be required to analyze a case study on leadership and present a one-page diagnosis and prescription of the case study.

Resources

Chapter 2 of the course textbook should be read, and at least one journal article of leadership should be acquired and read.

Session Five: Motivation in the Workplace
Description of Session

The next step in preparing oneself to be an effective administrator is to adopt an approach to motivate one's colleagues to attain the educational vision that has been jointly developed. To begin the process, you might ask yourself: What motivates individuals to behave, think, or feel in certain ways? What factors make you or others more willing to work, to be creative, to achieve, to produce? Theory and research in the area of motivation provide a systematic way of diagnosing the degree of motivation and of prescribing ways of increasing it. There are basically two views of motivation. One view posits that individuals are motivated by inherited, conflicting, and unconscious drives. This view, which was popularized by Freud and Jung, and more recently by Skinner, Maslow, and Glasser, is operationalized through the so-called content theories of motivation.

The other view of motivation says that an individual is basically rational and is normally conscious of his or her pursuit of goals. Plato and Aristotle, and, more recently, Jerome Bruner, are associated with this view. This perspective has spawned the so-called process theories of motivation, including the equity theory, expectancy theory, and goal-setting theory.

Competencies Involved

After completing this session, the student will be able to:

- Identify, compare, and contrast the major needs theories.
- Discuss the application of equity in educational settings.
- Comment about the used of various types of schedules of reinforcement.
- Use expectancy theory and goal-setting theory to diagnose motivational deficiencies.
- Describe the design and incentive system.
- Discuss the role of employee ownership in the reward system.
- Specify the characteristics of an effective reward system in an educational setting.
- Describe what is meant by a situational theory of motivation.
- Engage in the process of analyzing and diagnosing the effectiveness of the motivational techniques present in an institution and prescribe ways of improving it.

Evidence of Mastery

Students will effectively analyze a case study involving the motivational practices of a school and suggest ways of improving any motivational deficiencies.

Assignments

Students will submit a one-page analysis of a case study on motivation.

Resources

Chapter 3 of the course text should be read and one journal article on motivation should be acquired and read.

Session Six: Organizational Communication
Description of Session

One of the perennial complaints of school personnel is a lack of communication between themselves and another segment of the school community. Oftentimes, the greatest perceived "communications gap" is between the faculty and the administration. Therefore, if an administrator is to be effective, he or she must master the skill of effective communication.

In this session, we examine the nature of effective communication, a central organizational process that can occur at the intrapersonal, interpersonal, intragroup, intergroup, institutional, and public levels. As a linking mechanism among the various organizational subsystems, communication is a central feature of the structure of groups and organizations. It builds and reinforces interdependence between and among the various parts of the institution.

In this session, we first describe the communication process and then its five components: encoding, transmission, decoding, noise, and feedback. Next, we look at downward, upward, and lateral communication and discuss how interpersonal relations and attitudes affect the quality of communication, as well as issues of informal communication. We continue by presenting a set of strategies for improving communication accuracy.

Competencies Involved

After completing the reading and activities in this session, the student will be able to:

- Describe, illustrate, and identify the communication process and diagnose dysfunctions in it.
- Discuss the role of language, listening, noise, and feedback in communication.
- Discuss how interpersonal relationships affect the accuracy of communication.
- Specify the barriers to effective communication and propose strategies for reducing them.

- Specify and illustrate the dimensions of a supportive communication climate.
- Compare an assertive style to aggressive and passive styles and illustrate its use.
- Offer guidelines for increasing the effectiveness of interviews in educational institutions.
- Engage in the process of analyzing and diagnosing the effectiveness of the communication process in an institution and prescribe ways of improving it.

Evidence of Mastery

Students will be able to accurately analyze a case study on communication in an institution.

Assignments

Students are required to submit a one-page analysis of a case study on communication.

Resources

Chapter 4 of the course text should be read and one journal article on communication should be acquired and read.

Session Seven: Conflict Management
Description of Session

Several years ago, we invited Dr. Janet Baker, a well-known authority on conflict, to address a group of principals at a Principal's Academy offered at Saint Joseph's University in Philadelphia. We introduced Dr. Baker's topic as "conflict resolution." Upon taking the podium, Dr. Baker quickly corrected us and said that she was there to talk about "conflict management," not conflict resolution. "If your goal as a principal is to resolve conflict, you will be doomed to frustration and failure," she said. "The best that you can hope for is to *manage* conflict.

In this session, we begin our study of conflict management by considering the nature of conflict in organizations, especially schools. We will look at its levels, stages, and consequences. We then introduce special issues associated with intergroup relations. After describing the typical ways groups interact, as well as the behavioral and attitudinal consequences of these interactions, we examine three influences on these interactions: perceptual differences, task issues, and power differences between groups. The chapter concludes with an examination of prescriptions for dealing with conflict and improving the relations between groups.

Competencies Involved

After completing the readings and activities in this session, the student will be able to:

- Predict the outcomes of conflict in an organization.
- Diagnose the level and stage of conflict in an organization.
- Describe four types of interdependent groups and their behavioral and attitudinal consequences.
- Show how the nature of task relations can create conflict.
- Comment about the way power differences influence intergroup relations.
- Describe a range of strategies for dealing with conflict and intergroup interactions between groups.
- Offer a protocol for managing relations between culturally diverse groups.
- Engage in the process of analyzing and diagnosing the effectiveness of the management of conflict in an institution and prescribe interventions for improving it.

Evidence of Mastery

Students will be required to analyze a case study dealing with conflict management and diagnose the occasions of conflict in the institution in the case study and suggest interventions that would manage the conflict.

Assignments

Students will be required to analyze a case study on conflict management and present a one-page diagnosis and prescription of the case study. One journal research article on conflict management should be acquired and read. A copy should be included with the case study analysis.

Resources

Chapter 5 on the course textbook should be read, and at least one journal article on conflict management should be acquired and read.

Session Eight: The Strategic Planning Process
Description of Session

Strategic planning is a process that was first developed and refined in business and industry, but has been adopted by a variety of educational institutions throughout the nation. In some states, the process is mandated for all public schools. In this session, we discuss the components of the planning process and some successful planning models.

Competencies Involved

After completing this session, the student will be able to:

- Develop and utilize an academic planning process.
- Describe and define the components of a system planning process.
- Describe a typical strategic planning process.
- Recognize the primacy of the planning process over the plan itself.
- Engage in the process of analyzing and diagnosing the effectiveness of an institution's strategic plan and prescribe ways of improving it.

Evidence of Mastery

Students will be required to analyze a case study on leadership and present a one-page diagnosis and prescription of the case study.

Assignments

Chapter 7 of the course textbook should be read, and at least one journal article on strategic planning should be acquired and read. A copy of the journal article should accompany the one-page case study analysis.

Resources

Chapter 7 of the course textbook and the journal article will be the resources for this session.

Session Nine: Decision Making
Description of Session

Suppose Will Smith was appointed to the position of superintendent of schools for the Rose Tree School District with the express purpose to rightsize the school district in light of its declining student population. Having been successful in a similar situation in another school district, how should Will Smith proceed?

In this session, we begin by examining the nature of decision makers. Next, we look at the types of decisions managers and other organizational members make and the information they use to make decisions. Then, we specify the characteristics of effective decisions, including issues of quality, acceptance, and ethical decision making. We also compare and contrast individual and group decision making. Finally, we propose ways of improving decision making.

Competencies Involved

After completing this session, the student will be able to:

- Delineate the context of the decision-making process.
- Identify the types of decision-making processes used in educational institutions.

- Cite the criteria of effective decisions and apply them to decision making.
- Comment about the characteristics of an ethical decision.
- Trace the steps in the rational decision-making process.
- Contrast the rational process to alternative decision-making processes.
- Compare and contrast the value and use of individual and group decision making.
- Offer at least three strategies for improving individual decision making.
- Engage in the process of analyzing and diagnosing the effectiveness of an institution's decision-making processes and prescribe measures to improve them.

Evidence of Mastery

Students will be required to analyze a case study dealing with decision making and diagnose the strengths and weaknesses of the institution in the case study and suggest interventions that would address the decision-making weaknesses.

Assignments

Students will be required to analyze a case study on decision making and present a one-page diagnoses and prescription of the case study. They will also submit a copy of a journal article on decision making that they have researched.

Resources

Chapter 8 of the course textbook should be read, and at least one journal article on decision-making should be acquired and read. A video on the decision-making process used by President Kennedy in the Cuban Missile Crisis will be shown and discussed.

Session Ten: Employee Empowerment
Description of Session

Charlotte Burton is the new principal of Springfield High School. She met Marie Wilson, the teacher union representative, on her first day at the school. The two women were both strong-willed individuals who had reached their respective positions by aggressively pursuing their professional goals. They were both intent on showing the other who was "boss."

This scenario is not unlike many that occur at educational institutions of all levels. This situation reflects the exercise of power in an organization. Power is the potential or actual ability to influence others in a desired direction. An individual, group, or other social unit has power if it controls information, knowledge, or resources desired by another individual, group, or social unit.

Who has the power in the situation described at Springfield High School? Recognizing, using, and dealing with power differences is implicit in negotiation, which is a process for reconciling different, often incompatible, interests of interdependent parties. At Springfield High School, both Charlotte Burton and Marie Wilson have power. How well each uses her power and negotiation skills will determine her effectiveness.

In this session, we examine power and the negotiation process. After considering the reasons individuals or groups exert power, we examine the sources from which they derive power. Next, we explore the use of negotiations. We describe two bargaining paradigms, the negotiation process, and strategies and tactics of negotiations.

Competencies Involved

After completing this session, the student will be able to:

- Show the relationship between power and dependence.
- Diagnose the extent, location, and types of power in an organization.
- Cite courses of powerlessness and strategies for empowering others.
- Offer ways of securing more power and discuss the ethical issues involved.
- Compare and contrast the distributive and integrative bargaining paradigms.
- Develop an effective collective bargaining process.
- Engage in the process of analyzing and diagnosing the effectiveness with which the power is distributed in an institution and prescribe ways of improving its distribution.

Evidence of Mastery

Students will be required to analyze a case study dealing with power issues and diagnose the power relationships in the school and suggest interventions that would address any power inequities.

Assignments

Students will be required to analyze a case study on power issues and present a one-page diagnosis and prescription of the case study. They will also read at least one journal article on power and negotiations.

Resources

Chapter 9 of the course textbook should be read, and at least one journal article on power distribution should be researched and read.

Session Eleven: The Change Process
Description of Session

Changing an educational institution or system has been described as being like making a U-turn with the Queen Elizabeth II. In some cases, resistance to change is so extreme that this is an understatement.

Despite its difficulty, the process of change is absolutely necessary if an organization is to continually improve. Thus, to be an effective leader, especially in the transformational style, an administrator must become a change agent and master the process that can bring change about effectively. In this session, we discuss a variety of processes and techniques that enhance the administrator's chances of effecting change successfully. One of these is a ten-step process that I have personally found effective.

Competencies Involved

After completing this session, the student will be able to:

- Describe an approach to changing organizations.
- Diagnose the forces that affect change and offer ways of strengthening or weakening them.

- Identify possible change agents and the advantages and disadvantages of using each type.
- Offer a protocol for implementing changes in organizations.
- Identify the key issues in transforming an organization.
- List steps in evaluating an organizational change.
- Suggest ways of institutionalizing successful change.
- Engage in the process of analyzing and diagnosing an institution's tolerance for change and prescribe measures for improving it.

Evidence of Mastery

Students will be required to analyze a case study dealing with the process of change and diagnose the strengths and weaknesses of the plan in the case study and suggest interventions that would address the weaknesses in the plan.

Assignments

Students will be required to analyze a case study on the process of change and submit a one-page diagnosis and prescription of the case study. They will also be required to research a journal article on change.

Resources

Chapter 6 of the course textbook should be read, and the book *Ten Steps to Educational Reform* by Robert Palestini should be read.

Session Twelve: Leading with Heart
Description of Session

How the leader utilizes the concepts contained in the first eleven sessions of this course depends largely on his or her philosophy of how human beings behave in the workplace. The two extremes of the continuum might be described as those leaders who believe that human beings are basically lazy and will do the very least that they need to do to "get by" in the workplace. And those who believe that people are basically industrious and, if given the choice, would opt for doing a quality job. I believe that today's most effective leaders hold the latter view. I agree with Max DePree, owner and CEO of the highly successful Herman Miller Furniture Company. Writing in his book *Leadership Is an Art,* DePree says that a leader's function is to "liberate people to do what is required of them in the most effective and humane way possible." Instead of catching people doing something wrong, our goal as enlightened leaders is to catch them doing something right. I would suggest, therefore, that in addition to a rational approach to leadership, a truly enlightened leader leads with heart.

Competencies Involved

After completing this session, the student will be able to:

- Describe what leading with heart implies.
- Understand the importance of the concept of "employee owner- ship" in the effectiveness of decision making.
- Understand the importance of trust and respect in the effective or- ganization.
- Comment on the concept of "employees as volunteers."
- Identify the signs of heartlessness in an organization.
- Prescribe strategies for building trust and respect in an organiza- tion and setting the stage for leading with heart.

Evidence of Mastery

Students will be required to analyze a case study on leading with heart and diagnose the strengths and weaknesses in that regard and suggest interventions that would address those weaknessess.

Assignments

Students will be required to analyze a case study on leading with heart and submit a one-page diagnosis and prescription of the case study. They will also read *The Human Touch in Educational Leadership,* by Robert Palestini.

Resources

Chapter 11 of the course textbook should be read, and *The Human Touch in Educational Leadership* should also be read.

Session Thirteen: Organizational Effectiveness (Putting It All Together)
Description of Session

In this session, we draw together the concepts discussed in the earlier chapters and use them in an integrated fashion to engage in an organizational diagnosis that will evaluate the institutional health of an educational entity. An organizational diagnosis requires the educational administrator to systematically analyze the various aspects of the educational institution. Periodic review and analysis of the structure, culture, leadership, motivation, communication, conflict management, process of change, strategic plan, decision-making, and the distribution of power in an institution need to take place if the institution is to remain viable.

Competencies Involved

After completing this session, the student will be able to:

- Suggest a model for organizational diagnosis.
- Use the organizational concepts learned in previous session in an integrated fashion to engage in the process of systematically analyzing and diagnosing the organizational health of an education institution and prescribe ways of improving it.

Evidence of Mastery

Students will be required to develop their own case study and diagnose the organizational strengths and weaknesses in their study and prescribe ways of addressing the weaknesses.

Assignments

Students will be required to develop their own comprehensive case study and to analyze it according to the process of organization development presented in this course. They should read Chapter 10 in the course textbook to aid them in developing and analyzing the case study.

Resources

Chapter 10 of the course textbook should be read.

Please reflect on the teaching strategies you will use in your online course.

- Classroom discussion around the case study that is prepared for each session.
- Very limited lecture to clarify the more complex processes covered.
- Individual and group presentations.
- Audio/video and Power Point presentations.

Learning Activity	**Please select one of your level-3 competencies. Describe the learning activities you will use in your online course to teach the competency. Below indicate how you will apply the cognitive apprenticeship strategies.** Competency: The change process as it affects the organizational structure, culture, leadership, communication, motivation, power structure, decision making, and conflict management.
Modeling *How and where will you demonstrate the thinking process needed to master this competency?*	Initially, I will demonstrate how to analyze a case study and then compose a sample analysis. Once the students have mastered the format for composing a case study, my comments regarding the case studies that they submit will model for them what the ideal analysis would look like.
Coaching *How will you guide students as they try to complete tasks?*	I will make extensive comments and corrections on the one-page case studies that will be submitted for each session of the course. I will, in effect, be coaching them regarding how they should have analyzed the case study. This is a developmental process whereby the last case studies should be accepted without any corrections by me.
Scaffolding *How will you incorporate hints and tips that will help students remember how your want them to think?*	The method of analyzing a case study is to be consistently applied. I will see to it that in my comments I constantly stress this consistency.
Reflection: *How will you encourage students to look back over their*	I will encourage students to use what they learned in one case study analysis on the next one. Thus, by the end of the course, they should be submitting flawless analyses.

efforts to complete a task and analyze their own performance?

Articulation
How will you encourage articulation among students to give reasons for their decisions and strategies, thus making their domain and strategic knowledge more explicit?

The case-study method of analysis, which includes a diagnosis of the situation presented and a prescription to improve the situation, requires that students provide the rationale for their recommendations and suggestions. They will share their analyses with the other students and elicit feedback.

Exploration
How will you promote explorative opportunities for students to try out different strategies and hypotheses and observe their effects?

The opportunity to try different strategies is included in the prescriptive portion of the case study, where students are asked to speculate on ways in which the organization can be improved.

Fading
How will you gradually reduce the amount of support you provide to students, shifting more and more of the control to the learner?

By the end of the course, I will have weaned the students away from a dependence on the instructor, and they will become independent learners who can address an organizational problem and suggest appropriate interventions without the assistance and facilitation of the instructor.

Please reflect on how you will use the "storyboard" technique to design media elements for your course.

Session I	Introduction
Session II	Organizational Structure
Session III	Organizational Culture A. Prima Donna Video
Session IV	Leadership Theory
Session V	Motivation
Session VI	The Planning Process
Session VII	The Decision-Making Process A. The Cuban Missile Crisis Video
Session VIII	Conflict Management
Session IX	The Distribution of Power
Session X	The Process of Change A. Paradigms Video
Session XI	Leading with Heart

SCENE	VIDEO	AUDIO/NARRATIVE
One	Prima Donna	Soundtrack on video
One	Cuban Missile Crisis	Soundtrack on video
One	Paradigms	Soundtrack on video

⬛

INTERSTATE SCHOOL LEADERS LICENSURE STANDARDS FOR SCHOOL LEADERS

Standard I

A school administrator is an educational leader who promotes the success of all students by facilitating the development, articulation, implementation, and stewardship of a vision of learning that is shared and supported by the school community.

- Facilitate the development of a shared vision for the achievement of all students based upon data from multiple measures of student learning and relevant qualitative indicators.
- Communicate the shared vision so the entire school community understands and acts on the school's mission to become a standards-based education system.
- Use the influence of diversity to improve teaching and learning.
- Identify and address any barriers to accomplishing the vision.
- Shape school programs, plans, and activities to ensure that they are integrated, articulated through the grades, and consistent with the vision.
- Leverage and marshal sufficient resources, including technology, to implement and attain the vision for all students and all subgroups of students.

Standard 2

A school administrator is an educational leader who promotes the success of all students by advocating, nurturing, and sustaining a school culture and instructional program conducive to student learning and staff professional growth.

- Shape a culture in which high expectations are the norm for each student as evident in rigorous academic work.
- Promote equity, fairness, and respect among all members of the school community.
- Facilitate the use of a variety of appropriate content-based learning materials and learning strategies that: recognize students as active learners, value reflection and inquiry, emphasize the quality versus the amount of student application and performance, and utilize appropriate and effective technology.
- Guide and support the long-term professional development of all staff consistent with the ongoing effort to improve the learning of all students relative to the content standards.
- Provide opportunities for all members of the school community to develop and use skills in collaboration, distributed leadership, and shared responsibility.
- Create an accountability system grounded in standards-based teaching and learning.
- Utilize multiple assessments to evaluate student learning in an ongoing process focused on improving the academic performance of each student.

Standard 3

A school administrator is an educational leader who promotes the success of all students by ensuring management of the organization, operations, and resources for a safe, efficient, and effective learning environment

- Sustain a safe, efficient, clean, well-maintained, and productive school environment that nurtures student learning and supports the professional growth of teachers and support staff.

- Utilize effective and nurturing practices in establishing student behavior management systems.
- Establish school structures and processes that support student learning.
- Utilize effective systems management, organizational development, and problem-solving and decision-making techniques.
- Align fiscal, human, and material resources to support the learning all subgroups of students.
- Monitor and evaluate the program and staff.
- Manage legal and contractual agreements and records in ways that foster a processional work environment and secure privacy and confidentiality for all students and staff.

Standard 4

A school administrator is an educational leader who promotes the success of all students by collaborating with families and community members, responding to diverse community interests and needs, and mobilizing community resources.

- Recognize and respect the goals and aspirations of diverse family and community groups.
- Treat diverse community stakeholder groups with fairness and respect.
- Incorporate information about family and community expectations into school decisionmaking and activities.
- Strengthen the school through the establishment of community, business, institutional, and civic partnerships.
- Communicate information about the school on a regular and predictable basis through a variety of media.
- Support the equitable success of all students and all subgroups of students by mobilizing and leveraging community support services.

Standard 5

A school administrator is an educational leader who promotes the success of all students by modeling a personal code of ethics and developing professional leadership capacity.

- Model personal and professional ethics, integrity, justice, and fairness, and expect the same behaviors from others.
- Protect the rights and confidentiality of students and staff.
- Use the influence of the office to enhance the education program, not personal gain.
- Make and communicate decisions based upon relevant data and research about effective teaching and leaning, leadership, management practices and equity.
- Demonstrate knowledge of the standards-based curriculum and the ability to integrate and articulate programs throughout the grades.
- Demonstrate skills in decision-making, problem solving, change management, planning, conflict management, and evaluation.
- Reflect on personal leadership practices and recognize their impact and influence on the performance of others.
- Engage in professional and personal development.
- Encourage and inspire others to higher levels of performance, commitment, and motivation.
- Sustain personal motivation, commitment, energy, and health by balancing professional and personal responsibilities.

Standard 6

A school administrator is an educational leader who promotes the success of all students by understanding, responding to, and influencing the larger political, social, economic, legal, and cultural context.

- Work with the governing board and district and local leaders to influence policies that benefit students and support the improvement of teaching and learning.
- Influence and support public policies that ensure the equitable distribution of resources and support for all subgroups of students.
- Ensure that the school operates consistently within the parameters of federal, state, and local laws, policies, regulation, and statutory requirements.
- Generate support for the school by two-way communication with key decision makers in the school community.

- Collect and report accurate records of school performance.
- View oneself as a leader of a team and also as a member of a larger team.
- Open the school to the public and welcome and facilitate constructive conversations about how to improve student learning and achievement.

INDEX

ABOUT THE AUTHOR

Robert Palestini has been dean of Graduate and Continuing Studies at Saint Joseph's University in Philadelphia for the past fifteen years. He has spent more than forty years in basic and higher education. He has been a high school biology and general science teacher, a principal, assistant superintendent, and superintendent of schools. He is the author of seven books on various topics in educational administration. In addition to being dean, Dr. Palestini teaches two education leadership courses in the doctoral program that he developed seven years ago at Saint Joseph's (rpalesti@sju.edu).